SPIES AND HOLY WARS

Spies and Holy Wars

THE MIDDLE EAST IN 20TH-CENTURY CRIME FICTION

◆ REEVA SPECTOR SIMON ◆

UNIVERSITY OF TEXAS PRESS ⋎ AUSTIN

Requests for permission to reproduce material
from this work should be sent to:
Permissions
University of Texas Press
P.O. Box 7819
Austin, TX 78713–7819
www.utexas.edu/utpress/about/bpermission.html

∞ The paper used in this book meets the minimum
requirements of ANSI/NISO z39.48–1992 (R1997)
(Permanence of Paper).

Library of Congress Cataloging-in-Publication Data

Simon, Reeva S.
Spies and holy wars : the Middle East in 20th-century crime fiction /
Reeva Spector Simon. — 1st ed.
p. cm.
Includes bibliographical references and index.
ISBN 978-0-292-73757-0
1. English fiction—20th century—History and criticism. 2. American fiction—
20th century—History and criticism. 3. Spy stories, English—History and criticism.
4. Spy stories, American—History and criticism. 5. Detective and mystery stories,
English—History and criticism. 6. Detective and mystery stories, American—History and
criticism. 7. Middle East—In literature. 8. Jihad in literature. 9. Espionage in literature.
10. Spies in literature. 11. Politics and literature—Great Britain—History—20th century.
12. Politics and literature—United States—History—20th century. I. Title.
PR129.M54S58 2010
823'.08720935856—dc22
2010019019

FOR RICHARD BULLIET

Contents

Acknowledgments

It is a pleasure to have the opportunity to thank those who have helped bring this book to completion. The excellent reference staffs of a number of public libraries in Nassau County put at my disposal the resources of the New York State Library Systems and provided copies of hundreds of novels from libraries all over the state. The Interlibrary Loan Departments of the Columbia University Libraries and Yeshiva University Libraries facilitated borrowing materials not easily accessible through the public library system. In 2000, a stay at Oxford University put British imprints housed at the Bodleian Library at my disposal. Without the cheerful assistance of the librarians at these institutions, this book never would have been possible.

Through the years, many friends and colleagues served as sounding boards for ideas expounded herein and have read parts of the countless revisions. They include Ruth Burian, Bryan Daves, Ethel Goldberg, Barbara Gombach, Jean-Marc Oppenheim, Lawrence Potter, Ellen Schrecker, Sheila Spector, Eleanor Tejirian, and Terry Walz. Their input and critiques have been greatly appreciated; and, of course, all opinions and errors are entirely my own.

Many thanks to Jim Burr, Victoria Davis, and Scott Anderson at the University of Texas Press.

As always, I appreciate the encouragement of family—my husband, Sheldon, and my children and grandchildren, Miriam, Meir, Yaniv and

Eliana, Benjamin, and Ezra, without whose patience and forbearance this work never could have been attempted.

Last, but not least, I am sincerely grateful to Richard Bulliet who supported the idea for this book through the years of its gestation and to whom this volume is dedicated.

A note on spelling: Arabic terms and proper names in general appear as they would in American newspapers unless they refer to characters or terms used in the novels under discussion.

◆ SPIES AND HOLY WARS ◆

ONE

Crime Fiction as Political Metaphor

Called "Allah's Arrow," Hamir, the ruler of a small sheikhdom on the Red Sea,
was educated at Caltech, where he was a brilliant student, but as a foreigner
on campus, he felt slighted by the Americans he met. After completing his
studies in the United States, he returned to Arabia, and with his self-esteem
revitalized, Hamir was determined to avenge the perceived insults to his
person, his faith, and his culture by nuking Washington—so that by the
end of Ramadan, with vengeance assured and his honor restored, the Arab
would vanquish the infidel West. Lacking an efficient delivery system that
would allow him to drop bombs directly on Washington, the villain concocted an unusually deadly scheme. Posing as a German photographer—
Hamir was a master at disguise and linguistic acuity—he received official
permission to photograph the Capitol. Armed with a camera and tripod, the
Arab slowly and methodically made his way to the halls of Congress and,
reaching the Senate chamber, prepared his assault. Suddenly, with deter-
mination and élan, Hamir fired a fusillade of radioactive paperclips aimed
at the senators' desks. Fortunately, the lawmakers had not yet entered the
chamber and the hero, an FBI agent, was able to stop the sheikh, deflect
some of the paperclips before they had a chance to irradiate the lawmakers,
and save the government of the United States and Western civilization.

Published almost thirty years before 9/11 and at a time when direct attacks on the United States were still a part of futuristic fantasy, this novel—*Cobalt 60* by Richard Graves—is a typical, if somewhat more imaginative example of the many crime fiction novels that appeared during the twentieth century that incorporated the basic components of the crime fiction genre: identifiable heroes and villains and a plot or conspiracy that either disrupts the social order at home or threatens it from abroad.[1] At the same time, it differs from much of the crime fiction produced in the United States and Britain because it does not draw upon the Cold War for material. Instead, Graves turned to the Middle East for inspiration. Writing during a decade when the Middle East was in the news because of war, and real terrorist attacks and oil boycotts were clearly perceived as existential threats against the West, Graves integrated these events in his novel to present a vicarious apocalyptic plot by Muslims against the United States and Western civilization. The hero is decidedly Western, but here, rather than Communists or Nazis, the villain is Arab and Muslim and the plot is Islamic fanaticism expressed as *jihad* or holy war against the West.[2]

Cobalt 60 is also a good illustration of what this book is about: namely, the way politics and popular culture interconnect—in this case through spy novels and thrillers published during the twentieth century that use the Middle East for plot, setting, or character. The theme—*jihad*, or a holy war or crusade against the West, whether by outright Islamic conquest, terrorist attack or economic takeover—is a plot device that has been consistently interwoven in the novels. As such, it provides a convenient matrix for illustrating the interconnection between popular culture and politics and is the thread we will follow from World War I at the beginning of the twentieth century to the Iraq War in the twenty-first.

Cobalt 60 is only one of more than eight hundred British and American crime fiction novels published during the twentieth century that concern the Middle East. These novels, either through plot or characters, illustrate the relationship between popular culture and British and American policy in the region. The Anglo-American connection is significant, not only because of British-American political consonance in the Middle East during the twentieth century, but also because British and American authors were writing for audiences on both sides of the Atlantic. As publishing firms continue to be bought up by conglomerates, British fiction "stars" publish in the United States and American authors sell in the United Kingdom.[3] Publishing trends are important because of the impact that the market has had on the production of crime fiction novels.

Although crime fiction is commercially produced for a mass audience, its popularity is difficult to quantify. Fiction book sales are not broken down into specific categories except for romance novels, most of whose publishers specialize in producing them.[4] Publishers generally do not divulge sales figures, and best seller status—the popularity barometer—did not take into account crime fiction for most of the period under consideration because mysteries were not included on best seller lists until the 1960s.

Nevertheless, as early as the turn of the twentieth century, publishers understood that readers wanted to read detective stories and spy novels. In Britain, where popular fiction became more accessible with the shift from the publication of multi-volume novels to single volume books, book clubs specializing in mysteries and spy novels appeared. In the United States, detective novels and thrillers were serialized in magazines and later appeared in book form. With the emergence of private lending libraries in Britain and the United States, it soon became apparent that many patrons wanted to read classic mysteries and tales of espionage. This demand provided publishers with assured sales, and libraries became an important market for hardcover fiction sales.[5] In the United States today, public libraries are the largest mass purchasers of fiction and in 2005 accounted for a nationwide circulation of some 2.1 billion materials. The more than ten thousand libraries with their numerous branches and bookmobiles base their book purchases on reviews and public demand. In one suburban public library, for example, seven patron requests generate the purchase of one new copy of a book, and depending upon wear and tear, the book could have an average of ten to twelve readers before being discarded.[6]

Paperback books generated even more sales. Independently marketed, paperbacks had been around since World War II, when they became important vehicles for popular fiction in the United States. American Pocket Books began publishing and the Council on Books in Wartime released more than forty books a month in paperback through the Armed Services Editions that also reached a British audience. Many of these were detective novels. At first, American publishers saw the market for paperback originals as predominantly males, who were more inclined to read action stories than intellectual puzzles of detection. Publishers such as Fawcett, Lion, Popular Library, Berkley, Bantam, and Pocket Books soon took over this market niche, featuring varieties of hard-boiled detective fiction with sensational art covers to distinguish them from the more staid hardbacks that dominated library sales.[7] These books were independently marketed and did not rely on publisher-owned book clubs or lending libraries for sales. By 1965 the British paperback imprint Pan Books had sales of 21 million copies that included some six million Ian Fleming James Bond novels. As paperback originals and reprints of popular fiction reached multimillion copy sales, crime fiction, even though sales of its more expensive hardcover copies were lower, made up the largest group of paperback best sellers.[8]

With the adoption of such mass-marketing techniques as multimedia advertising and book promotions, British and American publishers reached people who did not necessarily frequent the neighborhood bookstore. Circumventing the traditional bookseller, publishers racked up sales of millions of paperback books by placing them on shelves in supermarkets, drug stores, newsstands, bus stations, and airports. As a result, many books, like Mario Puzo's *The Godfather* and Frederick Forsyth's Gulf War thriller *The Fist of God*, which had not been best sellers in hardcover, became paperback best sellers. Often, potential commercial success was calculated even before books were written. Publishers commissioned writers to produce formulaic novels or created multi-authored series that were then marketed aggressively.[9]

It is generally estimated that crime fiction accounts for one quarter of popular fiction sales whose readers, an editor commented, were "voracious and always looking for fresh meat."[10] Add used books to sales of new books, as well as multiple readers of books lent to friends and library circulation figures, and we can begin to get a picture of their popularity.

Crime fiction, then, is a commercially produced commodity. The mysteries, spy novels, and thrillers that are included in this category of popular fiction are not part of the canon of high culture imposed from above. In academic terms, they are included in the discipline of popular culture. The novels are reader generated: readers choose what *they* want to read as opposed to what they are told they ought to read. Indeed, despite their own political predilections, publishers are often ready to produce what is reflective of public opinion or what they determine the public will buy.[11] As the book industry grows, these stories and public perceptions of reality connect, because books are most marketable when authors and their publishers play on the conspiracies that society fears. As society's fears change, the industry feeds on it.

That is because the plot or conspiracy is the key component of all crime fiction novels, whether they are mysteries, spy novels, or thrillers. The plot concerns a crime or a disruption of the social order. The characters are a hero and a villain. The villain, the social miscreant, threatens the hero and his society. The reader, vicariously by reading the book, restores domestic stability or international order as the hero solves the mystery or thwarts the villain's conspiracy or attack.

In the classic detective novel, a crime is committed and the perpetrator must be identified. Popularized by the British and reaching its "Golden Age" during the 1930s and 1940s with the work of Agatha Christie among others, the classic detective novel has an august and classic provenance descending from Edgar Allan Poe and Sir Arthur Conan Doyle. The key character is the detective who, whether a professional or an amateur, male or female, is the conveyer of society's moral norms and must put the situation right or restore domestic stability. The reader works with the detective toward the solution of the crime so that reading these novels is an involved and active pursuit along with the detective in solving the puzzle or mystery. To ensure the correct process and inevitable outcome, authors must follow certain rules of presentation so that the reader will be able to analyze the situation logically from the clues provided and solve the mystery with the knowledge that there will be no unexplained suspects or bizarre last-minute actors who have not been previously introduced into the plot who suddenly appear at the denouement.[12] Often, plots are set in "closed" rooms to ensure that the suspects and clues can be easily accounted for and the focus can be on the puzzle which will be neatly solved at the end of the book.

Because of the stylized nature of the traditional detective novel, changes in location, setting, method of the murder, and ethnicity of the detective and the criminal are used to add spice to the script, so that the author can increase his output using the same formula without boring his audience.[13] Tiring of English country gardens and dining rooms, authors may turn to settings that are located almost anywhere on the globe. The "exotic East" is clearly one of them.

Authors have set their murders in most Middle Eastern countries, often using archaeological digs as the locale because of the confined nature of the sites. Egypt, Israel, Iraq, and Turkey—and cruise ships on the Nile, for that matter—have offered convenient backdrops for crime.[14] As a rule in these predominantly British and American novels, detectives and criminals have almost always been Westerners. Peoples of the region, much like the setting, are incidental props or part of the exotic scenery. Bellboys at Shepheard's Hotel in Cairo, workers on an archaeological dig in Mesopotamia, or the ubiquitous *fellah* with donkey stationed along the riverbank are often used to provide an exotic backdrop. In Agatha Christie's *Death on the Nile,* which takes place on a cruise to Luxor, the internationally renowned detective Hercule Poirot and his friend sip lemonade on the terrace of the hotel and, gazing at the rocks of the Nile, note how they resemble the "vast prehistoric monsters lying half out of the water" and the *"pays sauvage"* that was Egypt.[15] A frantic final chase through scenic Cairo provides exotic relief from a murder on a Mediterranean cruise ship in Manning O'Brine's *Corpse to Cairo*.[16]

Explicit sex and overt violence are replaced by Orientalist exoticism or sensuality.[17] For books set in the Middle East, the Casbah of Morocco automatically elicits a sense of intrigue: Anonymous, red-roofed, walled houses in the narrow alleys of Tangier, Casablanca, or Fez evoke both the mysterious and the fascinating: "The pink-brown city walls stretched as far as I could see to the right and to the left. Beyond them and the palms that topped them, a crowded mass of white, narrow, irregular, flat-topped buildings spread down the hillside and across a slanting valley and rose again. The minarets were like square candles, their tiles glinting in the sun. That was Old Fes."[18]

Even more so, North Africa brings to mind foreign agents and exudes the sensuous heat, beaches, cloudless blue skies, and danger: "There was a mystery in the gaping blackness behind the iron-grilled windows of the houses. I had the feeling that we—white-skinned and briefly dressed—were watched secretly and with curiosity as we walked in a town which had not yet been opened to tourists."[19]

It is also the place where Levantine millionaires and European expatriates spend their Swiss-banked illegal currency, living in luxury behind their bougainvillea-bedecked white stucco walls. In contrast to European cities, the Casbah is at once a magical land where one can escape from "Occidental vulgarity." At the same time it is the heart of the mysterious other,[20] much like Istanbul's Seraglio when the city was under Ottoman rule: "It was just off that point that ladies of the harem who happened to be in disfavor were put into sacks and dropped into the Bosporus . . . . 'At least it's a custom you've discontinued,' Tracy said dryly. The Turkish girl shrugged. 'The Bosporus has always invited tragedy.'"[21] This kind of descriptive Orientalism is common in the detective novels that make up approximately ten percent of the total crime fiction output related to the Middle East.

Most of the crime fiction books set in the Middle East, however, are spy novels and thrillers, novels that have an emotional rather than an intellectual appeal. These novels are the focus of this book. Spy novels and thrillers draw on the exotic, but unlike detective stories, they are *not* cerebral chess games that presume the rational use of intellect to solve a well-defined problem. They do not describe the solution of a simple crime that occurs within a small physical space allowing the reader to participate cerebrally in the solution process while rarely experiencing any apprehension or dread. To the contrary, spy novels and thrillers draw on the emotions. More often than not, the plots of these novels rely on brute force by an odious villain or an apocalyptic, irrational conspiracy that draws on the primordial fear of an assault on the national psyche and threatens the survival of the nation or even the very existence of the Earth itself.

While reading them, readers are under constant, steady tension and may even feel terror related to the graphic depiction of brutality, murder, or unspeakable torture that is an integral component of many of these formulaic novels of international conspiracy. They are propelled through the story by means of a series of tense episodes or by the constant threat of cataclysmic disaster. The objective of the novel is for the hero to thwart the evil designs of a criminal, rather than to unmask his identity. Often, the criminal and his evil intentions are identified even before the hero is introduced.[22]

Readers are drawn to the books by sensational book jacket illustrations: a foreign-looking man with a knife holding a woman at bay or a mushroom cloud over Washington, D.C.; a note on the cover that describes the gruesome horrors to come. Using the news as fiction fodder, writers have for more than a century baldly enticed readers to purchase thrillers that promise "the real inside story behind this morning's newspaper headlines" with tales "more astounding than fiction."[23] The books are packaged with lurid covers and promises of exposés of sensational hijackings, terrorism, assassinations, bombings, and kidnappings. Political events have provided instant scenarios for thriller writers who are able to transform stories widely circulated by the media into easily marketable fiction.

Readers begin the novel, become engaged, and are tied to the story through such literary techniques as an outrageous plot, suspense, a simplistic hero-villain confrontation, and a satisfying ending that ties all of the pieces together. The solution to the puzzle is either incidental or of no account because the reader knows that the hero with whom he identifies somehow or other will save the day. No gimmick is too outlandish, no setting too foreign for the story's twists and turns. Authors frequently introduce unexplained poisons, weapons, and characters who appear at the last minute. In the classic spy novel, for example, the double agent, unmasked at the end like the criminal in the detective novel, is usually someone whose thoughts the reader is allowed to follow, but the spy frequently uses unaccountable intuition. The reader understands that villainy is not based on reason, but rather on the stereotypical caricatures authors employ as signifiers of evil.

The villain is usually physically repulsive, a homosexual, or pathologically mean. There are no series of intelligible clues and the hero frequently uses his "gut feelings."[24]

As such, the books are much like other forms of escapist entertainment—movies, epic tales of heroes, fairy tales, superhero comic books, science fiction, television, or video games. They have emotional appeal and fill the need for vicarious experience and the desire to escape from reality into a more exciting life: sexual fantasy and sudden wealth, interaction with other cultures, victory over great and unconquerable odds, or even vengeance against a perceived enemy. People can fly—first class, of course—to chic cafés in evocative Beirut and Pahlavi Tehran, in order to undergo, perhaps, the hardships of jeep and camel travel to the bleak Arabian Empty Quarter. Readers become a part of the jet-set life in Swiss ski resorts and partake of the opulent life of a lush Riviera estate overlooking the Mediterranean, where they might be entertained at an elegantly catered party for the American secretary of state and the king of Jordan.

For many, the appeal of the modern spy novel and the thriller that developed soon after is not only their disregard for all of the official rules to provide surprise and thrill with every turn of the page, but also their educational nature. There are long, detailed explanations of technology, planning, and execution of a "crime" or conspiracy that provide tutorials on esoteric subjects. Before the Internet and cable television, one could read Paul Erdman as a primer on international finance in *The Crash of '79* or Stuart Jackman for a course on desert warfare. Other writers provide instruction on how to create a false identity, construct aircraft, missiles, and atomic bombs; use explosives and ordnance; and arm and disarm nuclear devices. "Today's spy stories undoubtedly require a high degree of precision," author Paul Henissart tells aspiring writers. "Because the readers are better informed, they have traveled, and they like to read about places they have visited."[25]

Because of high reader expectations for the inclusion of specialized knowledge and accurate description, most novelists research their books thoroughly and since the 1970s, experts from many fields have joined professional writers to author spy novels and thrillers. Because of their "inside" knowledge, their expertise is valuable and taken seriously. Journalists Marvin Kalb, Eric Pace, and David Ignatius put their coverage of the Arab-Israel Conflict, Ba'thist Baghdad, and the civil war in Lebanon to use in their novels. Academics, ex-CIA agents, Peace Corps volunteers, and military professionals have also written spy novels and thrillers.[26] Trusting that the books ring true overall—after all, planes were hijacked, hostages were taken, and sightings of weapons of mass destruction were reported—readers are drawn in by familiar news events and follow authors' musings about what might have happened as they unravel the plots in their thrillers to explain the mysterious. Today, talking heads on news programs provide instant news commentary; in the past, authors such as Nelson DeMille or Daniel Silva have used the genre to propose such scenarios as the reasons for the mysterious 1996 crash of TWA Flight 800 over the Atlantic near New York's JFK Airport.[27]

At the end of the novel, all of the major characters' personal problems developed in the narrative and the political intrigues generated by the plot must be resolved so that when the reader finishes the book, he feels satisfied and safe. At the same time, writes author Ken Follett, "he must feel as if he just got off a roller coaster. It was fun, it was scary, he's relieved it ended okay, and one day soon he's going to take another ride."[28]

The books under examination here are part of a genre of formulaic, escapist literature with wide appeal that, by definition, requires heroes readers identify with, villains they despise, and frightening apocalyptic plots that draw on atavistic paranoia. Readers are attracted to the novels by a modicum of reality, become hooked on the conspiracy, and willingly follow the author even as he forces them to suspend reality and move into the fantastic, resolving the seemingly unsolvable dilemmas by the end of the book. Presenting a parallel political universe where conspiracy against the hero and his world is pervasive and limited only by the author's creativity, the genre provides an emotional outlet where conflicts between good and evil can be acted out vicariously. Plots are apocalyptic conspiracies designed to generate terror and require a hero who will thwart them by defeating, smiting, or obliterating the enemy: the "other," whose nefarious schemes threaten the very existence of the hero, his culture, and his civilization. Readers identify with the hero because he embodies the national ethos or mirrors the nation's image of itself through a binary relationship with the villainous "other," and reflects nationalist perceptions of peoples and events through the lens of popular cultural myths. As a result, these novels are a natural vehicle for the presentation of a simplistic, dualistic view of the universe where, in the Anglo-American novels under scrutiny here, only the hero remains constant. The villains change, and with them, a reflection of the public's shifting perceptions of political reality. Appearing most often on best seller lists during domestic or foreign crises, spy novels and thrillers can lend themselves to political advocacy or merely reflect political perspectives that publishers believe echo views of the marketplace. For these reasons, plots and characterization have shifted as British and American views about the Middle East and policy interests have changed over the years.

Publishers understand the connection as do politicians: Winston Churchill lauded the heroic ethos of the British spy during World War I, and J. Edgar Hoover used popular culture to enhance the image of the FBI.[29] In the 1950s and 1960s, CIA operatives were encouraged to write spy novels, and the fiction had a large following that included U.S. presidents John F. Kennedy and Ronald Reagan. Government agencies, professional writers and ex-intelligence officers, politicians, military, financial, and academic experts alike have all exploited this genre of popular fiction as a vehicle not only to advance political and religious ideologies, but to warn of the danger of imminent invasion or global financial crisis; to vilify the non-Western Other; to romanticize the Middle East; to criticize American foreign policy; or to perpetuate the fear of an apocalyptic Islamic *jihad* against the West.

With the onset of the millennium, during the 1990s, even evangelical Christians used the thriller format, but in their case, to meet a religious agenda, to warn of the impending Armageddon. Volumes in the Left Behind series written by Rev. Tim LaHaye and Jerry Jenkins appeared in first place on the *New York Times* Best Seller list. With an initial print run of 2.75 million books, the series already has sales of more than 50 million copies and counting. The books have generated comics, children's books, movies, audio tapes, radio drama, books clubs, and internet chat rooms.[30] When the books first appeared in 1995, there was little notice. After all, the series was published by Tyndale House, whose readership is predominantly evangelical Christians, and books produced for that market are generally not listed on the mainstream best seller lists. Academics were for the most part unaware of the novels and their success, despite the intense interest generated about the ideological perspectives of the Religious Right and how they are being manifested in US foreign policy today.[31] Publishers, however, took the sales figures of the series seriously, and LaHaye's subsequent contract with Bantam Dell in 2002 did make *The New York Times*. His $45 million dollar advance from the publishing division of the giant Bertelsmann publishing empire for worldwide rights to four planned novels was among the highest paid to a novelist and was a clear signal that the international publishing conglomerate believed that the religious readership already hooked on the novels would not only continue to buy them, but that the series would also attract more mainstream readers.[32] Marketing has been reminiscent of the publishing phenomenon that occurred in the mid-1960s when Ian Fleming's James Bond novels hit the bookstores. Now, as then, thrillers that tell of an apocalyptic conspiracy featuring heroes firmly anchored in Anglo-American culture thwarting the evil designs of demonic villains fit neatly into the thriller category.

At the time that they are written and because of the nature of the genre, spy novels and thrillers are expressions of popular political belief and are in a sense translations of a political reality that is believed to be acceptable to the general reading public. As such, they can be used as a source for insight into current perceptions of events.[33]

As crime fiction literature developed over the course of the twentieth century, spy novels and thrillers increasingly reflected the "reciprocal" relationship between culture and foreign policy. Just as "Film and events 'speak' to each other," events lend political resonance to fiction, and fiction provides the "mythological justification for the particular scenarios of real-world action."[34] Spy novels and thrillers, in particular, not only project the public myth and mirror the nation's view of itself, but also reflect the assumptions of the culture of which they are a part. The genre "help[s] to shape the public sense of what is appropriate in confronting the crises of national and international life."[35]

Given the nature of crime fiction—spy novels and thrillers in particular—whose essential ingredients are hero, villain, and plot, it is surprising that, unlike literature or film, both of which have been analyzed thoroughly by scholars focusing on the Euro-centric bias in Western culture, these books about the Middle East have remained below the radar of academic scrutiny. Edward Said, concerned more with the impact of high culture and the influence of academia on European and American foreign policy, does not examine popular culture in his works on Orientalism. His analyses and Norman Daniel's expositions of how the portrayal of the East in literature and academic discourse have impressed the perspective of Western superiority and perpetuated the stereotypical view of the sensual, irrational, inferior, and immutable East, or in the words of Rudyard Kipling—"East is East and West is West"—have become the starting point for studies of imperialism.[36] Cultural theorists and historians look at the methods used to impose this imperialist domination through the production and control of knowledge by Orientalists, anthropologists, and historians, who, they maintain, were complicit in the creation of an imperial tradition that was inculcated through an educational and cultural apparatus of novels, museums, international fairs, and expositions, stories for boys, toys and youth move-ments.[37] Despite hints of both throughout this book, whether all popular culture has been part and parcel of imperial design or a convergence of political and commercial interests I leave for readers to decide.[38]

Where crime fiction related to the Middle East is just beginning to re-ceive its due, however, is in studies that, by and large, have stated the ob-vious: namely, that the plots are conspiratorial, the characters are stereo-typical, and the onus for evil is on Arabs and Muslims.[39] As this study will illustrate, how spy novels and thrillers about the Middle East connect with Western politics is more complicated, because not only did the nature of the imperial game change, but the relationship between East and West evolved over time. At the beginning of the twentieth century, authors described a supine, malleable Middle East controlled by the imperial West. By the 1970s, worldwide technological advances in the military, computers, and economic markets forced authors to depict Middle Eastern conspirators as intelligent as their Western antagonists. If their plots were to be believable, heroes and villains had to operate on a level playing field. At that point, in the throes of decolonization and Islamism, Arabs and Muslims became threats to the West on their own and did not require Western assistance.

As we look at British and American novels under study here, it soon becomes apparent that the Western heroic national ethos expressed in spy novels and thrillers initially connoted British imperialism and American mission. The work of God's chosen peoples against the infidel is reflected in British and American policy in the region, whether it be fostering Brit-ish imperial interests in the Middle East and preventing the collapse of the British Empire or, in the wake of decolonization, supporting the American imposition of Western values on what has been seen as an increasingly re-calcitrant Middle East. Opposition to Western hegemony in the region was translated in crime fiction as conspiracy. By the last third of the twentieth century, as the peril drew closer to home, the threat became existential.

While over the years, these plots against the West have appeared in many guises, one of the most consistent conspiratorial threads to permeate spy novels and thrillers about the Middle East throughout the twentieth century has been *jihad* expressed in terms of a religious takeover of the West or the destruction of Europe or America by political or economic ter-rorism. In this context, fictional plots and their perpetrators are portrayed and interpreted through the lens of British and American policy. A good example of this is Richard Graves's *Cobalt 60*. The hero is American, the vil-lain is an Arab Muslim, and the plot concerns *jihad* against the West.

That Arabs and Muslims have merited a place among the galaxy of world conspirators should come as no surprise given historical circumstance. This is because today, after a three-hundred-year hiatus, Muslims from the Middle East once again are seen to menace Westerners, either as international terrorists or as religious fanatics. A look at how the theme of *jihad* in crime fiction has consistently connected with the developments in the crime fiction genre and marketing, politics, and Anglo-American policy in the Middle East over the course of the twentieth century from the Great War to the millennium is the subject of the following pages.

We begin with World War I.

Spies and Holy War

JIHAD AND WORLD WAR I

The story begins during World War I with John Buchan's novel Greenmantle
and the plot to bring down the British Empire: "There is a dry wind blowing through the East," we read, "and the parched grasses await the spark
and the wind is blowing towards the Indian border. . . .

> I have reports from agents everywhere—pedlars in South Russia, Afghan
> horse-dealers, Turcoman merchants, pilgrims on the road to Mecca,
> sheikhs in North Africa, sailors on the Black Sea coasters, sheep-skinned
> Mongols, Hindu fakirs, Greek traders in the Gulf, as well as respectable
> Consuls who use cyphers. They tell the same story.

With these facts, Sir Walter Bullivant of the British Foreign Office briefs
Richard Hannay, who has just returned from the Western Front. "The East
is waiting for a revelation. It has been promised one. Some star-man, prophecy, or trinket—is coming out of the West. The Germans know and that
is the card with which they are going to astonish the world."[1] Hannay's
mission, should he agree to undertake it, is to find the mastermind, foil the
plot, and save England. Armed with three clues obtained at great cost from
an agent who died near Kut in Mesopotamia, Hannay agrees and the first
British spy novel about the Middle East gets underway.

Accompanied by colleagues, who include Sandy Arbuthnot, a multilingual Orientalist who resembles T.E. Lawrence and wanders throughout

Anatolia as a Sufi dervish impersonator gathering intelligence, and John Blenkiron, a pragmatic American capitalist who, despite American neutrality in the war, wants to "get let into the game somehow,"[2] Hannay works out a plan and the group decides to meet in Constantinople. Sandy disappears for parts East, and Hannay and Blenkiron take a European route to the Ottoman capital where they discover that not only are the Germans behind the plot, but that the mastermind is an unlikely character. Their nemesis is not the German military embodied in the repulsive Colonel Stumm, but, surprisingly, a German woman, none other than the notorious Hilda von Einem, an archaeologist, who was once married to a German diplomat. Von Einem tries to recruit Arbuthnot into her anti-British conspiracy to unite Muslims across the Ottoman Empire in a strike at the heart of the British Empire. She needs him to impersonate her Muslim "Mahdi," Greenmantle, who has inconsiderately forsaken her by dying before the onset of the holy war. She tempts Sandy with greatness and the prospect of leading millions, but he, in typical British form, decides to save the Empire instead.

The novel *Greenmantle* was published in 1916 in the midst of World War I and presents a conspiracy—an Islamic *jihad* against the British Empire in the Middle East. Buchan's fictionalized account of the "plot to bring down the British Empire" is the first real spy novel to use the Middle East and its peoples for plot and character. It drew on popular late nineteenth century British imperialist views of the Middle East. These included the key elements that readers had come to expect from the popular fiction of the day, creating a paradigm that would be incorporated in political thrillers and spy novels throughout the twentieth century: namely, a conspiracy by the Arab/Muslim world to destroy the West—thwarted, in this case, by a British hero. Successful when it first appeared, by 1960 the novel had sold more than 350,000 copies.[3]

For his fiction, Buchan (1875–1940) drew upon a Scottish Calvinist upbringing that taught the moral imperative of serving good as well as love of Empire.[4] Before World War I, he worked in South Africa on post-Boer War refugee and repatriation issues and returned to England to work in law and politics. Like many civil servants in precarious financial situations, he added to his income by writing fiction, biographies of great men, and popular history. In 1913, too ill to serve in the military because of ulcer problems, he also decided to write "shockers"— *The Thirty-Nine Steps* remaining one of his most popular. Buchan spent the war years working first for the Intelligence Corps and then, in 1917, was appointed director of propaganda for the Ministry of Information. His connections with the British secret service during that time are reflected in his spy novels, as well as his history of

World War I, which was first serialized in the *Spectator* and later published as a multi-volume work. This nonfiction work reflects Buchan's contact with such wartime prime ministers and cabinet members as Edward Grey, David Lloyd George, and Arthur Balfour.[5]

Buchan's third spy novel, *Greenmantle*, illustrated the sorts of British insecurities about fears of external threat that had been building for decades. In the first, *The Power House* (1913), a young lawyer chances upon a conspiracy to destroy Western civilization by a group of scientists working in the English countryside. His second book, *The Thirty-Nine Steps* (1914) contains hints of a Jewish conspiracy and highlights the fragility of Western civilization, while *Greenmantle* presents a conflict of civilizations, not so much between the Muslim world and the West as between Britain and a Germany that Buchan considered barbaric. A believer in the righteousness of the British Empire, Buchan deplored the cynical manipulation by Kaiser Wilhelm II's Imperial Germany of "Islam" as a vehicle for the destruction of British hegemony in Central Asia. He used this theme in the context of plots and counterplots directed from the European continent, thus reflecting the concerns British novelists and policymakers since the 1880s had about endurance of the empire.

While one can trace stories about spies back to the Bible and Homeric literature, until World War I, espionage, the second oldest profession, was considered unsavory but necessary. Its professionals, therefore, were not the stuff of which literary heroes were made. European warfare had been governed by a code of honor inherited from the Middle Ages, with its emphasis on knights in shining armor and chivalry, not deception. Clearly, spies had been in common use: Queen Elizabeth I used them; Nathan Hale and Aaron Burr operated during the American Revolution. Although Napoleon is said to have claimed that one spy in the right place was worth thousands of troops on the battlefield and established the first French intelligence service, his spies were not accorded heroes' honors. To the contrary, no one officially recognized the use of spies, although everyone knew that the other side had them, because in European society it was unthinkable that a gentleman would degrade himself by becoming a spy. It was a job that automatically presupposed the dishonorable traits of lying and cheating, even though it was understood that the essence of a good spy embodied the quality of loyalty to one's employer—at least while his credit was good.[6]

This abhorrence of the dishonorable went to ridiculous lengths on the battlefield, where it was against the rules to use camouflage. For years, British units in fire-engine red uniforms stood in straight lines opposite French soldiers in scarlet and blue, either awaiting mutual slaughter or offering irresistible targets for Americans fighting guerrilla-style, firing from behind rocks and trees. The furtive business of spying, with its need for lying, cheating, and blackmail, was obviously not as honorable as real soldiering. It was not until 1884 that the British changed their field uniforms to khaki. The French retained their colorful uniforms in some units until the end of World War I.

Towards the end of the nineteenth century, however, there was a sudden resurgence of interest in spies and spying. During an era of political turbulence in Europe, terrorism and acts of anarchism abounded and the all too real presence in England of foreign revolutionaries, anarchists, and nihilists from Russia and Ireland gave the British pause. During the 1880s such events as the Fenian bombing campaign and the discovery of an Irish bomb factory in Brooklyn, New York, that included caches of dynamite sticks, exploding cigars, and explosive walking sticks; the suicide bombing of a French anarchist in London's Greenwich Park; the assassination of Tsar Alexander II; and an attempt on the life of Kaiser Wilhelm II were all clear reminders of the threat of international terrorism.

The press warned that Britain did not exist in splendid isolation and that incipient globalization threatened the empire and the West. Although *The Times* acknowledged that progress yielded the industrialization and modern technology that united the world, in 1883 the newspaper also warned that there was real danger as well because now all Europe was "bound together by a wide network of railways and steamers and telegraph lines, and a blow struck at any one part diffuses itself over all the rest, and is felt in its degree by all."[7] An empire like Britain, threatened by economic competition, politicians were quick to point out, would have "to fight to the death against successive rivals."[8]

In response to domestic terrorist threats, the British established Scotland Yard Special Branch and a Secret Service to combat bombings by the Irish. They also instituted a Directorate of Military Intelligence and a British Naval Intelligence Board to combat what the military saw as an increasingly apparent German threat after the Prussian victory over France in 1870.

When the French spy scandal of 1894 broke, people were once again focused on espionage, especially when the unpalatable truth came to light that two supposedly civilized countries had been engaged in espionage against each other. The Dreyfus Affair, as it was called, shocked the French and, by extension, the British. It made clear the fact that French officers lied in order to defend the honor of their officer corps, some of whose members had manufactured and falsified evidence against Jewish officer Alfred Dreyfus. He was condemned to Devil's Island on charges of spying for Germany. Although Dreyfus was later exonerated, the "Affair" remains a controversial political subject in France. In Britain, repercussions from the case prompted anxiety over enemy espionage on its soil.

In England, invasion stories and war prophecy novels abounded.[9] These had been popular for more than a decade, some in response to the military technology introduced during the Franco-Prussian War (1870). Others dwelled on Britain's increasing political involvement in European affairs and Germany's entry into the race for colonies, a competition that had until then occupied primarily Britain, France, and to a lesser degree, Russia. Fictionalized accounts of a future conflict with either France or Russia appeared at the end of the nineteenth century. In 1893, William Le Queux's serialized novel *The Great War in England in 1897*, prophesied an invasion of the southern coast of England by the French accompanied by evil Russian soldiers who impaled babies on their bayonets. Although the invasion is ultimately thwarted by a valiant and successful British counterattack, the novel underlines the danger of the foreign spy operating on British soil.[10] The book went through sixteen editions, was endorsed by the military strategist Lord Roberts,[11] and was followed by a spate of terrorism and invasion tales. Another author, George Griffiths, warned in *Angel of the Revolution* (1893), of an international conspiracy by a brotherhood of nihilists, anarchists, and socialists to bring America into a war on the side of Germany and Britain against France, Russia, and Italy—an alliance of Anglo-Saxon genius against the East and ending this time with a final battle against Islam.[12]

With Kaiser Wilhelm II's move into the imperial arena, German challenges were perceived as threats against Britain, and writers translated them into fiction. Three years after the Germans passed a Fleet Law that provided money for the construction of a battle fleet, Erskine Childers published the first real British spy novel, *The Riddle of the Sands* (1903), a tale of a British patriot who, while out sailing, discovers that the Germans are preparing to invade England by means of troop-carrying barges. Childers wrote the book as a plea for the establishment of a British North Sea fleet. He was, in fact, the first of many to use the spy story and thriller as a method for warning the public of imminent danger through fictitious military scenarios. It should be emphasized here, however, that although Childers wrote a bona fide tale of espionage and his hero acts like a spy, his hero is not a professional, but an amateur who chances upon the knowledge that will aid his country—spying was still a dirty business.

From 1903 to World War I, novels of espionage-conspiracy were published in Britain every year, and although still nonprofessionals, heroic agents, like detectives, came to represent stability in an age that was becoming increasingly insecure. In the public mind, villains had already shifted from the French to the Germans after German support for the Boers against Britain (1899–1902) and the invasion scare of 1900. Reflective of this policy shift, Britain signed treaties with the French (1904) and the Russians (1907). At the same time, writers depicted German hordes crossing the English Channel by tunnel, plans for which were loudly opposed when construction was first proposed in the 1880s. In W. W. Jacobs's *When William Came*, a tale of Teutonic-conquered Britain, Russians drop bombs from gas balloons over Edinburgh.

As they would throughout the twentieth century, marketing methods played an important role in popularizing these stories, but they also fueled the paranoia that the British Empire was going the way of Rome in the fifth century. Authors explained that the public needed information— what to look for and where to look—and they undertook to supply it. After all, Le Queux complained, there were German spies in all of the cities of England—some even on "golfing teams with the ruler of Great Britain."[13] Novels were commissioned by such press barons as Lord Northcliffe, the founder of the London *Daily Mail*, who serialized Le Queux's *The Invasion of 1910* (1906) in his newspaper and advised the author to adjust the route of the invaders so that it included towns where the newspaper sold well. Later published as a novel, the book was translated into many languages, including German. Advertised as providing real intelligence on military matters, instead of French villains, it featured Germans who impaled babies. Stalwart British guerrillas were the heroes.[14] For their part, the Germans, also worried about a future war, responded with a counter-novel, *Seestern*, about a British preemptive strike against the German fleet. The *Daily Mail* serialized more novels by Le Queux and even appointed a Spy Editor. It also offered a reward for information about foreign spies in Britain which was said to have been a factor in the spy panic of 1908–1909 that pressured the government to establish an official inquiry into espionage in Britain.

Real spying became a more active endeavor. In 1905 the British included an intelligence department in their reordered chain of military command, and in 1906, military intelligence was moved into the War Office building in Whitehall.[15] By 1910 a professional service was in place with domestic and foreign capabilities; a year later the Official Secrets Act was passed.[16]

Each international crisis of 1911–1912—Agadir, the Balkan Wars, and the uncovering of a small network of German agents—worried the director of the Home Section of British intelligence, who feared that he had underestimated the presence of German agents in England and, by extension, the threat to the empire.[17] German economic and military encroachments in Turkey and the Persian Gulf led the British government to worry not only about the Middle East, but even more about the possible invasion of India. The British had had their eye on Mesopotamia (Iraq) at the head of the Persian Gulf and when the war broke out in 1914, troops from the India Army took Basra and moved northward, only to be stopped and besieged at Kut—where John Buchan's tale, *Greenmantle*, picked up the story.

> We have had our agents working in Persia and Mesopotamia for years— mostly young officers of the Indian army. They carry their lives in their hands, and now and then one disappears, and the cellars of Baghdad might tell a tale. But they find out many things, and they count the game worth the candle. They could give us no details. All but one—the best of them— he had been working between Mosul and the Persian frontier as a mule-teer and had been south into the Bakhtiari Hills. He found out something, but his enemies knew that he knew, and he was pursued. Three months ago, just before Kut, he staggered into Delamain's camp with ten bullet holes in him and a knife slash on his forehead. He mumbled his name, but beyond that and the fact that there was a Something coming from the West he told them nothing. He died in ten minutes.[18]

What was later revealed and the story that Buchan told was based on a real German plot to bring down the British Empire that became operational during World War I. It was an extension of Kipling's "Great Game," played at the end of the nineteenth century by the Russians and the British, whose agents infiltrated the vast areas in Central Asia unknown to Europeans in order to explore and map the terrain and to spy on each other. Dressing as Afghans, Hindu horse traders, and Armenian merchants, British India army officers were sent on solo missions through the Northwest Frontier and beyond, traveling from the Caucasus to China. With Russia on the northern border, they strove to gain the confidence of tribal leaders in anticipation of a Cossack-led Russian military thrust southward to India. Although the Russian threat to India was always of primary concern to policy makers during the nineteenth century, after the 1907 Anglo-Russian agreement to partition Persia, the British turned to what they saw as German mischief in the region. During the run-up to World War I, the British worried about the Reich's political, economic, and military machinations in the Middle East that seemed to be growing daily.

A latecomer to the colonial competition, Germany was not included when most of the non-Western world was divided up by the colonial powers. England was ensconced in India, the Persian Gulf, and in Egypt astride the Suez Canal; France occupied most of the rest of North Africa while it eyed Syria, dreaming of its Crusader past. For its part, Germany looked to Turkey and the Ottoman Empire for future imperial spoils, but not for outright occupation. The German "Drive to the East," or *Drang Nach Osten*, as it was called, was played out diplomatically, economically and militarily. In the 1890s, German specialists were sent to prepare a survey of Ottoman economic potential. Kaiser Wilhelm II visited the Middle East in 1898 and laid a wreath at the tomb of the Muslim "Crusader" hero, Saladin, in Damascus. His speech supporting Ottoman Sultan Abdulhamid II at a time when the Sultan was in bad odor in the West because of the Armenian situation was covered in Arabic and Turkish newspapers and distributed throughout the Middle East on "brightly coloured postcards." The British were worried about Wilhelm: cartoonists and satirists wrote of his visiting *"Abdul the Damned"* and spoke of *"Deutschland über Allah."* A German military mission had already begun to train Ottoman officers in Istanbul. Travelers, Orientalists, and archaeologists were recruited to go east to work and to observe. The British knew about Max von Oppenheim, who became chief of German intelligence working through the Institute of Archaeology and reported to the German Foreign Office. They called him "the spy." [19]

The British responded to increasing German business in the Middle East, which included plans for a railway to link from Berlin to Baghdad, by sending reconnaissance missions made up of military personnel and inveterate travelers who went to Turkey, Mesopotamia, and Arabia to check on German progress. In 1904, Percy Cox, then a major in the Indian British army (later Sir Percy Cox of Mesopotamia), was sent to the Persian Gulf to check out German deliberations with the Sheikh of Kuwait over the construction of the terminus of the railway and the possibilities for opening German business offices in Bushire, Basra, Mohammera, and Bandar Abbas. Cox was "near his prime of life, tall and spare, blond and blue-eyed. He moved lithely, and he shot straight. He could manage a difficult horse and a fast camel."[20] Gertrude Bell, who was later to play an important political role in the region, traveled to the Middle East in 1899 and returned before the war to report on Turkish military operations in Syria, where she took pictures and watched the railroad construction.[21]

The British also recruited Arabists and archaeologists. David Hogarth worked for British Naval Intelligence, and Leonard Woolley, later renown for his research on the Sumerians, were joined in 1911 by T.E. Lawrence, who would achieve popular acclaim after his exploits in the Arab Revolt in Arabia, at a dig on the Syrian side of the Euphrates where they watched German engineers construct a bridge. While discussing pottery shards and linguistics, the British academics looked through their field glasses and photographed the Germans, while the Germans used identical Zeiss binoculars and cameras to photograph them.[22] There were British officers in Arabia, and late in 1913 Lawrence and Woolley turned up in the Sinai "walking the footsteps of Moses." The British were concerned about the security of the Suez Canal, but danger also lay in eastern Turkey, Mesopotamia, and Afghanistan—the gateway to India.

Once the Ottoman Empire entered World War I on the side of Germany and Austria-Hungary, a month after the outbreak of the war, the British had to become involved in the Middle East directly, not only because of territory but also because of Islam. Using the "Islam card," German Orientalists worked with their government to persuade the Turks to have religious authorities declare a holy war against the British. Were this to happen, they plotted, Muslims from Turkey to India would rise up in one great movement against British rule, and if that movement could be controlled by the German Foreign Office, all the better.[23] The German government had already sent agents to lay the groundwork under the leadership of Oskar von Niedermayer, a Persian Bahai, and Wilhelm Wassmuss, who was fluent in Persian and Arabic and had connections with some of the sheikhs of the area. Before the war, the British did not take Wassmuss seriously, but once hostilities between Britain and Germany began, the German agent seized British hostages, worked with the tribes against the British, and became a constant nuisance to British forces in Mesopotamia. Repeatedly throughout the war, Wassmuss escaped British capture and earned their respect. The British described him as a "blond, manly-looking Saxon of agreeable manners and good character." Wassmuss was also known as the "German Lawrence."[24]

To a twenty-first century reader, the idea of German manipulation of Muslim surrogates to bring down the British Empire is both audacious and patronizing, but in truth, the plot reflected contemporary European views of Muslims under Turkish rule. Nineteenth and early twentieth-century Europeans viewed Muslims on the one hand as a supine people waiting to be used by a great power like Germany, yet on the other hand as a group capable of occasional outbursts of violence against the West. Muslims were at once seen as both noble savages in the guise of the biblical Bedouin residents of the Holy Land and the enemies of Christendom to be conquered politically or economically.[25] By the early twentieth century, the West had overcome the fear of Islam that had been a part of the European historic memory from the time of the Muslim conquest of Spain and the later Ottoman forays into Central Europe. Europeans now looked east to conquer and dominate. Islam was viewed as an inferior faith or even quaint. What did it say about a people who could be swayed into holy war by some "starman, prophecy, or trinket?" [26]

For the British, the threat was real enough. They already had a fairly recent experience with "Mahdis, mullas and imams." After all, the memory of the rebellion of the Sudanese Mahdi, Muhammad Ahmad ibn Abdalah (1881–1885), against British rule was still fresh.[27] It was formulated in terms of a *jihad* against the British who occupied Egypt and the Sudan in 1882. At home, Englishmen read factual accounts including one by Buchan about the Mahdi's siege of Khartoum, the failure of the British relief column to reach the city in time to prevent General Charles George Gordon from dying a martyr's death. The events later resurfaced in fiction. Heroic tales such as A. E. W. Mason's *The Four Feathers* reinforced the view that "primitive" peoples can be swayed by religious fanaticism to revolt: "Mohammad Ahmed marched," the public read, "preaching with a fire of a Wesley the coming of a Saviour. The passionate victims of the Turkish tax gatherer had listened, had heard the promise repeated in the whispers of the wind in the withered grass, had found the holy names imprinted even upon the eggs they gathered up."[28] The British press condemned "Mahdism" as an anachronistic, cruel, destructive tyranny which ruined the Sudan and its peoples and described its perpetrators as lustful fanatics.[29]

But the memory lingered. Despite Ottoman Westernization programs undertaken during the nineteenth century, featuring German military advisors and Krupp guns, the British thought and Buchan wrote in *Greenmantle* that the Turks were still susceptible to "Islam" and to German manipulation:

> The Sheikh-ul-Islam is neglected, and though the Kaiser proclaims a
> Holy War and calls himself Hadji Mohammed Guilliamo, and says the

Hohenzollerns are descended from the Prophet, that seems to have fallen pretty flat. The ordinary man again will answer that Islam in Turkey is becoming a back number, and that Krupp guns are the new gods. Yet—I don't know. I do not quite believe in Islam becoming a back number.[30]

Acknowledging that they had scoffed at the idea of an Islamic *jihad*, the British were slowly concluding that the Germans were instigating a holy war that Muslims were innately susceptible to. Buchan has Sir Walter question how the Germans

> got some tremendous sacred sanction—some holy thing, some book or gospel or some new prophet from the desert, something which would cast over the whole ugly mechanism of German war the glamour of the old torrential raids which crumpled the Byzantine Empire and shook the walls of Vienna? Islam is a fighting creed, and the mullah still stands in the pulpit with the Koran in one hand and a drawn sword in the other. Supposing there is some Ark of the Covenant which will madden the remotest Moslem peasant with dreams of Paradise? What then, my friend?

"Then there will be hell let loose in those parts pretty soon," Hannay responds. And, concludes Sir Walter—"Hell which may spread. Beyond Persia, remember, lies India."[31]

How, then, to save the empire? In the real war, the focus of hostilities was Europe, where the stalemate on the Western Front persisted. Armies faced each other, casualties were horrific, and soldiers were like cogs in a machine with little possibility for independent derring-do. What Bullivant in *Greenmantle* offers Hannay and his comrade-in-arms, Sandy Arbuthnot— two sides of the same coin: both British to the core, believers in Empire, and products of public school education—is the opportunity to become a hero, a special person. He offers them action, possibilities to perform lone, exceptional duties and the ability to make a difference.

For the British, this would be the war that not only professionalized the secret service but created the heroic ethos of the spy that would be translated into fiction. The "actual facts, in many cases, were in every respect equal to the most fantastic inventions of romance or melodrama," Winston Churchill would later write. "Tangle within tangle, plot and counterplot, ruse and treachery, cross and double-cross, true agent, false agent, double agent, gold and steel, the bomb, the dagger and the firing party were interwoven in a texture incredible and yet true. The Chief and the high officers of the Service reveled in these subterranean labyrinths and amid the crash of war pursued their task with cold and silent passion."[32]

Buchan's Hannay is a veteran from the Western Front, where he has experienced modern warfare firsthand—warfare that "asks for the average rather than the exception in human nature" and "is like a big machine where the parts are standard."[33] Summoned to the Foreign Office, Hannay is offered an opportunity to be extraordinary, to undertake a mission that only he could accomplish, one that would task all of his abilities and involve deadly risks with no government backup. He could save England and his operation could mean the difference between defeat and victory.

> I may be sending you to your death, Hannay—Good God, what a damned task-mistress duty is!—If so, I shall be haunted with regrets, but *you* will never repent. Have no fear of that. You have chosen the roughest road, but it goes straight to the hill-tops.[34]

Here is a British everyman, albeit of a certain class, who is an amateur, called into service, and performs as he is expected: to ride off to war to save the empire and civilization. He is an ordinary man who becomes an extraordinary model for later heroes who arise, like the knights of old during times of adversity or crisis. We will encounter him again later not only in the character of James Bond, but also in American heroes who emanate both from Bond, American Westerns and superhero comic books—figures who embody the ethos of imperium and mission.

For Hannay, the mission is reflective of a philosophy propagated by the British public school education that encouraged young stalwarts to serve God and country and prepare for life in the Empire. To accept the "White Man's Burden," and, as a later critic would write, "unhesitatingly the beneficent gift of the Almighty—the glorious iron crown of Duty," to carry the "banner of the cross to the colonies, and with strong arm, iron will and earnest purpose guard the empire from those dual evils of degeneracy: effeminacy and vice" were the goals of the day.[35]

The themes of inculcating the imperialist ethos and extolling the "White Man's Burden" along with "The Great Game"—securing Afghanistan for the British Raj, in the British public school tradition—come together in the boys stories that were published during the nineteenth century. These are tales of adventure, pursuit, and escape in the midst of omnipresent danger in exotic imperial locales, as in the stories of Robert Louis Stevenson, Henry Rider Haggard, author of *King Solomon's Mines* (dedicated to "all the big boys who read it"), and Rudyard Kipling, all published during the height of the Empire. The stories glorify British imperialism and exhort young Britons to sail off to far-off places, to convert, educate, and modernize the backward.[36] Heroes not only save the world, but, even more important, they also enrich their own characters by the quest and the adventure.[37]

This mission was carried over into the spy novels and thrillers that became a staple of the popular culture coming of age in the twentieth century. Richard Hannay, like his later incarnations—James Bond, for one—is the individual embodiment of this British ideal and operates on a global stage. In other novels, Buchan has Hannay thwart an attempt by the Germans to transmit a scourge of anthrax, prevent a revolution in South America, and retrieve British defense plans stolen by German agents. In each case, he performs his duty admirably, and although he is a spy, Hannay fulfills his patriotic commitments with a character and spirit inculcated in the British public school. Traditions of team sports, disdain for ideas, unblinking loyalty, a "certain hauteur," and even cold showers were cultivated for future rulers of the Empire.[38] In the course of duty, the British agent will be morally and physically tried; when he wins, he will not only be victorious, but also, an "improved" person. Spying, like school games, is deemed a sport and, like school games, the mission must be played out to the end of one's endurance for the good of the experience. In this war, the boys would be ready when spying became an honorable enterprise.

This view of self—"Britishness" and spying—was encouraged by Sir Robert Baden-Powell,[39] founder of the Boy Scouts, who compared military scouting to games, and suggested that the skills be taught in school. He had served in most of Britain's imperial wars at the end of the nineteenth century, operated as a military spy in Dalmatia, Turkey, Germany, Austria, and Russia, and collected information on troop movements, fortifications, and weapons before World War I. Like Buchan, Baden-Powell wrote books to supplement his income, but he emphasized his experiences as a spy and as a guerrilla. In books such as *Aids to Scouting, Scouting Games, and My Adventures as a Spy*, Baden-Powell likened military scouting to games (hide and seek) and encouraged educators to instruct boys in the skills of observation, camouflage, and deduction, which he would later inculcate through the Boy Scout movement. He stressed the art of detection and frequently compared the art of war to the solution of puzzles and the detection of crime. "The instructor should read to the would-be scouts a detective tale from Gaboriau or Conan Doyle (Sherlock Holmes)," he wrote, "laying special stress on the clues to the crime, and deduction therefrom."[40] He should examine the boys to see that they have grasped the idea of drawing conclusions from small signs.

Moreover, warfare was like a game and spying was a most private sport practiced by boys of every nationality—creating a brotherhood much like the military officer corps. "There is a fascination which gets hold of anyone who has tried the art," he maintained.[41] Therefore, every spy is a good spy, even the enemy. In the best school spirit, Richard Hannay, Buchan's spy extraordinaire, declares of his loathsome adversary in *Greenmantle*, the infamous Colonel Stumm: "My anger had completely gone and I had no particular ill-will left against Stumm. He was a man of remarkable qualities." After all, Stumm is an officer who plays the game, plays it well, and even though he loses and Hannay despises his life-style, the British officer has to respect the German for his effort.[42]

This camaraderie, the *esprit de corps* among the officer class no matter whether or not they are allies or enemies, is played out time and again in spy novels. In the series by J. Railton Holden written later about World War I, Australian fliers stationed along the Suez Canal allow the Turkish pilot Suliman to escape after an amicable discussion over tea about their common bonds as officers who, regardless of nationality, fight according to the proper rules of engagement: "Do you think, my friend, that others would have taken the same sporting action as you?" queries Suliman. "We of the Air Force play cricket as you say, we use not poison gas, nor the flame thrower, nor the poisoning of wells. We kill in fair fight, man to man." When Spider reports to his commanding officer that he allowed the Turk to escape because it was "he who pulled my pal out of the blazing machine, not me," his commander tells him that he would have "done exactly what you did."[43]

We see the behavior again when the British Captain Miller, in Rex Adams' *Star of Persia*, which refers back to events in 1918, must release Wadmuss [read Wassmuss] after capture at the Khyber Pass.

> "Some day, when this war is over, perhaps we shall meet again—in Heidelberg or London—and drink a toast to each other, but until then, good-bye and good luck, Captain Miller," he concluded as he held out his hand. Miller gripped it hard; he could not but admire this man's courage and patriotism.
>
> "Good-bye, Herr Wadmuss, and good luck to you. I sincerely hope we shall have the pleasure of meeting again under better circumstances than this . . . ."[44]

We encounter it again in the military tech novels that appeared at the end of the twentieth century—a respect almost begrudgingly expressed by Americans for their Arab pilot counterparts.

It is clear that Buchan's hero Hannay will agree to save Britain from danger and will surrender his chance at participating in the big show for a lone adventure that no one may ever know about. In the end, viewing the results of his detection and analysis of the clues along the site of the last battle between the Russian Cossacks and the German led Turks at Erzerum, Hannay becomes energized, glorying in the fact that his and his colleagues' work will live on. "It's the job that matters," he declares, "not the men that do it . . . We have won, old chap—won hands down—and there is no going back on that."

But Sandy Arbuthnot needs more. After all, he is the quintessential mole, that undercover agent who has that special British ability, notably exemplified in Rudyard Kipling's novel, *Kim*, which enables him to absorb alien cultures without being assimilated by them. "He rode through Yemen," Bullivant explains to Hannay,

> which no white man ever did before. The Arabs let them pass, for they thought him stark raving mad and argued that the hand of Allah was heavy enough on him without their efforts.

The Turks know about him; but, after every mission, he disappears into thin air: "You say he's in your battalion. I was wondering what had become of him, for we tried to get hold of him here, but he had left no address . . ."[45] When Sandy reappears in England, he is a complementary character to Hannay—an undercover agent who can meld with the locals without totally "going native," but who also has the ability to carry off ethnic dissimulation that makes him invaluable for the mission. This uniquely British trait stands them well—Bullivant continues, resulting in the British Empire, for

> we are the only race on earth that can produce men capable of getting inside the skin of remote peoples. Perhaps the Scots are better than the English, but we're all a thousand per cent better than anybody else. Sandy was the wandering Scot carried to the pitch of genius. In old days he would have led a crusade or discovered a new road to the Indies. To-day he merely roamed as the spirit moved him, till the war swept him up and dumped him down in my battalion.[46]

Whether or not he was modeled on T. E. Lawrence or Aubery Herbert, or Percy Cox, for that matter, Arbuthnot is cut of the same cloth. After all, it was John Buchan who sent Lowell Thomas to the Middle East to find the stuff of heroic propaganda. Thomas returned with Lawrence of Arabia who had been sent to lead the Arabs in rebellion against the Turks.[47] Like these bearers of British cultural imperialism and racial superiority, Sandy uses "the badge of Britishness as a passport to all kinds of cultural feasts and voyages of self-discovery."[48]

A throwback to nineteenth century chivalry before the dehumanizing industrialization of warfare, Arbuthnot embodies Lord Curzon's belief in the ennobling and invigorating stimulus for youth in imperial service "on the outskirts of Empire, where the machine is relatively impotent and the individual is strong . . . saving them alike from the corroding ease and the morbid excitements of Western civilization."[49] He combines adventure, linguistic expertise, and daring on his mission to the Ottoman Empire: "The Turk and the Persian wouldn't follow the ordinary new theology game," he tells Hannay. "He must be of the Blood. Your Mahdis and Mullahs and Imams were nobodies, but they had only a local prestige. To capture all Islam—and I gather that is what we fear—the man must be of the Koreish, the tribe of the Prophet himself."[50]

Left to his own devices until the heroes meet in Turkey, Sandy joins a secret dervish order, is tapped by German agent Hilda von Einem to be her candidate for Mahdi, and is able, almost single-handedly, to thwart the conspiracy in the end. Through it all, and despite the challenges and enticements to join the other side, he never forgets who he is. Even though the German agent tries to convince him to join her—"You are of my household in spirit, and you alone of all men I have seen are fit to ride with me on my mission. Germany may fail, but I shall not fail." She offers him the "greatest career" that any mortal has ever known, yet he tells her that he is a British officer. "You can offer me nothing that I desire," he said. "I am the servant of my country, and her enemies are mine. I can have neither part nor lot with you. That is my answer, Madam von Einem."[51]

Where Hannay, who, when the conspiracy is thwarted, is content to leave the arena after the game is over and his team has won, Arbuthnot cannot resist becoming Greenmantle, if only for a little while, to see the ruse through to the end, and to sense the adulation of control. Turban on his head, he leads his troops in the charge against the Germans and the Turkish armies riding "like one possessed." "And as he rode, it seemed that the fleeing Turks were stricken still, and sank by the roadside with eyes strained after his unheeding figure . . . ."[52]

Hannay and Arbuthnot, Buchan's spies, moles, and double agents created the paradigm for later heroes in spy novels throughout the twentieth century. The "Islamic conspiracy" that he introduced in *Greenmantle* evolved through the twentieth century in crime fiction. For Buchan, while "Islam" was clearly a possible threat to the West, it could also be channeled and controlled by it—if not by Germany, then certainly by Britain. Muslims were waiting for a leader. "I knew that the prophecy had been true," Hannay exclaims upon seeing the mob follow Sandy at Erzerum, "and that their prophet had not failed them. The long-looked for revelation had come. Greenmantle had appeared at last to an awaiting people."[53] The idea that Muslims were supine and ripe for domination and that *jihad* could be used by others for their own interests is a theme played out in novels until the Iranian Islamic Revolution.

Greenmantle **was an instant success.** Published in 1916 on the heels of his *The Thirty-Nine Steps*, the initial print run sold 30,000 out of the 35,000 copies printed. More than 50,000 copies were sold of a cheaper edition, published two years later. It was the most popular of Buchan's books and was said to have provided solace to the incarcerated Tsar Nicholas II who read the novel while awaiting his doom.[54] Sir Robert Baden-Powell, creator of the Boy Scouts, was a fan, as was U.S. President Theodore Roosevelt. The novel delivered what readers wanted, to the point that during the interwar period, everyone fantasized about being Richard Hannay, the amateur turned professional spy. By that time, the exploits of T.E. Lawrence, managed by Lowell Thomas for mass receptivity, had become part of Anglo-American popular culture and his wartime adventures as a British agent actively participating in the Arab Revolt against the Turks—blowing up trains and bridges in an exotic locale while in Oriental dress—together with his work as a spy and participant in the peace conference at Versailles that ended World War I—all coalesced with the growing popularity of the fictional government agent whose exploits took him far from England throughout the reaches of the British empire.

Despite the plethora of real spies, conspiracies, and action during World War I, and despite the success of *Greenmantle*, the "war to end all wars" generated only a few spy novels set in the Middle East.[55] By the 1920s, the "Great Game" in the Middle East and Central Asia was over, imperial politics changed, and with them, so did fictional plots. The World War I victors redrew the map, and instead of colonies, they granted themselves mandates: The French occupied most of North Africa and controlled Syria and Lebanon; the British ruled directly or indirectly Palestine, Trans-Jordan, and Iraq. In the real world, policing rather than espionage held sway; there was scant opportunity for Lawrencian adventures in newly emerging states ruled by bureaucrats and the regular military.

Buchan's model for the spy novel survived throughout the interwar years because of the empire and the rising power of Soviet Russia and Nazi Germany. Very few crime fiction novels about the Middle East appeared, however, and for the most part, they are mysteries that could be set anywhere in the region. After all, British readers were quite familiar with events occurring in Egypt and Palestine from newspapers served with their morning tea and breakfast. They read about the tens of thousands of boys serving the flag throughout His Majesty's Empire in the Fertile Crescent, the Gulf, Asia Minor, and North Africa. These lands were already familiar to the British upper-class traveler whose well-honed cultural snobbery persisted and could be activated at any point: "Who do you suppose would take a soapbox? Certainly not a native. They aren't bothered with cleanliness or godliness either for that matter."[56] Plots stressed the political and were only related to the fear of Islamic unity and *jihad* when the British perceived that "Islam" had crossed the line from religion to politics. The idea of a religious/political way of life was an alien concept. In these novels, British rule and political policy in the area are taken as givens. It is only when Muslims threaten British power that they cannot be tolerated. Then it is the job of the agent, in spite of his empathy for local custom, to protect British interests in the area. It is in this context that the next significant manipulation of Islam occurs in Sax Rohmer's *The Mask of Fu Manchu.*

THREE

Holy War and Empire

FU MANCHU IN CAIRO

Buchan created the paradigm for spy novels that appeared during the interwar period. With their heroes smiting foes of the British Empire throughout the world, novels could be set anywhere—in essence presaging the thrillers that emerged during the 1960s with the popularity of James Bond.

When the theme of a Muslim holy war against the West did appear in fiction published after World War I, authors, more often than not, set their plots in North Africa, evoking the rebellion of Abd al-Qadir who led a *jihad* against the French conquest of Algeria in 1838. Largely unread today, these novels spun tales of anti-Western uprisings and British-backed conspiracies against the French. One author, John Henry Harvey, writing under the pseudonym "Operator 1384," drew on his service in the French Foreign Legion and added holy war to his tales of gunrunning, slave auctions, and drug smuggling. Swaggering "devil-may-care" legionnaires in their bright uniforms are juxtaposed with "the naked, dirty Arab children playing in the white heat, the flea-ridden curs which slunk along the streets snapping and snarling at all who approached them, the soft shuffle of slippered feet served to remind the young men that this was indeed the changeless East . . . ."[1] His "mahdi" villain in *The Son of Allah* (an unlikely title for a Muslim to be sure) bids his followers to be "strong and faithful to Allah and Mohammed, His Prophet, and surely shall the blood of the Infidels flow in torrents and only their corpses be left in our land for the vultures to feed on."[2]

Author Graham Seton sets a more fanciful tone. His hero, Colonel Grant, is given the opportunity to get back into the "Great Game", "to be fated as a victorious Roberts at Kandahar, a Kitchener at Khartoum . . ." by leading an anti-French mahdist conspiracy was an irresistible offer. The twist here was that the Colonel, a Scot, would command a tribe composed of descendants of Scottish mariners shipwrecked off the coast near Tangier in the seventeenth century who subsequently dominated tribesmen in the Atlas Mountains and led them to fight France, Britain's historical imperial competitor in the Middle East and North Africa.[3]

For the most part, however, in the few novels about the Middle East, British heroes are more concerned with keeping peace in the territories they awarded themselves as victors in World War I—that is, unless the Empire itself is threatened.[4]

In the 1930s, however, fiction fans read once again that tribes were on the march on the Afghan border and that a dangerous movement was "creeping south day by day." During his travels from Iraq and on his way to India and then to Iran, former assistant commissioner of Scotland Yard Sir Denis Nayland Smith in Sax Rohmer's *The Mask of Fu Manchu* heard rumors about an Islamic movement threatening British interests. "Heaven knows we had tough trouble before," he reports, "but now that the tribes are rising in response to a mad rumor that El Mokanna, the Masked Prophet, has come out of his tomb to lead them . . . ."[5] The British are truly worried, because a "religious revival is overdue among the Moslems, and this business may fill the bill . . . Superstition is never very far below the surface in even the most cultured Oriental. And these waves of fanaticism are really incalculable. It's a kind of hypnotism, and we know the creative power of thought."[6]

Could this cataclysmic threat be related to the murder of a British Orientalist found lying in a pool of blood in the city of Isphahan? Were the relics he found—"a sword or scimitar of Damascus steel inlaid with gold having a curved, double-edged blade and the hilt encrusted with emeralds, rubies, and pearls . . ." and "a mask of thin gold finely engraved; and fifteen thin gold plates sixteen inches long by twelve inches wide, bearing the text of the New Koran of El Mokanna"[7]—that were now missing, real or copies made by master Isphahani craftsman Solomon Ishak? The trail leads Smith from Persia to Cairo where the leader of the holy war is waiting to secure the authentic relics. In this novel, *The Mask of Fu Manchu*, the plot does not concern Turkey during the World War I; rather, it is Cairo, cultural heart and seat of British Middle East imperial rule during the interwar period, that comes under attack. The puppeteer attempting to dupe the Muslims into *jihad* against Britain is not a Westerner but a most unlikely villain—the Chinese "devil-doctor," Dr. Fu Manchu.

What is significant about *The Mask of Fu Manchu* is not only that it builds on the *jihad* plots but that it provides an illustration of British colonial rule in the Middle East just before de-colonization. It was also written by a best-selling author, Sax Rohmer, who, despite the fact that he wrote a number of works about Egypt, was hardly associated with novels about the Middle East. Better known for his anti-Chinese caricatures ("Yellow Peril"), Rohmer, *nom de plume* of Arthur Sarsfield Ward (1883–1959), was one of the most adept practitioners of the art of the Gothic and a master of fantasy and the occult. He is most closely identified with his series of novels that feature the Chinese super villain—the evil "devil-doctor" Fu Manchu, whom he introduced to his readership in 1912. His plots rely on the exotic and use outrageously stereotypical villains. Most of his novels focus on Asia, calling to mind the fear of the "Yellow Peril," and are grounded in the battle for supremacy between the Asian East and the European West.

By the time *The Mask of Fu Manchu* appeared in 1932, Rohmer already had a devoted readership on both sides of the Atlantic. The Fu Manchu novels about the Chinese arch-villain—leader of an international conspiratorial mafia and master of disguises who employed unique methods of murder, were later made into films, comic strips, and radio and television serials.[8] His detractors label his work racist and "absolute rubbish."[9] Rohmer's defenders maintain that writing about the Chinese instead of Russian anarchists or the Mafia allowed the author the use of characters, customs, backgrounds, locales, dress, and modes of death that were opportunities for the exciting writing that drew in his readers.[10] Ian Fleming was a fan and his James Bond novels reflect Rohmer's influence.[11] The Fu Manchu novels not only remain popular today, but they are collectables. The number of websites devoted to the exploits of the Chinese villain is on the rise.

At twenty, Rohmer, who was born in Ireland and raised in England, was already publishing short stories drawing on his life-long fascination with Egyptology, Islam, Arabic, Richard Burton's version of *The Thousand and One Nights*, the occult, the work of the magician Houdini, and other esoteric disciplines that he would later incorporate in his work about the Middle East.[12] One of his first stories, "The Mysterious Mummy," told of secret societies, medieval alchemy, and the transmission of esoteric knowledge.[13] For these and his later work, Rohmer drew on the Gothic literary tradition from such early practitioners of the art as Wilkie Collins (1824–1889) and Edgar Allan Poe (1809–1849) who played with the fanciful and the fantastic.

In Collins' *Moonstone* (1868), credited with being the first full-length English detective novel, there is the juxtaposition of reality with fantasy. The detective-hero encounters "Orientals" and a jewel with a curse. Poe's graphic "The Mask of the Red Death" engenders terror evocative of Gothic novels and horror stories that were evolving on a parallel track. These are not the love stories of modern romance novels which transport readers to a glamorous world where the heroine finds true love in the arms of a handsome sheikh. Rather, they are books of "violence, shootings, and stabbings, of wild chases by land, sea, and air," set in places like "frowning castles on the Appenines . . . [the] world of villainous monks, imprisoned beauties, magic potions, and jeweled daggers."[14] The Fu Manchu novels combined elements of these tales of the occult with espionage. Using relics as objects of power, Rohmer presents supernatural villains that were fantastic, almost like fairy-tale giants and witches who seemed to be an easy match for the Western hero who operates within the confines of scientific rationalism. The docile and almost inept British officer barely saves the West from the "Yellow Peril" or worse.

In 1911, after working at a bank and for a gas company, writing some fiction, newspaper articles and lyrics for music hall productions, Rohmer was asked to write an article on a notorious crime figure in the Chinese neighborhood in London called the Limehouse.[15] For British readers, the East End of London was like the "Dark Continent," the "microcosmic battlefield of Imperial neuroses." During the last decades of the nineteenth century, it had become the "Empire" for journalists and fiction writers and was as inscrutable to their readers as China itself. Tales of British heroes fighting against international crime, white slavery, and drugs in the city were popular at a time when Chinese and Japanese illusionists, jugglers, and acrobats played the music halls.[16] Two Chinese characters, Ching Ling Foo and Ching Ling Soo (later discovered to be an American imposter) were popular on both sides of the Atlantic. So, too, were the exploits of Harry Houdini, the master illusionist, with whom Rohmer corresponded as early as 1915. London's Chinatown and the music hall provided the material that would later be incorporated into the Fu Manchu stories.[17]

Other "Sinister Orientals" had already been developed by such writers as Edgar Wallace (1875–1932) and Roland Daniel (1880–1969), but Rohmer's Fu Manchu is a genius of villainy and head of his own world-wide criminal organization, the Si-Fan, dedicated to the dominance of the Orient and the conquest of the West. Fu Manchu has at his disposal esoteric knowledge unknown to Western science, including potions to increase longevity and bizarre agents of death—worms, scorpions, pythons, fungi, bacilli, and spiders—as well as an international coterie of cutthroat followers: dacoits from Burma, thugs from India, *hashishin* from Syria and Iran, and zombies from Haiti. Combined with the occult, an ever-popular element in escapist literature, the "sinister Oriental" plots that Rohmer used were popular reading of the day.

Asians were easily digestible villains both in Britain and in the United States, where experience of the "Yellow Peril" was part of a Sino-phobic historic consciousness more potent than Muslims or Islamic holy war. The Chinese were at once strange, unknowable, foreign, and culturally threatening while Islam had been dominated and was supposedly controllable. The Chinese had defied the British during the Boxer Rebellion and Asian immigration was so threatening to America that plots depicting the potential control of the West by the diabolical Chinese mad scientist were perfectly believable. Asians evoked images of yellow hordes overrunning Europe or California. These were the stereotypical Chinese coolies, virtual slaves living together in barracks and thus a threat to white women, who competed with honest American workers and morally corrupted the Christian Anglo-Saxon Westerners. Rooted in Christian historical memory of the Mongol invasions some seven centuries earlier, these stereotypes were immortalized by medieval monks who wrote of atrocities committed by the unstoppable Genghis Khan and his mounted horsemen, who overwhelmed eastern Christendom as if delivering a punishment from the Almighty.[18]

Fu Manchu, the super-villain, captivated Anglo-American imaginations, and Hollywood exploited his villainy: He had "menace in every twitch of his finger, a threat in every twitch of his eyebrow, terror in each split-second of his slanted eyes."[19] "Imagine," we read in *The Insidious Fu Manchu*

> a person, tall, lean and feline, high shouldered, with a brow like Shake-speare and a face like Satan, a close-shaven skull, and long, magnetic eyes of the true cat-green. Invest him with all the cruel cunning of an entire Eastern race, accumulated in one giant intellect, with all of the resources, if you will, of a wealthy government—which, however, already has denied all knowledge of his existence. Imagine that awful being, and you have a mental picture of Dr. Fu-Manchu, the yellow peril incarnate in one man.[20]

He was merciless, adept at torture, revengeful, a master of unknown drugs, and "lord of a vast army of thugs and slaves ready to do his worst bidding. He was so evil that periodically he had to be killed off, and was so mysteriously super powerful that he always reappeared in time for the next episode." He also disappeared and returned as American relations with China waxed and waned.[21] At the end of the first three books, Fu Manchu is apparently killed, but re-appeared only to retire during the 1920s. In 1930, he re-emerged with *Daughter of Fu Manchu* and, two years later, *The Mask of Fu Manchu*. He then "hibernated" during World War II,[22] only to return as an anti-Communist in the 1950s.

Rohmer's *The Mask of Fu Manchu* is significant because it continues the *Greenmantle* theme of the malleable Muslim easily manipulated by a superior cultural force to commit *jihad*, albeit, in this case, an Asian instead of a European. In the novel, Rohmer combined the modern espionage novel with the occult, and added the villainy of Fu Manchu to the threat of Islamic Holy War against British rule in Egypt. Except for *Daughter of Fu Manchu* and *The Mask of Fu Manchu*, however, both of which take place in Egypt, Rohmer's earlier works set in the Middle East have been largely ignored to the point where the seeming incongruity between the Chinese villain and a Middle Eastern setting is best illustrated by the changes Hollywood made to the film version. Released soon after the book appeared, *The Mask of Fu Manchu* film starring Boris Karloff omits all hints of an Islamic Holy War and the action occurs in Asia instead of Egypt. American filmmakers substituted the mask of the Muslim El Mokanna, for the funerary mask and sword of Genghis Khan with which Fu Manchu plans to unite Asia and take over the world. It is clear that to Hollywood, the Chinese manipulation of Muslims and the threats of Islamic holy war would not sell as many tickets as would a movie about the "Yellow Peril." Americans had not yet entered the Middle Eastern political arena.

Much like *Greenmantle*, Rohmer's *The Mask of Fu Manchu* presents Muslims as part of the British colonial worldview: that is, both as a defeated Islam that is at once docile and supine, awaiting manipulation by a superior race, and the belief that rational Muslims under colonial tutelage could be prepared for admittance into the modern Western world. Rohmer, who also worked for British Intelligence during World War I, introduces agents in the Hannay mold who stand as bulwarks of Western civilization against the Oriental threat. Here, however, the comparison ends. Where Buchan was influenced by his Presbyterian upbringing and the British mission of empire, Rohmer drew on his interests in Egyptology, the occult, magic, Oriental studies, and his own recollections of a British imperial Cairo that ended with World War II.

Unlike China, which he never visited, Rohmer did travel in 1913 to Egypt where he honeymooned in Cairo, visited the pyramids, Luxor and Thebes, and began to write about the region. In the *Brood of the Witch Queen*,

Ancient Egyptian sorcery is at work, but the characters are all European. In *Hassan of Aleppo* or *The Quest of the Sacred Slipper*, published first as short stories and later in book form, the ancient Order of the Assassins (*Hashishin*) operates in England where they punish those who have stolen from Mecca a slipper believed to have been worn by the Prophet Muhammad. The theft of sacred relics is a common theme in successful Oriental thrillers.[23] Surprisingly, Rohmer did not capitalize on the discovery in 1922 of King Tut's tomb with horror stories and mummy tales. Instead, the two books with Egyptology themes, *She Who Sleeps* and *The Bat Flies Low,* involve a scam perpetrated against an American antiques collector and the use of ancient esoteric Egyptian knowledge to produce cheap electricity.

Throughout his life, Rohmer retained a nostalgic affection for colonial Egypt—refusing to return after World War II because the "gracious life of Cairo had vanished forever."[24] By 1950, other authors would describe Cairo's atmosphere not as romanticized exoticism, but as menace, where the "swarming natives in their mud hovels" were only a few moments from the best hotels and the fantastic pyramids. "You felt it in the *Mouski,* the native bazaars where you could buy anything you could name if you had the price," Stephen Hunt, Bruce Kneale's hero, says in *Appointment in Cairo,* where he is sent to stop a British Nazi bent on spreading anti-British propaganda—

> where you rubbed shoulders with men of many races who jostled you as they went by. At night, maybe, more than any other time, you felt it as you walked the banks of the Nile, watching the feluccas, their clumsy outlines softened by darkness, drifting down its dusky waters, masts and great sweeping sail boats slashing the clear high sky with sharp black outlines. While in shadows tiny lights flickered and river men sang softly the eerie tuneless songs of their country and natives brushed past you in the darkness.
>
> There is a feeling about the place, Hunt thought, remembering these things, and I don't like it. I don't like it because in some way it's evil.[25]

For Rohmer, however, the city still had its quasi-Western cosmopolitan flavor. Like most British turn-of-the-twentieth-century travelers to the region, he stayed at Shepheard's Hotel, visited the tourist attractions, traveled to Luxor and Thebes, and was thoroughly taken with the gracious life of 1913 Cairo, which at that time had become a Europeanized city, leaving just enough local color so that the European traveler could report that he *saw* the Orient, but without having become a part of it. With the onset of the tourist season, "this quiet spot in which we sat would be bustling with busy, international life . . . Dragomans, sellers of beads, of postcards and of scarabs would be thick as flies around the doors of the hotels. Thomas Cook's dahabîyehs would moor at the landing places; fashionable women would hurry here and there, apparently busy, actually idle; white-suited men, black-robed guides—bustle—excitement."[26]

After the British occupation of Egypt in 1882, the city was split physically between Islamic Cairo and British Cairo, reflecting East and West—the medieval, Oriental Casbah and the European city given its *belle époque* veneer by French and Italian architects.[27] Focused on the Opera Square, the Azbakiyya Gardens, the government buildings of Ataba Square, and the banks, hotels, and luxury shops filled with European goods in the Ismailia Quarter, the tourist could easily ignore the unsightly if he wished. After all, "to whatever government, Turkish, French, British, or Egyptian, the people may from time to time acknowledge obedience, everybody knows that Egypt really belongs to Thomas Cook & Son."[28] By 1908, visitors reported that there was nothing "native" in the Ismailia Quarter except perhaps for a "Sudanese porter seated on the bench outside a sumptuous mansion, half-hidden by palms and tropical shrubs."[29] One had to venture into the Oriental part of the city in order to see native Muslims and whirling dervishes.[30]

As the British intensified their rule, they transferred their class system to the European part of the city. For the expats, being invited to dinner and dance at the Residency was the greatest mark of prestige. With polo, dancing, racing and riding, Cairo was more like "an English town in which any quantity of Oriental sights are kept for the aesthetic satisfaction of the inhabitants, much as the proprietor of a country place keeps a game preserve or deer park for his amusements."[31] The British may have worked with the more westernized Egyptians, but generally they were able to ignore them outside of the office. Social professionals—much like Mr. Wendover Wright in Percy White's mystery *Cairo*, published just before World War I—designated which ladies and gentlemen would make the *Gezirah Gazette* and who should be invited to dine and dance at the Residency. Mr. Wendover Wright knew their "places, their marriages, the extent of their incomes. Unless lost in a dim middle-class environment, he could generally give outlines of their careers."[32] He was most concerned with Anne Donne's taking up with one Abdul Sayed, an obvious Egyptian social climber who, although he might be a Pasha and an Oxford man, was, nonetheless," Wendover tells Mrs. Donne, "a native. You can't change that, and this chap has managed to get out of his place."[33]

This fictional encounter echoed the view of British historian Stanley Lane-Poole writing in 1892 about Westernized natives: "They dance with foreign ladies, wear Frankish clothes, smoke cigarettes, enjoy French plays and, but for their Eastern habits of tyranny, peculation, insincerity and corruption, they might for all the world be Europeans."[34] But beneath it all, they revert to type during a crisis: When Ann refuses his offer of marriage, Sayed Bey sheds his Westernized rational veneer and can only think emotionally—of vengeance against the West that had drawn him in only to reject him once he had succeeded, or so he thought, in becoming part of it.[35]

Despite considerable investment in the westernization process, the anglicized, Western-educated Muslim native is not accepted in British society. Not quite an opposite, he is not quite English either, despite the Oxford education, the title, the car, and the clothes. He may have redeeming qualities, but there is "slippage"—something is lacking. Instead of the "Other," he is, to borrow a term from Homi Bhabha, a "Mimic," the "subject of a difference that is almost the same, but not quite." He at once resembles the Westerner, but is at the same time a menace to the West.[36] We meet him time and again as the colonial tradition was rendered in fiction in the form of a certain hauteur toward "natives," who were not necessarily villains, but objects of British slur—frequently rendered "niggers" or "coolies," even if they were Westernized Oriental gentlemen: "The fellow talked like a book," we are told in Jepson's *The Death Gong*. "Your Oxfordized foreigner usually does—and loves to hear himself at it." Only reluctantly does the young English lord Sir John Perrin accept the Arab's assistance in his escape—for a substantial contribution to the Arab's French bank account, of course, for Hafiz was a "suave polished Europeanized Moslem, sporting a monocle through which he surveyed me critically. His black hair was brushed back from his high forehead, and glistened with a perfumed brilliantine which assailed my nostrils unpleasantly. An oily brute, altogether. He fingered a string of lapis beads and smiled ceaselessly."[37]

By the turn of the twentieth century, Cairo demographics made the social situation even more complicated. In addition to the Egyptians who were receiving a Western education in mission and foreign schools and then taking their places in the burgeoning government bureaucracies or retaining their places among the Ottomanized elite that was in power through most of the nineteenth century, the number of foreigners in general was growing. The British had taken over fiscal and political control of the country from a dynasty permitted to govern the country by the Ottoman Empire and the Great Powers. Muhammad Ali, a former Albanian officer, who remained in Egypt after the defeat of Napoleon's army in 1801, consolidated power, jump-started the economy and tried through the creation of factories and schools to bring Egypt into the modern world. He experienced military defeat, however, upon reaching too far in his occupation of Syria (1832–1840). Also, a spending spree—his grandson Isma'il built opera houses, palaces, and new neighborhoods—forced the Egyptian government to sell Egypt's stock in the Suez Canal. Defaulting on loans to its European creditors, in 1882 Egypt was occupied by British forces. The British governed Egypt through the illusion of an independent government, but in truth, the British agent and consul general, the first of whom being Evelyn Baring (later Lord Cromer), ruled the country through British advisors and a cadre of bureaucrats attached to Egyptian ministries. Statesmen and diplomats implemented official policy while soldiers and policemen obeyed orders and did their duty, often to the ire of the local population. With the British occupation came civil servants, businessmen, venture capitalists, and speculators of all nationalities.[38] They joined the Christians and Jews who had already gravitated to Cairo from the eastern Mediterranean since the time of the United States Civil War, when Egyptian cotton became king on the world market.

By 1910, an eighth of the city's 700,000 people were from some place else, many arriving from Italy, Greece, and Central European capitals looking for economic opportunity in British occupied Egypt. As part of the newly emerging middle class, they were the tailors, dressmakers, pharmacists, photographers, physicians, and translators. They opened department stores and ran luxury boutiques. Some became bankers and many staffed the colonial bureaucracy and the offices of British agencies that imported cars, textiles, and sold insurance. Often they served as intermediaries between the British occupiers and their Muslim subjects. Their children attended Italian, French, and British schools while the parents aspired to social connections with the *haute bourgeoisie*, membership at the Gezirah Sporting Club, and dinner at the Residency.

These people were the Levantine class that lived in the Mediterranean coastal cities along the southern and eastern shores. The term "Levantine," probably coined by the French in the sixteenth century from the word *levant* or from a rising sun in the east, connoted neither Muslim nor Copt, but rather the children of Italian, French, or English parents who intermarried with Greeks or Armenians, Syro-Lebanese Christians, Cypriots, or Middle Eastern Jews. By the early twentieth century, the term had accrued pejorative connotations of profiteering, distasteful business dealings, and déclassé social climbing. Such characterizations are played out in the crime fiction of the period. Once again, a look at White's novel *Cairo* provides a glimpse of British disdain for these poseurs. Committing another faux pas, Mrs. Donne attends a dinner party hosted by an attorney, Mr. Andrew Kepple. Also known as "Colquhoun Kepple," he is a "flamboyant product of the Levant, whose late father had been known to the police and the liquor traffic as Andrea Keppalos" and whose grandfather, a Yorkshire navy man who had become a contractor and swindled the Egyptian government in Ishmail Pasha's time, only to be found drowned in the Suez Canal a few weeks before its opening.[39] Kepple had a "dubious Order of Merit awarded by the hooknose secretary of an obscure Legation whom he had helped to a loan of 2,000 francs in Paris. . . ."[40] The dinner was quite funny, she recounts:

> You should have been there to see the Comtesse in flame-coloured chiffon eating peas with her knife! They were all so full of surprises, too! Captain Tosti tells me that his mother was born at Cork and he at Corfu. Irish wit, he says, and Italian subtlety are splendid ingredients in character. He takes quite an eugenic view of his personal value . . . . Mr. Levy told me he wasn't sure whether his father would welcome his approaching marriage with the distinguished member of the old French nobility whom he was about to make his bride, and the young Syrian wife of Mr. Stavros, the white-bearded patriarch, was so ashamed of her bare plump shoulders—it was, she confessed, her first low dress—that she hid as much of her bare skin as her plump hands could cover whenever Captain Tosti rolled his eyes in her direction. I wouldn't have missed the dinner for anything, Mr. Addington. I hadn't a dull moment. Think of what you've missed . . .[41]

The British viewed the Levantines not only as not quite European, but also as transmitters of the worst of Western civilization's greed. They corrupted the "purer, more spiritual and more wholesome" bona fide Arabs. The British idealized the pure Arab and demonized those of mixed or indeterminate lineage or ethnicity.[42] In fiction, they are portrayed at best as distasteful characters, though more often as outright evildoers. In Alex Weigall's novel *The King Who Preferred Moonlight*, for example, the hall porter in the Ismail Pasha hotel, of faded magnificence but once "a palace of that mid-Victorian potentate, which stood within its overgrown, untidy gardens on the sun-baked Egyptian sea coast," is a Levantine of mixed Hungarian and Polish ancestry. He:

... combined with the appearance of a broken-hearted Balkan bandit the speech of a Cockney, having been born and bred in Soho, London, where his father had opened a very small restaurant, and having come to Egypt in the days of Sir Garnet Wolseley in connection with the commissariat of the British army. He had a large bird-like nose, moody dark eyes, a black and drooping comic mustache, and an olive complexion, but his uniform of white duck did not become his lean figure: he would have looked better in the black cloak and hat of a stage conspirator.[43]

It is the Levantines, not the Arabs, who remain villains through the interwar period. Cosmopolitans, be they the Hebrews in the novels of Dennis Wheatley or Sapper, both authors who wrote from a right-wing perspective, or even the Armenian Mr. Samarkan in *The Mask of Fu Manchu*, either work for the enemy or corrupt the pure Englishman.[44]

Although Rohmer incorporates all of these standard character types in his Fu Manchu novels, it is important to note here that in other books largely unread today, he introduced his readers to a modern Muslim detective—an Arab hero, a Sufi mystic who uses reason to solve mysteries, a Muslim embodying both East and West.[45] In these *Tales of Secret Egypt*, Rohmer simultaneously incorporates the occult and the rational—providing material about pharaonic Egypt so popular in the horror and adventure tales of his day—as props for the plots and tempers the stories with a dose of the rational through the interplay between the Sufi Abû Tabâh, who solves the mysteries, and the British "victim," Kernaby, who loathes the sheikh when he meets him, but grows to respect him more and more with each mystery.

The British agent for a Birmingham company that exports cheap British goods to Egypt and imports authentic replicas in the form of copies of antiquities, Kernaby stays at Shepheard's while in Cairo and is part of the British social scene. A man of moderate intelligence and naiveté, he comes into contact with all sorts of people reflective of pre-World War I Cairo: Egyptian dealers in antiquities, Jewish merchants, Levantine hashish smugglers, Muslim harem women and Christian belly dancers, and Islamic "fanatics" including dervishes of all varieties. These interactions are the catalysts for danger through which Kernaby comes into contact with Abû Tabâh, the "evil magician"—a man who strikes fear in the souls of Egyptians, and at once intrigues and repels the Englishman but in the end gains his respect:

He was, then a young man, probably under thirty, with perfectly chiseled features and a slight black mustache. He wore a black *gibbeh*, and a white

turban, and brown shoes upon his small feet. His face was that of an ascetic, nor had I ever seen more wonderful and liquid eyes; in them reposed
a world of melancholy; yet his red lips were parted in a smile tender as that
of a mother. Inclining his head in a gesture of gentle dignity, this man—
whom I hated at sight—addressed me in Arabic.

And yet, he was "poisonously suave. Beneath the placid exterior, beneath
the sugar-lipped utterances, in the deeps of gazelle-like eyes, was hid a cold
and remorseless spirit for which the man's silken demeanour was but a
cloak. I hated him more and more."[46]

In each tale, Kernaby is coincidentally thrown together with the Imam,
who first warns him of danger and then saves him from a horrible fate
when, despite precautions and despite being an Englishman, Kernaby finds
himself in trouble. Once, disguised as a street Arab in order to infiltrate
the business of a perfumer and retrieve the ingredients of the exotic perfume "Breath of Allah," Kernaby is arrested for drunkenness. He has really
been drugged, and upon awakening in jail, is enraged at not being treated
as an Englishman should be.[47] Released to the custody of Abû Tabâh, the
Imam warns him about and proceeds to rescue him from poisoned pharaonic signet rings, stolen Islamic relics, and the "strange rites" of the Black
Darwishes who induce their victims to commit suicide.

Though mystical and occult appurtenances appear throughout the tales,
Abû Tabâh uses only reason to solve the mysteries of theft and murder.
Nevertheless, Kernaby constantly wonders at his "uncanny power akin to
second sight"[48] and ponders his real identity: "That Abû Tabâh was some
kind of agent, recognized—at any rate unofficially—by the authorities,
I knew or shrewdly surmised; but the exact nature of his activities, and
how he reconciled them with his religious duties, remained profoundly
mysterious."[49]

This paradox—how to reconcile religious tradition with modernity—
shows up time and again in Rohmer's fiction. That he respected modern
Islam as practiced in the Egypt he knew is hardly in doubt. The Muslims,
such as Abû Tabâh in *Tales of Secret Egypt* and Hassan es-Sugra in *She Who
Sleeps*, are portrayed as practicing Muslims operating in the modern world.
The Englishman respects Hassan es-Sugra, the Egyptian who found the
tomb in *She Who Sleeps*. He is devout and made the pilgrimage to Mecca.
"He's quite a lot of mystery," we are told. "But he holds some kind of posi-
tion in the Moslem world that gives him complete control of the natives.
He's the best man at the job in Egypt."[50] The Englishman is "learning to

look with less satisfaction upon the hurriedly grasped successes of modern life, and to experience an unpleasant sense of inferiority in the company of this dignified, placid, yet majestic Arab."[51]

With Rohmer's stories about *Bimbashi Baruk of Egypt*, the hero may be Egyptian, but he is no longer a strict Muslim. Written more in tune with the pulp fiction of the day, Baruk is a bifurcated East-West personality who is an agent during World War II, the product of an Arab father—a sheikh of pure lineage, and an English mother. In many respects, Muhammad Ibra-him Brian Baruk, is a typical public school product, but there also "ran in his veins the blood of Muslim captains who had slain the infidel and spared not."[52] At home in both cultures, but in truth more Western than Eastern, Baruk works for British intelligence and foils Nazi plots in Syria, subverts the pro-Nazi Rashid Ali regime in Baghdad, and thwarts a holy war to be perpetrated by another imam moving west from Khorasan—not unlike the villain in Buchan's *Greenmantle* or Rohmer's own *The Mask of Fu Manchu*. "He's just an ordinary imam, or parish priest, from a mosque in Kasha, on the Khorasan frontier," Colonel Roden-Pyne tells his protégé BB, "but it seems that he thinks he has a Mission." As a result, the Germans had got hold of him. "He does his howling under cover in mosques and in the houses of sympathizers," the colonel continues,

> so that the action is difficult. It would be dangerous, too. His followers pretend to look upon him as a sort of evangelist. As I need not tell you, Islam is solidly with us against the Germans. Freaks like this fellow no more reflect upon Moslems than the Oxford Movement reflects on the Church of England. Those who listen to him are either disaffected, slightly cracked, or they are ambitious crooks. Every creed at one time or another has served as a cloak for such.[53]

Bimbashi Baruk impersonates the "Mad Mullah" and breaks up his ring of followers; removes the Japanese agent, the "infamous Mr. Ko" who financ-es the pro-German Rashid Ali in Iraq; and rescues the British correspondent when she is caught in the Libyan Desert by the Germans.

To return to The Mask of Fu Manchu, we can see how Rohmer combines the divergent British impressions of the Middle East of his day—both the positive view of the subaltern who is being Westernized or molded into a little European and the fear of the irrational, the primitive masses, whom he saw as susceptible to any charismatic leader. Despite his later disgust at

Hollywood's racist depictions in the film versions of his Fu Manchu novels, Rohmer's repugnance for the irrational masses who can be easily manipulated into *jihad* by a charismatic individual is the legacy left by his Fu Manchu series. The natives can be duped by Fu Manchu and his dervishes in *The Mask of Fu Manchu*, much as the Germans could manipulate them in *Greenmantle*. They fear curses at pyramids, relics, and omens. Modern Egyptians are graphically juxtaposed against whirling dervishes who hypnotize themselves into ecstatic trances, the Syrian leader of the Hashishin with his "fiercely hooked nose,"[54] and fanatics visiting Egypt from Isphahan.

Nayland Smith and his companion Dr. Petrie find themselves in a never-ending battle with the evil doctor: They are threatened, captured by his agents, or must thwart a scheme to foil the murder of someone else. Assisted by one of Fu Manchu's agents, the beautiful Karamaneh, who has fallen in love with Petrie, the villain is aided by dacoits and thugs and his extensive knowledge of mysterious poisons, disgusting insects, and drugs. It soon becomes clear that Sir Lionel Barton was murdered by one of Fu Manchu's minions who steals the relics from Isphahan and brings them to Cairo. It is in Cairo, the heart of British Middle East imperial interests, where Fu Manchu challenges the British and where the West meets its match. By appearing in the "golden mask," concealing his true identity as did the ancient El Mokanna (meaning "veiled one" in Arabic), the Chinese villain intends to exploit Muslim naiveté by stirring the dervishes from Shiraz to Cairo to revolt, thus simultaneously dominating Islam and toppling the British empire as he extends the diabolical reaches of his criminal organization Si-Fan ever further westward.

Obviously, in order to achieve full psychological effect, the denouement must be set in Giza, site of the Sphinx and the pyramids. There, Fu Manchu once again astounds his perennial adversary, Nayland Smith, who, standing transfixed, watches an incredible scene that unfolds before his very eyes as the top of the Great Pyramid lights up the darkness:

> I saw a tall, majestic figure, wearing either a white or a very light green robe. The face was concealed by a golden mask and surmounted by a tall turban. Upraised in the right hand glittered a sword with a curved blade
>
> . . . .
>
> A weird chanting arose from the dervishes. I didn't even glance back. I was staring—staring at that apparition on the Pyramid. Distant shouting reached me—orders, as I realized. But I knew, had known all along, that no climber could reach that point.

Then, as suddenly as it had appeared, the apparition vanished.

The lights had been extinguished, or covered; such was the conclusion to which we came later. But at the same time the effect was most uncanny. And as the figure vanished, again, from the dervishes, came a loud and now triumphant shout:

"*Mokanna!*"[55]

Of course, in the end, the British save the Muslims from themselves and the "Evil Genius" escapes only to wreak havoc yet again somewhere else.

The idea of Western manipulation of Islam lingered in fiction. Almost fifty years after the appearance of Rohmer's novel, we find this scene revisited in another political context and with a space-age update required for a novel that was written in the wake of the Iranian Islamic Revolution. The theme of A. J. Quinnell's *The Mahdi* is explicit and expressed outright in the dedication of the novel: "For all believers of Islam: that the simplicity and totality of their faith not blind them to the dangers"—in this case, the danger of being manipulated even by an empire long gone from the region. Instead of Egypt, Quinnell sets the climax of his story in Saudi Arabia where at the appointed time, and despite the anticipated malfunctions that must occur to add spice to the novel, mission control has the miracle ready. Abu Qadir (hints of Abd al-Qadir of Algeria) and his followers have assembled for the hajj (religious pilgrimage):

> There comes a moment when quivering expectation demands satisfaction, and that demand now flowed in a foaming wave from three million souls and flooded into the circle and onto the rigid man and the sacrificial goat.
>
> Slowly Abu Qadir sank to his knees, once again raised his arms, looked imploringly into the sky, and called:
>
> "A sign, Allah! Give your Mahdi a sign!"
>
> Three million pairs of eyes looked up in the clear blue evening sky and at that moment saw a perfect column of shimmering green light which bathed the valley and centered on the scrawny goat and held it illuminated for two heartbeats. Then the goat disintegrated in a cloud of expanding green smoke which rolled slowly over the rigid figure of Abu Qadir.
>
> . . . .
>
> Abu Qadir was the first to move. The green smoke had dissipated, leaving a shallow black cavity in the desert sand. He placed his hands flat down in front of him, and slowly pushed them forward until he was prostrate.

Like a wind blowing across a vast field of corn the pilgrims followed his example until the valley of Minā was carpeted in white bodies, all facing inward.

A low moaning word reverberated down to the circled figure: "Mahdi!"[56]

Though reminiscent both of *Greenmantle* and *The Mask of Fu Manchu*, despite the simplistic dedication, the 1980s update includes more sophisticated special effects for a reader exposed to James Bond movies, as well as an ingenious plot that places a British mole in "Islam." A mere apparition at the Pyramids would not suffice to motivate the obedient, seething masses, whom the cynical British, learning from the Germans and the Chinese Devil Doctor, seek to manipulate in the afterglow of empire.

Quinnell has the British prepare for the future. By the end of World War II, the British Empire was in crisis. Under siege by nationalist movements from India to Palestine, the British government slowly began to disengage from imperial rule. Spies were nostalgic and tended to hold on to the notion of empire and control. They became obsessed with nationalist coups and revolutions in North Africa, Lebanon, Syria, and Arabia, but the *jihad* plot did not disappear entirely.

Reluctant to relinquish control to the United States even in fiction, British authors must have thought, in the 1970s and 1980s, why not revive the *jihad* conspiracy? It was a time when they could fantasize about placing a Mahdi mole inside Islam so that they could control it.[57] Just after World War II, in Quinnell's version, the British implant their own Mahdi sleeper agent who is to be reactivated at the appropriate time in the holy city of Mecca. For maximum effect, they decide to use the United States and American space-age technology of lasers and satellites to "sting" both the Americans and the Russians, and have Britain retake control of the Middle East in one fell swoop.

An old British Middle East hand contrives the scam and sets the scene for Hawke, the American CIA agent who will be manipulated by Pritchard, an Englishman who worked in the area in the 1930s and disappeared from sight shortly thereafter: "It was rumored that he had fallen out of favor with the British authorities in Cairo, even that he had committed the then cardinal sin of 'going native', of marrying an Arab woman, who had borne him a son," only to resurface later in Saigon and Indonesia. The British retain his services, we are told, "presumably knowing something about which everyone else was ignorant," despite the fact that he has attended the wrong schools and his loyalties are suspect.[58]

The solution to the Middle East problem, Pritchard tells a skeptical Hawke, is Islam, because, unlike Christianity, Islam "is a religion that demands total obedience of believers." If the Muslims can be unified, the immense power of Islam can then be controlled, possibly by the West. Ignoring the younger man's sarcastic retorts to this analysis, Pritchard calmly sips his cognac and replies that it only requires a "miracle." "Are you telling me," he taunts Hawke, "'that a country which developed nuclear weapons, a country which put a man on the moon'—faint smile—. . . 'a country which built Disneyland, couldn't produce a full-blown, Lloyd's registered, copper-bottomed A-one miracle?'"[59] The plan is set and, predictably, the Mahdi appears in Mecca, but later, at the postmortem held deep in the jungles of Malaya, the British agent who has acted as liaison with the manipulated Hawke commiserates with Pritchard because the British agent had never seen his son, Abu Qadir, nor would he ever be able to. "That's true," Pritchard agrees solemnly, "but I have given him the greatest gift any father could give a son: the total devotion of a billion people."[60]

Despite Quinnell's fantasy, clearly by the 1980s Western manipulation of Islam was wishful thinking. Both the spy novel genre and Middle East politics had undergone profound changes in the more than half-century since Buchan's tale of German-controlled *jihad*. Until the 1960s, British authors and British heroes dominated the field of espionage fiction. Like the turn of the century novels, those of the 1920s and 1930s dealt with domestic fears. Sapper's fascist Bulldog Drummond, the "Leader," was a popular hero who led his black-uniformed cohorts to violent elimination of those they disliked for political or racist reasons. Villains are drug dealers, criminals, and white slavers and reflect the cornucopia of nonwhite villains in popular fiction through the 1950s. They embody the racism, Social Darwinism, and xenophobia that dominated British "boys' literature" of the inter-war period leading straight to the villains in Ian Fleming's novels that illustrate racial subversion of the white hero.[61] Hostages, captures, escapes, torture, and violence are integral parts of the story. Bulldog Drummond is not involved in the Middle East, but he is a model for later operatives who appear after World War II and are sustained through the Cold War.[62]

What Buchan and Rohmer introduced to the spy novel before World War II—namely a heroic spy becoming increasingly professional, caricatures of stereotypical anti-European villains, and threats to British political hegemony in the Middle East—would be amplified and mutated during the 1960s when Ian Fleming introduced James Bond to the reading public. The Bond novels appeared just when the publishing industry was undergoing a marketing revolution and Anglo-American policy in the region was changing.

FOUR

The Publishing Explosion
and James Bond

Between 1950 and 1969 more than one hundred ninety-five crime fiction novels about the Middle East were published—almost four times the number of spy novels that appeared from 1916 through 1939 when Buchan's *Greenmantle* and Sax Rohmer's *The Mask of Fu Manchu* first appeared. Of the titles published before World War II, twelve were murder mysteries and fourteen concerned crime; five used World War I plots; four dealt with *jihad*, and twenty-one with military coups or mandate politics. World War II and its immediate aftermath were the subject of seventeen novels that followed the military campaigns and the nefarious activities of German/Nazi spies, more often than not in Cairo, where one of the villains is Egyptian.[1] There were few novels about the Cold War or the Arab-Israel conflict.

Because of the numbers of books that began and continued to appear after World War II, we can no longer talk about one prototypical author or analyze one novel. Rather, we need to look at the trends that emerge due to changes in the genre and the coalescence of political events that began to occur during the 1950s and 1960s and continued through the twentieth century. Novels began to reflect new political contexts: policing the mandates, the world of the Cold War, de-colonization, independence movements and pan-Arab nationalism. Although British troops retreated from the region, British spies in fiction did not. They perpetuated the notion of empire and control, and became obsessed with nationalist coups and communist-inspired revolutions in North Africa, Lebanon, Syria, and Arabia.[2]

PLOTS: 1916–1949		PLOTS: 1950–1959	
Murder Mysteries	17	Murder Mysteries	14
World War I	8	Jihad	3
Jihad	7	World War II	3
Mandate Politics	21	Cold War	9
World War II	17	Coups	17
Cold War	4	Arab-Israeli Conflict	3
Arab-Israeli Conflict	2	Crime	12
Crime	14	Other	5
Oil	1	TOTAL	66
Other	7		
TOTAL	98		

By the 1950s, political circumstance forced a marriage between the imperialists and those westernized Middle Easterners whom they first created and later disdained. In detective novels, when British officials are murdered and the suspects may be British, instead of the imperial representative, the efficient, modern, punctilious Arab policeman arrives on the scene and takes charge. The British must defer—after all, they no longer rule these countries directly—and Zaki Bey or Khalil Hadid solves the crime.[3] These men have been well educated; some have even attended Oxford, drawing a response of begrudging admiration from the British who remained in the country and who now had to cooperate in investigations conducted by the people they once ruled. Abdul Wadoud, an Iraqi senator and one of the suspects in Ruth Wadham's *Weekend in Baghdad*, is dressed in pajamas and *aba* when he meets with British civilian Peter Shaw who investigates the murder *ex-officio* in order to clear his Iraqi friend. The Arab may be in local dress, but on the bookshelves in his salon, the Iraqi has a complete set of Sherlock Holmes, including short stories published in magazines that appeared during the turn of the century that he picked up on a visit to London.

Often the villains are not evil; rather, they are on the wrong side politically. As westernized Arabs, they are products of British education, and have become nonpracticing Muslims with a nostalgia for tradition, who enjoy quoting English poetry. In the context of Cold War politics, they are either secular communists or Arab nationalists, in either case, though, clearly opposed to British imperial rule in the region.[4] In novels about pre-revolutionary Iraq, which ended in 1958, Oxford-educated Iraqis or pro-British Kurds are the heroes, while Arab nationalist supporters of Nasser or nationalist Iraqis and Egyptians are the villains.[5] None of the embassy staff could believe that Ibrahim killed the British ambassador in John Sherwood's *Undiplomatic Exit*. After all, how could a devotee of Western classical music who regularly visited the home of the embassy official to enjoy this pastime, and who was perceived to be a man of honor by all of his acquaintances, be suspected of indulging in an Arab-type murder—here defined as marching up to one's enemy at a public occasion and shooting him, or hiring someone else to knife him in the back in a dark alley? It was also difficult to believe that Ibrahim was actually involved in a coup against the pro-British government.[6]

While there is no talk of Islam, Muslim "fanaticism," *jihad,* or differences in culture, these Arab characters are not seen as "mimics," either. Neither Third World imitations nor malleable Muslims, they are British creations who had been under imperial tutelage for a generation and were products of British schools. Arab detectives and villains were quick to discuss issues within a Western mindset, reminding both British and American readers that the Arabs, too, were participants in the development of Western civilization: "'We should not forget the philosophers from Iraq. There was al-Kindi, for example. He was born in Kufa. Was not your Roger Bacon perhaps influenced by his writings?' The light of charity was burning rather less brightly now in Coleman's eyes."[7]

Despite the occasional political confrontation, however, British expats retain a love for the area if not for the inhabitants or even for the Islamic/ Arab civilization. They miss the exoticism of the Middle East and the opportunity it provided for adventure and financial gain. During the interwar years, authors produced a number of "Lawrencian" wartime missions in "mufti" to Egypt and Palestine; after World War II, they have British agents return once again to the Middle East after short-lived careers at home as real-estate agents, solicitors, or inheritors of the family business.[8] Another taste of action in the "Great Game" or a physical challenge in an exotic environment may have whetted the appetite of these "accidental" heroes, who, at the end, only wish for one more chance at getting back into action.[9] There are treks through the Empty Quarter in Arabia to find pre-Islamic artifacts: The lost treasure of the leader of the medieval Assassins, Hasan-i Sabah, somehow finds its way south to Arabia. Some bitten with the oriental bug, live in the Gulf and invest in salvage operations or engage in outright smuggling. Others rescue unfortunate Western victims of white slavery or plane crashes. At bottom, however, there is a residual romanticism, a love of the harsh existence undergone by the Bedouin, and then internalized by British boys raised on tales of endurance of physical hardship, if only for the challenge.[10]

Author William Haggard's character Colonel Charles Russell, former head of the British "Security Executive,"[11] personifies this nostalgic approach to former British hegemony, with an understated lust for vengeance peppered with critiques of British policy and politicians. Officially retired from active service, Russell is drawn back into battle to prove that Britain never should have relinquished imperial rule in the first place. He sees his duty in assisting or putting back on keel those former colonies that had once enjoyed British tutelage, but were now transformed into "half-barbaric," independent states. He must save a Gulf sheikhdom from revolution or Communist *putsch*, solve the Arab-Israeli dispute, rescue Malta from Libyan clutches, or Egypt from the threat of imminent war.[12] All the while, in his heart of hearts he knows that just a few years ago, the villains *never* would have dared to take on the British. Today, however, things just are not the same.

The Egyptian president remembered Russell from colonial service: "Captain Smith, I recollect you called me, since my real name tied your tongue in knots. I suppose I should have been greatly offended but in fact I was greatly flattered. I knew what you British thought of our army and 'Smith' somehow suggested that I was really a soldier." Russell then recalls that

> this Captain had been no chocolate soldier. He came from a background of military incompetence unequaled since the Habsburg Empire, but though he'd been too loyal to admit it Russell had been aware that he knew. Technically they'd been equals, liaising, but Smith had made it clear from the start that he'd be happy to take Captain Russell's orders. Suggestions if you insisted, then. They had gotten on extremely well.[13]

The colonel enters the fray. He assists the Egyptian president in thwarting the Libyan threat and the Gulf sheikh in counteracting the plot against him because even though they are Middle Eastern leaders, they nonetheless have some Western sensibility. In *Visa to Limbo*, he even shares the sheikh's mistress. Nevertheless, at the same time, we seem to sense throughout that he is always thinking: You see they still need us; they really cannot do anything for themselves.

In the real world, however, politics intervened. The Suez debacle (1956) and the arrest or defection of British agents George Blake and Kim Philby to the Soviet Union in the early 1960s, occurring during the period of bureaucratic reorganization brought on by a post-World War II socialist government in England, took crime fiction genre in two directions. The imperial mission interpreted by Buchan and William Haggard's heroic perpetuation of empire persisted, albeit with declining readership, only to be revived a decade later by the publication of Ian Fleming's James Bond novels.

At the same time, on a parallel genre track, writers began to humanize the spy novel, to examine political issues instead of merely solving tactical problems through violence. These authors, some of whose work achieved literary and best-seller status, used the spy novel as a device to critique Cold War policy and to probe questions of policy, loyalty, and deceit.[14] The fiction of Eric Ambler, Geoffrey Household, John le Carré, and Gerald Seymour, to name just a few, portrayed disillusioned British operatives acting in an atmosphere of overall British malaise, raising questions about policy and treachery. While the Buchan school had used the genre to warn about international conspiracy, these authors used the genre as a vehicle for advocacy—a platform from which to caution policy makers or to warn the public about ecological danger or imminent terrorist threat.[15]

Even before World War II, author Eric Ambler had questioned the chauvinistic approach of writers who penned secret agent tales. He introduced the concept of the "neutral"—the innocent man caught up in a web of circumstance in plots that dealt with shades of gray. Emerging as a thriller writer in 1937, Ambler told an interviewer that

> *having failed* at playwriting, *having failed* as a songwriter, *failed* as an engineer, I looked around for something I could change and decided it was the thriller/spy story. I would do something different. The detective story genre had been worked over, but no one had looked at the thriller. It was still a dirty word. So I decided to intellectualize it. I changed the genre and couldn't write the books fast enough.[16]

As a counterpoint to Sapper, who was writing "solid right-wing" fascist stories, whose heroes even appeared in black shirts, and in contrast to Buchan, "an establishment figure, so fuddy-duddy," Ambler decided to make his heroes left-wing and popular-front figures, and introduced the average man who is accidentally thrust into the web of intrigue. The hero's attempts to extricate himself from the "web of circumstance" provide authors with the opportunity to examine political issues.

Ambler's heroes are English businessmen traveling abroad who become enmeshed in local politics. They refuse a bribe, after which odd occurrences start to happen, bureaucratic red tape entangles and trips them so that they are caught in political intrigue not of their making. Istanbul, a World War II nest of international spies, is the setting in *Journey into Fear*. In *The Levanter*, Ambler uses an innocent neutral to provide a skeptical look at terrorist groups, a technique similar to John le Carré's character Charlie in *The Little Drummer Girl* or Geoffrey Household's Anglo-French ingénue Armande Herne in *Arabesque*. These neutrals are accidental heroes who become the lens through which the reader is exposed to all sides of a complicated issue. Ambler's hero, a local businessman of mixed Middle Eastern and English parentage living in Lebanon, discovers that his battery and ceramics factories have been infiltrated and are being used by Palestinian terrorists, members of a new group who wish to upstage Yasir Arafat by firing rockets into Tel-Aviv. Ultimately caught up in the political quagmire and forced to become an actor in a plot about which he cares nothing, Michael Howell loses his business and his reputation in the Arab world.

Le Carré's potential agent, the British actress, Charlie, is the naive filter through which the reader is exposed to the perspectives of both the Israeli intelligence operative and the Palestinian terrorist leader but will find a solution from neither.[17]

Even earlier, through a variegated character study reflective of society in the immediate post-World War II era of decolonization and end of the mandates in the Middle East, Geoffrey Household's *Arabesque*, published in 1948, predicts the conflict to come: His heroine, Amanda, unwittingly becomes an agent in an arms-supply operation for the Jewish Agency in Palestine and at the same time falls in love with the British officer whose job it is to stop the gunrunning from Lebanon into Palestine. The British do not trust the Jews, a French officer becomes an outright anti-Semite after being betrayed in an arms supply scandal, and a westernized Lebanese Christian sheikh views Muslims as ignorant and unappreciative of Arab culture. The heroic Lieutenant Rashid er Rahman ibn Ajjeun, an Arab officer in the British army, places personal loyalty above politics, but is ever confident that the Jews will not succeed because there are too many Arabs. And the Middle Eastern Jew, David Nachmias, has no good words for the Eastern European Jews for whom he works, believing that they do not understand the Middle East.

Journalists, too, will use the spy novel and thriller as vehicles for questioning the motives and actions of all sides of political questions and will attempt to humanize the conflict through character development. "The genre," notes Gerald Seymour, who covered Ireland and the Middle East, "has the capability of informing an audience, giving them more insight into the problems we are all talking about, than a forest of newspapers and a cloud of TV newscasts."

> I would expect to tell my readership more about the real and human situation in Northern Ireland or the Middle East or Afghanistan than they can ever obtain from the dried up river of courses of nonfiction. This is the medium for getting into the skulls of *people*, of discovering attitudes, for pecking out the motivation of the few men and women who will make the headlines across our breakfast tables . . . . They are real individuals, not just the cardboard cutouts of my imagination . . . . If you want to know what is really happening in our world today, then cancel the newspapers, unplug the TV, and head down to the bookshop.[18]

In *The Glory Boys*, he situates the Arab-Israeli conflict in the context of cultural differences, pitting the British and the Israelis against the PLO and the IRA, examining the issue of terrorism through the eyes of Eastern and Western operatives—the "Oriental" and the "Celt" filtered through British and American eyes.[19]

Abdel al-Famy, a young Palestinian on his first mission, assisted by a veteran Irish assassin, McCoy, who "plays nursemaid to the Arab in exchange for arms for the IRA," are sent to England to assassinate an Israeli nuclear scientist invited to lecture in London. The murder was to be a symbolic act designed to prove to the world that the Arabs did not fear Israeli nuclear capability.

The Irishman is appalled at the Palestinian's total lack of training and at his fanatical unequivocal acceptance of the suicide mission tactic. To McCoy, al-Famy is an "Arab suicide merchant," and this realization causes him to ponder.

> "It's animal when you don't care . . . unnatural when you don't feel the tension, subhuman." The Irishman had read of these people when they went into Israel. "Suicide squads, kamikaze, there to kill and to be killed. Take the greatest possible number with you . . . . Madness or motivation?" McCoy didn't know which it was. "And the man beside him, with the vacant, contented eyes, would be one of them? Had to be, didn't he?"[20]

While it is all right to kill for a cause, it isn't worth dying for in McCoy's book. When the crunch comes, the Irishman saves his skin, proving the British assessment correct, that when technique confronts resolve, the unfathomable Arab was the greater threat.

Al-Famy, on the other hand, has only disdain for the Irishman. The Palestinian is contemptuous of IRA operations—"a pathetic cowboy world of animal heroics, shooting down one soldier and claiming that as a victory, killing one middle-aged policeman and believing that changed political strategy; that is no course to fight." They don't know what they are fighting for, al-Famy thinks, and that is why they cannot "steel themselves to acts that will shock and stagger on the grand scale . . . . He will understand what it is to kill when the diplomats of every major capital in the world will react. He will find out what it is to earn the hatred of one half the world, the gratitude and adulation of the other."[21]

So it is that when failure looms as the first attempt on the Israeli's life does not succeed, al-Famy presses forward, despite overwhelming odds. For him, the anticipation of recognition and the possibility of striking a blow for his people was enough to die for: "All would say his name when the next evening came. Some with adulation, some with resignation, some with detestation. The blow he prepared to strike would be mighty, it would shatter the fetid complacence of many millions, and to those who lived on the far side of the wire and the mine fields and who longed to cross over, he would bring hope and aspiration. There was a pounding of excitement, close to purest happiness."[22]

Al-Famy is killed by a British sharpshooter as the assassin tries to shoot the departing Israeli scientist at the airport, but incredible as it seems, the reader is left with an uncomfortable feeling—grieving for and yet understanding why al-Famy must complete a mission that will most certainly result in his death. For somehow, from the shadows, another villain has emerged—Israeli officials are smug: "they were the experts with these bastards. . . . Europeans did not understand them," and the Israeli government knows that the paunchy, fifty-year old scientist has a heart condition and that he has been targeted for assassination. Yet, they use him as bait and insist on sending him to London and probably ultimately, one way or another, to an untimely death. Who, then, is the guilty one?

Throughout the rest of the twentieth century, while some novels followed in the Ambler tradition and received critical acclaim, the Buchan-style spy capers retained their readership but were largely ignored by critics. As a legacy of colonial rule in the Middle East, the British retained a sense of responsibility that fiction exploited—as it does, of course—nostalgia for a once great empire, now only an evocative memory suitable for historical study. Through the 1950s, British soldiers continued to serve in the Gulf. In fiction, they suppress mutinies and save oil sheikhs from military coups in postwar holding actions, not so much out of specific British interest—this had long been relinquished by the mediocre leadership in London—but out of an intuitive duty to rule. Other old Middle East hands defended their turf against the invasion of businessmen and Americans, taking pride in their Orientalism, being able to deal peacefully and effectively with cantankerous sheikhs by accompanying them on falcon hunts and to camel races, by listening to tribal poetry, or by attending interminable Bedouin feasts where veterans of the British colonial enterprise could appreciate non-Western delicacies.

When in the 1950s, Ian Fleming introduced James Bond to the world of espionage, his variation of the classic spy novel not only revived but transmuted the Buchan tradition into what has become known as the political thriller. Inspired both by Buchan and Sax Rohmer, who was also popular in the United States, Fleming also incorporated the heroic characteristics of the American hardboiled detective, an agent acting alone who explored society's dark side, at times operating on the borderline of legality.[23] The character is a hardened professional—an urban, cynical, streetwise, calloused American who fights foreign villains. Less elitist than the classic tales of espionage, these detective novels found a readership both in America and Britain. Plots focused on corruption, and the hero/detective became a hardened professional, a cynic and a loner operating against foreigners and the dregs of society, avenging wrongs done against the average person.

Fleming combined elements of the mystery, the spy story, the gothic strains popular in Sax Rohmer's Fu Manchu novels and various forms of the crime book genre, added the ethos of the American hardboiled detective novel and created a formulaic paradigm that became popular immediately and is still going strong. Originally the Bond novels were written as a parody of John Buchan's Richard Hannay stories; but, in truth, Fleming perpetuated the Buchan tradition. Fleming's first James Bond adventure, *Casino Royale*, appeared in 1953 in a printing limited to 4,750 copies. It sold out in a month.[24]

The popularity of the book—a novel set in an exotic locale, featuring a handsome, urbane hero who faced an odious villain conspiring against western civilization—was immediate: Readers were drawn in by the conspiracy—"an 'unnatural' or a pathological disruption of an otherwise ordered world," a key component of what would become the thriller. As a throwback to pre-World War I Britain in the Buchan sense, in the 1950s and 1960s threats are not merely to the empire. Rather, Fleming presents a re-vivified conflict between the Anglo-Saxon West and the "Other." Fleming's James Bond, heir to Buchan and Rohmer, creates the hero readers identify with and through whose eyes they uncover the plot and save England. Create the conspiracy, fill in the villain and the exotic landscape, add sexual dalliance, capture and torture, escape and victory, and the formula can be perpetuated *ad infinitum*. Arcane and specialized information—detailed description of luxury as in the Bond novels or an analysis of the intricate workings of jet aircraft, advanced weaponry, the stock market, assassination preparations, or building a bomb—draws readers in, adds suspense, "rivets eyes to the page," as they are bombarded with an apocalyptic conspiracy.[25]

In 1953, when he appeared in *Casino Royale*, James Bond struck a receptive chord in Britain. Like Buchan, Fleming, a former member of British intelligence, introduced Agent Bond at a time when Britain was, in fact, threatened once again, not by war in the exotic outreaches of empire, but by Soviet moles and real conspirators in the drab bureaucratic corridors of the socialist post-World War II government. The Suez debacle (1956), the defection of Kim Philby to the Soviet Union in 1963—his co-members of the Cambridge spy ring Guy Burgess and Donald Maclean had defected a decade earlier—and French President Charles De Gaulle's rejection of British entry into the European Common Market only drew attention to Britain's loss of prestige in the international arena. Domestic malaise accompanied by the physical contraction of empire, beginning with the post-World War II independence of Egypt and Jordan, of India in 1947, and the creation of Israel in 1948 that ended a half century later with the end of the British Empire, sparked the comment by American Secretary of State Dean Acheson that "Great Britain has lost an empire but not yet found a role in the world."[26]

There is no doubt that when Ian Fleming began to publish, Bond was clearly seen as the patriotic antidote to British disillusionment at imperial retreat.[27] Some viewed him as a throwback to Lawrence of Arabia. He also exemplified the view that the British may have lost an empire, but they could emerge victorious through "super cunning."[28] What the Bond novels did was to create a fantasy world where the British Empire still existed and the defense of Britain, first against the communist threat and later against international conspirators of all stripes, was the key to saving western civilization.[29] Bond's task was to deflect actual British concern with real

Soviet spies, to provide safety valves for the negativity brought on by self-introspection and doubt, and to re-create British glory, if only imaginary. Thus, Bond was sent to chic locales in order to thwart the international plots of SMERSH, but also to combat alien ethnics—whiffs of Oriental and Jewish conspirators and sci-fi villains rather than actual Chinese, Pathans, or "Fuzzy-Wuzzies"—that were directed not against what was left of the crumbling empire, but rather against the civilized world, reckoned largely as Britain, the United States and their allies.[30]

Like Buchan, Fleming wrote with undeniable certainty of the innate superiority of Britain. Disgust at and scorn of foreigners is not limited to Japanese, Koreans, and Africans. Paris is singled out as selling "its heart to the Russians," and Bulgarians and Rumanians are described as "the scum of the world who had gradually taken the town over." None of the major villains is English; those who are British citizens are of German and Baltic origin.[31]

The Bond novels, however, went further in sanctioning outright stereotypical vilification of the enemy. If Fleming's villains were acceptable as evil incarnate, whether aliens or imaginary threats in an anti-white, anti-Semitic, or non-Western guise, then the genre provided opportunity for authors to spew venom in print against the Other and the thriller would become a convenient vehicle for the *jihad* conspiracy novels that would dominate the next two decades. It should be emphasized that in these novels, the villain lacks any positive traits that could mislead the reader into liking him and his cohorts. He could be a benign desperado, an authoritarian usurper of power, or a horrific manipulator of the naive. He might be the frightening stranger who does not fit into the mainstream either by culture or appearance, and who degenerates with time and frequency of appearance into the grotesque: the half-breed, the queer, the prowler, the monster, or the bogeyman whose evil is the stuff of fairy tales. He is the coward, the traitor, or the terrorist—the sneak attacker who preys on society in a cowardly manner, one who shoots the hero in the heel. And, last, he is all of those social undesirables who embody any traits currently out of vogue.[32] He is the Other, the one who must be smashed lest he conquer, pollute, corrupt, control, defeat, or destroy the good, who, in this instance, personify the best of the West. Because of the nature of the genre, therefore, despite decades of teaching against racial stereotypes, spy novels and thrillers have remained a bastion of unrelenting racist vituperation against any group out of fashion. Villains change and often quickly date the books: "This year it's chic to be wary of the Chinese;" notes critic Dilys Winn, "last year the Arabs; the year before, the South Africans."[33] Here, the reader quickly learns to mistrust everyone on all sides, even the spy's boss, his Control.

The Bond series was a new outlet for the depiction of stereotypical physical repulsiveness not seen since the 1930s, but which became almost commonplace in the 1970s and 1980s. In *Live and Let Die*, to pick a random example, Mr. Big, a Haitian whose head resembles a football, has gray-black skin, "taut and shining like the face of a week-old corpse in the river," and is hairless "except for some gray-brown fluff above the ears." The villain has no eyebrows, no eyelashes, and the wide-set eyes are so far apart that "one could not focus on them both, but only on one at a time... They were animal eyes, not human, and they seemed to blaze." Authors later drew pictures of Arab villains in much the same way. In Graham Lancaster's *The Nuclear Letters*, Al-Hata, the Arab sheikh, has white hair, eyes "pink like a rabbit's," and skin that should have been the "color of mahogany was a sickly white." Children mock and women are repulsed by his "ghostly" face. He is a "freak" in the "swarthy bearded world of Arabian masculinity," and the hero—rich, athletic, handsome Neil Janner, who is an internationally renowned society dentist to the rich and famous, as well as a British agent, notes that it could only be imagined how "being an albino in such a situation might have scarred and twisted the mind. . . ." Upon seeing him, Janner "shuddered involuntarily,"[34] a reaction much like Hannay's at his perception of Stumm's homosexuality, or the British at the sight of Fu Manchu.

As a hero, Bond was Richard Hannay taken to extremes. Operating in a masculine world of physical exertion and mystery, with a ruthless enemy and a just cause, he is at once the exemplification of the chivalric hero, rescuing damsels in distress and treating women subordinates—secretaries, for example—with respect. Unlike Buchan's hero, however, Bond is also a sexual predator and a materialist whose conquests and meticulously described hedonistic lifestyle are part of the appeal of the books. Bond appears, he is co-opted or assigned, he is recalled into service, or falls into a mission when danger threatens. He is proactive and combative, a knight on a quest. He tends to be a loner, more akin to the prototypical American hero, Superman or the cowboy—whether in Western garb, dressed as the lone detective "stalking these mean streets," or as a spy summoned by his Control to thwart the conspiracy.[35]

Other authors had used a similar formula to have their agents travel to different locales that usually reflected political hot spots or crises. Simon Harvester and other professional authors adopted a particular style and format to write for a devoted following. Between 1942 and his death in 1975, Harvester wrote some forty-four spy tales in addition to his other novels. His hero Dorian Silk had a large readership that followed him along numerous foreign and dangerous "roads." These included *Assassins Road* (Middle

East), *Battle Road* (Thailand, Vietnam), *Moscow Road*, *Nameless Road* (Mongolia), *Red Road* (Russia), *Silk Road* (Afghanistan), and *Treacherous Road* (Yemen). Books published in the 1960s reflected British fear of Communist subversion in those areas where Silk foiled schemes by KGB agents and Communist colonels bent on *coups d'état*.

But Fleming's success also generated American clones and imitators that dominated paperback publishing for decades. These included Edward Aarons's Sam Durell series, Philip Atlee's books featuring Joe Gall, and the more than two hundred titles in the Nick Carter series.[36] From 1955 until the death of the author in 1975, Fawcett published the Cold War exploits of Aarons's Sam Durell—a Yale graduate who was raised by his grandfather, a Mississippi riverboat captain, of the CIA's Section "K." Durell was "a man who could hunt after other men and who, in turn, was not afraid to be hunted. . . . It set him apart. He could have taken a desk job in Analysis and Synthesis at No. 20 Annapolis Street, working up extrapolations for Joint Chiefs and the White House, but he couldn't go back across the gulf that separated him from everyday life. Each year, the notations on his contract renewal offered a recall from field work, but he could not return. He had become different from other men."[37]

In *Assignment: Zoraya* (1960), Washington has a problem with the desert kingdom of Jidrat.

> In Jidrat, you've got the worst sort of paternalism added to the wildest brand of Arab nationalism. And it's mixed with that peculiar savagery the Arabs seem to specialize in. The place is in ferment—a microcosm of the whole world in this one Arab sultanate. Mud shacks and starvation and goats and camels next to air-conditioned palaces, foreign sports cars, and polo ponies. The old Imam can't hold out much longer. The Q'adi and our two-bit Hitler, Colonel Ta'arife, have temporarily allied themselves to get rid of the old man and take over. And the only one who can pull the country together is Prince Amr al-Maari, the playboy of the world.[38]

The "playboy" prince is called home to take control of the country. He was acquainted with Sam Durell from their college days at Yale, where Durell introduced the prince to the intricacies of poker. Durell enlists the aid of a beautiful, reclusive Arab maiden who was promised to the prince in a marriage that never took place, but which Zoraya still desires. The trio returns to the Middle East to face a stupefying concoction of problems, all occurring in one novel, that illustrate how Americans viewed Arab countries in the early 1970s: civil war, white and black slave trading, rape and mutilation of an English couple, vengeful Bedouin, and mysterious male Russian and female Israeli agents, who happened once to have been married. When the smoke clears, Amr assumes his emirship, marries Zoraya ("it is the will of Allah"), and promises that Jidrat will remain politically neutral. Washington is pleased, Sam Durell gets promoted, and all is well. Much like the Bond novels, these series are simplistic and reflect an unsophisticated view of the non-Western world.

Paperback publishers meticulously enumerated the heroic norms of their protagonists. Fawcett-Gold Medal touted Joe Gall in The Nullifier series that appeared from 1963 until it was withdrawn in 1977 as "(1) adventurous, (2) sensual, (3) worldly, (4) skilled in certain arts, and (5) patriotic."[39] Agents such as Nick Carter and Malko were created and their exploits were similarly written to formula and serialized. The multi-authored Nick Carter, Killmaster series was launched in 1964 by Award Books, a new paperback imprint that bought the rights to use the Nick Carter character from Condé Nast. Carter had begun as an important pulp fiction detective created in 1886 and later metamorphosed into dime novel form in the 1920s and 1930s. Now he was to be upgraded into an American James Bond. "I saw how big James Bond was in the United States," Lyle Kenyon Engel would later write, "and I figured if England has their special agent, why shouldn't America have its special agent?" "Killmaster" was to be a 007 designation; it meant that he had the license to kill.[40]

During the more than two decades of his published exploits, Carter thwarted more than two hundred attempts to destroy the United States through economic, military, chemical and biological, nuclear or terrorist warfare. Much like Simon Harvester's Dorian Silk, Carter operated in locales throughout the planet, and battled villains that included mad scientists, Communists, Japanese masterminds, ex-Nazis, and Arabs. In the books using the Middle East for plot or villain, there are Chinese attempts to take over North Africa, drugs in Istanbul, ex-Nazi and Arab schemes to destroy Israel, as well as plans by Berbers assisted by the Chinese to invade France by tunneling under Gibraltar. An Arab version of the Mafia steals microfilm to sell to the Communists, and an Arab sheikh uses a group of Bahamians in his plot to take over the world. As in the Fleming novels, the Nick Carter series exploits racist stereotypes and apocalyptic plots.

There were female versions, too. Peter O'Donnell took comic strip character Modesty Blaise and published a book length heroic female parody of Bond. It was time for a female James Bond, O'Donnell wrote, but not a "bra-burning Woman's Libber." The problem was that, unlike a male character whose martial arts and language acuity was self-explanatory, a woman hero required a background to explain her unusual talents. A World War II refugee, Modesty wanders south into the area of Iran and the Caucasus where, in one of the displaced persons camps, she meets a Hungarian Jew, a former professor, who teaches her to read, write, and speak several languages. He names her Modesty Blaise, a name evocative of early British tales of King Arthur and the magician, Merlin. When she is sixteen, the professor dies, and Modesty goes on to Tangier, joining a gang where she learns martial arts and all of the skills that men naturally possess. She takes over the gang, meets her confederate Willie Gavin, and together they spend the rest of their careers tracking down villains for the British Secret Service.[41] Another female agent, Dorothy Gilman's Emily Pollifax, is different: She is an elderly suburban lady who became a spy for want of something to do. Defending American interests as a CIA operative armed with an umbrella and martial arts expertise, Mrs. Pollifax shows up in Morocco to check on an American informant, in Turkey to aid a famous double agent, in Jordan to assist anti-Saddam intellectuals, and in Syria to prevent an assassination attempt on President Hafez al-Assad.[42]

Fleming's Bond hit a nerve, and his success generated demand for more product: that is, more spy novels featuring Western heroes thwarting cataclysmic conspiracies. Appearing at a time when the publishing industry was undergoing a marketing revolution, the Bond phenomenon, including film versions produced for the American audience, shot spy novels and thrillers to hitherto unforeseen commercial heights, accounting for the resurgence in popularity of the genre.[43] During the years Ian Fleming wrote the Bond books, more than 25 million copies in eighteen languages were sold. Sales figures more than doubled after Fleming's death, and once Bond received the imprimatur of United States President John F. Kennedy, "everybody under the sun wanted a Fleming book."[44]

Spin-offs included the "spy as serious mainstream fiction," the spy novel as "feminine romance," as "historical swashbuckler," science fiction, medical fiction and even the "spy novel cookbook." Added to these were anthologies of short spy fiction and nonfiction works of espionage. The "ultimate extension of the bubble," Anthony Boucher concluded in his "Criminals at Large" column in the *New York Times Book Review*, was the "appearance of cartoons devoted entirely to espionage intrigue," such as Antonio Prohias's "Spy vs. Spy" of *Mad Magazine* renown. Increasingly, the Bond phenomenon accounted for more than the number of copies of books sold.

During its heyday in the 1960s and 1970s, there were James Bond fan clubs, clubs dedicated to the cult of James Bond, hit records of James Bond movie theme songs, fashions, T-shirts, 007 toys, models of Bond gimmickry and technology, and, of course, films.

In Italy, the hysteria over Bond spilled over into reality. After an Italian weekly (circulation of over 700,000) published an article on espionage, thousands of people wrote to the publishers, asking how to join the ranks of the secret service:

> Housemaids, youths from the provinces, old-age pensioners, eager boys, businessmen, learned physicists, children, clerks, porters and waiters rushed in to take up the career of international spy, wanted to know where it was necessary to apply to become a secret agent, and sought all the relevant information: how much was earned, was the car supplied, what age must one be, must one know judo, was it necessary to be a bachelor, how much did a course in spying cost, was it possible to become a secret agent if one were scared to travel by air?
>
> No one thought to ask whether or not he had to kill; rather, the question raised was quantitative: If I entered the secret service, how many people exactly would I have to kill a year?[45]

With Bond, the spy took on a new image: He was neither brutal, venal, furtive (a traitor operating in dark and dishonorable corners), nor disingenuously amateur. Spying was now a glamorous profession. Bond worked only two or three missions a year and spent the rest of his time as an easygoing civil servant, enjoying the rewards of wealth and women. And for these missions, he had merely to be physically fit and violent.

With popular acclaim came commentary. Philosophers and literary critics began to write about the novels, albeit with snobbish disdain, and academics discussed the genre in the Academy. Social philosopher Jacques Barzun, who also had a critical interest in mystery and crime fiction, even initiated a literary controversy when, in his "Meditations on the Literature of Spying," he called the spy novel a contamination of the classic detective story. Diverting himself with "the tales of childish fantasy," Barzun wrote, the spy novel addict operates on a level of a preadolescent because the ubiquitous spy is nothing more than a nine-year-old boy. "The spy ingenuity (why not ship the fellow in a trunk?), his shifting partisanship without a cause, like his double bluffs, his vagrant attachments, and his love of torturing and of being tortured are the mores of the preadolescent gang." That

the adult reader consumes these works of childish fantasy is not a phenomenon, Barzun concluded. What is shocking is that the reader accepts the
fantasy as wiser than government, and that the modern civil world seems
to have "made official the dreams and actions of little boys."[46] These were
not works that would engage mystery fans who read the books as cerebral
chess games.

As paperback sales of Bond books in the British market leapt from the
initial 50,000 copies of *Casino Royale*, to more than 237,000 copies of his
books in 1959 to almost 28 million copies in 1977, and accounted for ten
of the first eighteen titles in paperbacks that sold well over a million copies,[47] authors required more original plots and villains to supply the readers' market. The overwhelming success of the genre with its distinctive
heroes legitimized the incorporation into fiction of increasingly stereotypical villains and apocalyptic plots. Books that appeared with a Middle East
plot reflected that popularity. Only 162 spy novels/thrillers had appeared
during the four decades since the publication of Buchan's *Greenmantle*. Of
these, some sixty-six titles appeared during the 1950s. During the 1960s, the
numbers of mysteries, spy novels and thrillers produced began to explode
when, in that decade alone, some 129 novels that used the Middle East for
plot, locale, or character were published.

PLOTS 1960–1969			
Murder Mysteries	23	Cold War	30
World War I	1	Arab-Israeli Conflict	14
Jihad	2	Oil	3
World War II	4	Crime	16
Coup	28	Other	8
TOTAL			129

Spy novels and thrillers also began to appear regularly on hardcover
bestseller lists. In 1964, some seventy-five spy novels and thrillers were published, noted Boucher in his *New York Times* column.[48] Two Bond novels
and John le Carré's anti-heroic antidote to Bond, *The Spy Who Came in from
the Cold*, made best seller lists, with le Carré's novel outselling all other
hardcover fiction that year. Within a decade, an average of two thrillers
a year appeared on best seller lists in the United States. These included

Frederick Forsyth's *The Day of the Jackal*—which created an assassination plot paradigm—and le Carré's *Tinker, Tailor, Soldier, Spy* and *The Honourable Schoolboy*. Paul Erdman's *The Crash of '79*, one of the first best sellers with a Middle East theme, made the top twenty for 1977. Although most authors plotted novels within the context of the Cold War, often using the imminent political coup as the emergency, bringing the Western spies into the region, the theatre of operations was extended internationally and included the Middle East and other non-European regions of the world.

What the genre now needed was plot material, and to fill that need, beginning in the late 1960s, more novels with Middle Eastern motifs appeared, as events occurring in the region took on global overtones that translated into attacks against the West. The overwhelming success of the genre and the adoption of mass marketing of fiction, especially paperback fiction, coincided with events on the international scene that would provide authors with almost unlimited plot material to sustain the spy novel/thriller genre for more than three decades.

FIVE

Secular *Jihad*

INTERNATIONAL TERRORISM AND
ECONOMIC DESTABILIZATION

By the 1980s, almost 600 thrillers and spy novels using the Middle East as a backdrop for action, characterization, or plot material had appeared in the United States either as British imports or as American originals. Suddenly, it seemed that supermarkets, drugstores, bus stations, and airports were inundated with spy novels whose covers depicted petro-sheikhs and terrorists held at bay by macho "avengers," "destroyers," "killmasters," "executioners," "peacemakers," and assorted James Bond clones.

That the books were included on best seller lists and formed the subject of academic discourse indicates the importance of the genre, perhaps not for literary critics, but certainly for publishers, who were aware of market share as they invested in authors who could produce spy novels and thrillers to satiate the appetite of an ever-growing readership. The popularity of spy novels and thrillers, coinciding with the paperback publishing explosion, generated demand for product, and authors complied, broadening the range of subjects from World War II to the Cold War and beyond. More and more titles were published and the numbers of American authors began to exceed the British.

Before the late 1960s, American authors writing in the context of American foreign policy used the Middle East as the scenic backdrop for adventures about retrieving microfilm or combating Communist-backed military coups. F. Van Wyck Mason, who began writing in the 1920s, had his G-2 agent Colonel Hugh North securing microfilm in Tangiers, rescuing

Americans held hostage in Turkey and solving murders in Cairo.[1] Unlike the British, who had been in the region for a century, however, Americans had little familiarity with the Middle East and its cultures. They read vicariously from the British spy novels that had been published simultaneously in America; but, for a good part of the twentieth century, the Middle East seemed to them more or less *terra exotica*. During the early years of the Cold War, deserts and casbahs were fascinating settings for adventure stories, replete with fantastic local color. They provided splendid opportunities for using picturesque adjectives, but unlike the Soviet Union, the Middle East did not yet present a physical threat to the United States.

Fictionalized American heroes appeared in plots where they were sent to the Middle East and North Africa to meet defecting Soviet scientists.[2] Of the heroes in 148 spy novels published between 1916 and 1959, fewer than a dozen, including three adventures featuring F. Van Wyck Mason's Colonel North, are American. Most authors had their agents defer to the British on more complicated issues. When American operatives did venture eastward, Middle Eastern characters waxed nostalgically for British experience in the region: "But the world is complicated these days," the prescient imam said in a novel published in 1960. "When the English were here, at least they kept order. Today, a stone cast in Jidrat can smash the skyscrapers of New York City."[3]

The Holy Land had always been a part of American consciousness, but only in mid-century did American policymakers and writers really discover the Middle East. Missionaries, travelers, and journalists wrote about the area, and Americans ventured into the region during the Barbary Wars in the early nineteenth century and through trade. American merchants supplied the Ottoman Empire with kerosene, prompting a diplomat to remark in 1879 that "even the sacred lamps over the Prophet's tomb at Mecca are fed with oil from Pennsylvania."[4] In the early twentieth century, as a result of America's entry into World War I, President Woodrow Wilson raised political consciousness about self-determination throughout the region. But for the most part, United States diplomatic involvement in the Middle East—both overt and covert—was of little consequence until the post World War II period. As late as 1939, with their stake in the region's petroleum production increasing, US oil executives had more influence in Middle East capitals, especially Riyadh, Saudi Arabia, than did American diplomats.[5]

Like the British during World War I, during World War II the United States began to institutionalize its own intelligence services. In 1942, with Americans involved in the war, President Franklin Delano Roosevelt created the Office of Strategic Services and placed it under the jurisdiction of the Joint Chiefs of Staff.[6] Directed by William J. Donovan, the OSS, manned both by military and civilian personnel, included a number of individuals who would later become prominent American academics. They and American operatives working with the British provided much of the intelligence in preparation for the Allied North African campaign in 1942. Direct involvement in the Persian Gulf came three years later after a private meeting between President Roosevelt and Saudi King Ibn Saud that focused on petroleum and the assurance of American participation in the Persian Gulf oil bonanza. Having been frozen out of most of the oil-rich Persian Gulf by the British, whose imperial presence in Kuwait, Bahrein, and the Trucial States dated from the nineteenth century, the United States staked its claim in Saudi Arabia, where oil was discovered in the 1930s. The FDR-Ibn Saud meeting, during Roosevelt's return from the Yalta Conference while on board an American battleship cruising through the Suez Canal ensured the free flow of oil to the United States. American Secretary of State John Foster Dulles's trip to the Middle East during the Eisenhower administration marked the beginnings of direct American involvement in the Middle East.

At the end of the war (1945), the OSS was officially abolished, only to be reestablished two years later by President Harry S. Truman as the Central Intelligence Agency. With the advent of the Cold War, the Agency was charged not only with data collection and evaluation, but also with the goal of extending American influence through covert action and regime change.[7] In 1953 there was the overthrow of the Mossadegh government in Iran and in 1957, an abortive plot to remove Shukri al-Quwatli as president of Syria. In 1958 the US Marines landed on the shores of Lebanon just after a bloody coup overthrew the pro-West monarchy in Iraq.

In terms of Middle East policy, however, Americans were new to the region, and authors had little material to drawn on. The United States had no imperial experience there, and Muslim immigration to America had barely begun.[8] The post-World War II Anglo-American partnership delegated the protection of oil fields in the Persian Gulf and defense of the Suez Canal to Britain, leaving the United States on the periphery with Greece and Turkey, positive relations with Israel, and a focus on the "Northern Tier" countries in order to outflank Egypt and Arab nationalism.[9] During the Cold War that engaged the West until 1989, the free flow of oil and the prevention of Soviet control of that important resource dominated American policy thinking. Americans set up signals intelligence stations (SIGINT) in Turkey on the southeast shore of the Sea of Marmara and the Black Sea coast to collect data on Soviet naval systems, tactics, and new equipment, as well as to monitor test launches of early Soviet missile programs and Soviet development of long range radar. Monitoring these sites, using U2 spy planes, and exchanging microfilm by legal travelers across borders were all part of US strategy to gather information on the periphery of the Soviet Union. [10]

Like Churchill before him, CIA Director Allen Dulles talked about the nobility of espionage in war. To him, the exploits of the attractive, highly motivated agents during World War II and the Cold War that followed reinforced a growing positive image in the mind of the American public. [11] Kermit Roosevelt exemplified this image. When he was sent off to overthrow the government of Iran in 1953 (Operation Ajax), agent Roosevelt was thirty-seven years old and the spy in charge of the CIA's department on the Middle East and Asia. Kim Philby, the Soviet agent, described him as the quintessential quiet American, a "courteous, soft-spoken Easterner with impeccable social connections, well-educated rather than intellectual, pleasant and unassuming as host and guest. An especially nice wife. In fact, the last person you would expect to be up to the neck in dirty tricks." Roosevelt, grandson of President Theodore Roosevelt, sounded much like Richard Hannay when he wrote that "I remembered what my father wrote of his arrival in Africa with *his* father, T. R., in 1909 on the *African Game Trails* trip: 'It was a great adventure, and all the world was young!' I felt as he must have felt then. My nerves tingled, my spirits soared as we moved up the mountain road." [12] Having accused the Democrats of being "soft on Communism" and "losing China," the Eisenhower Republicans decided to bolster the United States' presence in Latin America and the Middle East.

Dulles, and, later, CIA Director Richard Helms, thought that the use of spy novels featuring the exploits of Americans was a good way to "publicize" the work of the CIA, much as Ian Fleming, and Buchan before him, had provided positive exposure for British intelligence, just as J. Edgar Hoover did for the US Federal Bureau of Investigation. [13] In the early 1970s, agents and ex-agents, with the encouragement of their superiors, were writing spy novels, leading some to comment that now with agents writing the novels, the overall quality of the genre had improved. By the late 1980s, the CIA's Publications Review Board had vetted more than eighty-five works of fiction. [14] In 1964, E. Howard Hunt, a CIA operative who later achieved notoriety as one of the Nixon "plumbers" in Watergate, began to write about his experiences. He was stationed in Mexico at the same time as the Lee Harvey Oswald visit, worked in the Balkans, the Far East, and Uruguay, and was involved in the American-inspired coup in Guatemala. Writing under the pseudonyms of David St. John and Robert Dietrich, Hunt had his operative Peter Ward, who resembled Bond, engage in the good fight—the struggle of the West against the evil USSR.[15] Later, riding the wave of Middle East-inspired novels, he published *The Gaza Intercept* (1981) under his own name.

In the American mind, changes in foreign government were to be accompanied not only by a shift in political alignment, yielding a closer relationship with America, but also with the acceptance ipso facto of Western culture and norms. Not as direct as the French *mission civilizatrice*, American modernization theory prevalent in American academia during the 1950s and 1960s nonetheless discounted as primitive the Middle Eastern religious and cultural traditions.[16] This dissonance is clearly reflected in earlier American novels. In a fictional attempt at portraying realistic American involvement in the Middle East, American journalist Marquis Childs in *Taint of Innocence* (1967) not only depicts the clash of cultures but highlights American disingenuousness about the region that would later dominate the anti-heroic novels of the 1980s. The CIA agent stationed in a Persian Gulf sheikhdom has a sense of patriotism at odds with a US foreign policy that is in league with oil interests. Present at a riot at the oil field, he is appalled at the death of two Arabs when, against CIA orders, an oil company security man orders his men to fire on the rioters. He fantasizes that the Western-educated wife of the local sheikh is in love with him. How could she be happily married to a boor who merely wants the oil companies to leave his country? Completely misunderstanding the situation, the agent gets personal and is at a loss when the woman is shocked at his advances. Western educated or not, she agrees with her husband's politics and is satisfied with her marriage to the emir who, after the dust settles, is sent off on a diplomatic mission to London. The naive American is left in a quandary: He cannot believe that a Western-educated woman would remain with an Arab who is one generation from the camel and he is disgusted with the profligacy of oil-rich countries. What he cannot understand is why the Arabs fault the oil companies that are trying to modernize and westernize by bringing to the region air conditioning and education. Peace Corps volunteers and journalists will continue to write novels on similar themes.[17]

Another example, Edward Sheehan's *The Kingdom of Illusion* (1964), satirically illustrates the monolithic world outlook of American foreign policy makers and evokes the heavy-handed policy of Operation Ajax. Here, the conflict is between an ambassador who, as an Arabist, understands the local culture, and his bosses in Washington who send a CIA troubleshooter "fireman" to the region to straighten out a messy post-revolution situation. The new prime minister, Mustafa al-Mabrouk, is a Western-educated former Bedouin goatherd who tries to increase the amount of economic assistance from both East and West by playing the two against each other while still retaining his country's political independence. Impressed by British aristocratic values after his year of study in London, al-Mabrouk is still insecure in the presence of Westerners and reacts by giving vitriolic anti-Western speeches for home consumption. Ascetic and totally absorbed with his country's welfare, the prime minister likes Americans but will turn to the Soviet Union, if need be. He likes his country's handsome, but not very intelligent king and tries to save him from disaster, but cannot. An absurd attempt by the CIA agent to overthrow this too "liberal" prime minister results in catastrophe. Blamed for the fiasco he had no part in, the ambassador is demoted to a "Fourth World" country as punishment for failed diplomacy. The novel illustrates the American dilemma in dealing with newly independent countries in the era of decolonization. It did not have to be set in the Middle East; it could have been set almost anywhere.

For the most part, however, novels followed predictable form in the Bond era. Agents were sent to foil nationalist- or communist-inspired coups against Western-backed governments. The Middle East was also the setting for Cold War novels and mysteries.

There were very few novels about the Arab-Israeli conflict or attacks outside the region. By the late 1960s that would change when once again paranoia gripped the West. The British, in the grips of decolonization and the Suez debacle, were at the end of their imperial game, withdrawing from the Middle East even as an intelligence crisis hit London—when British spies, most notably Kim Philby, defected to the Soviet Union. Both the United States and Britain became increasingly worried about Soviet moles in their intelligence services. Americans, especially after the Tet Offensive (1968), were insecure over failures in Vietnam and were reluctant to become entangled elsewhere. The American Vietnam Syndrome, as it was called, coincided with anxiety generated at home by anti-war and minorities' rights movements and domestic conspiracy theories that stemmed from the assassinations of President John F. Kennedy (1963), Robert F. Kennedy (1968), and the Reverend Martin Luther King, Jr. (1968).

With the British preoccupied at home and the Americans mired in Vietnam at the same time that the publishing explosion of paperback spy novels created a demand for fictional heroics, there was a real vacuum that required new protagonists to fill the void. The confluence of publishing trends, international politics, and events occurring in the Middle East created a new fictional dynamic that would provide plot material for spy novels and thrillers for two decades. The Israeli victory in the June 1967 Arab-Israeli war created new Western heroes; Palestinians who decided to use international terrorism as a political method became villains, and terrorism and the OPEC oil boycott during the Arab-Israeli War of 1973 brought a Middle Eastern secular *jihad* against the West squarely into crime fiction.

Throughout the spring of 1967, coverage of United States military involvement in Vietnam was being broadcast daily into American living rooms. As the Vietnam War escalated, Operation "Rolling Thunder" was on and 200,000 American troops were fighting in the South while the United States Air Force bombed in the North. General William Westmoreland testified before Congress that the war could be won if the military applied more force and if the American public accepted more losses. At the same time, the Middle East was heating up for the third Arab-Israeli war. By mid-June, the Six-Day War was over. The Israeli military had defeated the combined forces of its Arab neighbors and emerged with territory three times its former size under its control.

American comedians joked that the US could use a general like Moshe Dayan in Vietnam and a military official remarked that "when a country decides to go to war, it goes in 'wham'—to win."[18] For novelists in fictional overload with Russian, Chinese, and Nazi villains, publishers and writers saw in the Israeli victory over the Arabs in 1967 and the subsequent Israeli intelligence triumphs a relatively unexploited arena for their operatives and agents. The war, as well as other subsequent Israeli successes such as the capture of Adolph Eichmann, the lifting of Soviet radar from Egyptian territory, the raid on Entebbe, the spiriting away of gunboats from the Cherbourg harbor, and the sudden acquisition of plans for the Mirage jet and material for nuclear weapons, gave the Israeli Mossad international stature equal to that of the Soviet KGB, the American CIA, the British MI6, and the French Sûreté, at the same time that the British and Americans were losing face internationally.[19] Spy novels and thrillers began to reflect Israeli invincibility, and for a short period, the Israeli hero entered the public arena.

In essence, what this fictional hero represented was the extension in fiction of the Americanization of the Israeli and of Israel, a phenomenon that had been developing since the emergence of the State of Israel in 1948. Just as the American view became a Jewish projection of what Israel ought to be, the Israeli hero in popular fiction synchronized an American/Israeli typology that operated in a world where American and Israeli interests co-alesced. This was a politically liberal Israel governed by the Labor Party, operating as the bulwark against Communism while struggling in defensive wars against the Arab Soviet clients bent on destroying her. So long as this synchronization lasted—essentially through tenure of the Israeli Labor government (1948–1977)—Israelis could be virtually synonymous with their American heroic counterparts.[20]

The Israeli victory over the Arabs in 1967 not only completed the transformation of Israelis into Westerners, but in the exuberant aftermath of the war, it triggered a new self-confidence among American Jews, especially when others confirmed it: "Incidently [sic]," White House special counsel Henry McPherson would cable to President Lyndon Johnson just after the fighting ended, "Israel at war destroys the prototype of the pale, scrawny Jew. The soldiers I saw were tough, muscular, and sunburned."[21] Notwithstanding the romanticized kibbutz farmer/soldier identification with the Israelis, the new perception of the Israelis and by extension, the Jew, whether he lived in Tel-Aviv or Brooklyn, suddenly shifted from Holocaust victim to soldier hero. The depiction of the Haganah agent in F. Van Wyck Mason's *The Cairo Garter Murders* (1938) had become outmoded. Instead of the sweaty man of the dirty hands and the moist and flabby handshake, the "fox-faced Bulgarian Jew with eyes like gimlets and a distressing shuffle,"[22] in Leon Uris's novel and later the film, *Exodus*, Americans were treated to the Israeli hero in the image of Paul Newman, the quintessential American. This tender-tough Sabra image of a victim who could now defend himself, introduced into American film and fiction by writers who were among the more than half a million World War II Jewish combat veterans, mirrored the American political culture of idealism and realism. Israelis were now welcomed as heroes in American popular culture.[23]

Dov Shalzar in Leonard Harris's novel *The Masada Plan* (1976) is a good example. The perfect choice for the New York post, Shalzar not only speaks the "language of the natives, but he had the medals, glamour, eloquence and sex appeal to woo Hadassah ladies and other friends of Israel at lunches, dinners, and receptions, or wherever funds had to be raised and Israeli positions explained."[24] This Israeli appealed to American Jews and Christians because he embodied recognized heroic characteristics and was more American than "Jewish." His girlfriend is a blonde Protestant, and the Israelis he defends do not eat lox and bagels. During a period when Americans were bogged down in Vietnam, *these* Israeli heroes could replace Americans who, in both fact and fiction, questioned the effectiveness of the United States in the world arena.[25]

Published about the same time, Thomas Harris's thriller *Black Sunday* (1975) demonstrates the impact of the Vietnam War as America stands politically and militarily impotent in the face of a major terrorist attack. Israel warns of a conspiracy in the offing plotted by an American Vietnam veteran and Palestinian Black September terrorists to kill 80,000 people, including the newly elected president of the United States, while the entire nation is watching the Super Bowl football game in New Orleans. At the same time, the Israeli Ambassador doubts that the Americans will act—"The salient fact will be that the atrocity happened *because* the United States has helped Israel. Because they got involved in another dirty war. Indochina has made them sick of involvement just as it did the French, and understandably so."[26] In the end, the attack is thwarted not because of American or even Israeli heroics, but because, just as the United States did not "win" in Vietnam, Michael Lander, the Vietnam veteran left impotent and physically handicapped by the war, is incapable of executing the attack. Detonation of the explosives is avoided due to malfunction.[27]

PLOTS 1970–1979			
Murder Mysteries	17	Oil	3
Jihad	3	Economic Threat	18
World War II	3	Terrorism	37
Cold War	14	Nuclear Threat	3
Coups	30	Lebanese Civil War	1
Arab-Israeli Conflict	79	World War III	1
Crime	23	Other	11
TOTAL			243

The Masada Plan and *Black Sunday* are but two examples of the hundreds of novels that directly or indirectly concerned the Arab-Israeli Conflict. Until the early 1980s, the Israeli fictional superspy was everywhere: authors had him in Kuwait foiling PLO terrorist operations or in Texas thwarting Arab destruction of American oil facilities. At first, he was so respected that he was even called in as a consultant on difficult cases: to find Soviet moles in British intelligence, and to save members of the United Nations General Assembly from the maniacal designs of a mad messiah who used the Biblical Ten Plagues in a plan to kill the Pope.[28] In more than forty American or

British novels with Israeli heroes, penned by American, British, and Israeli authors for the American reading market, he was busy saving the United States, New York City, Tel-Aviv, and California from nuclear holocaust; rescuing American presidents, the wife of the American Secretary of State, and the Israeli president from terrorist hijackers, and preventing the assassinations of the US president, the Shah's foreign minister, and the king of Jordan.[29]

Some authors made the Israeli hero even more sympathetic by adding a trace of vulnerability to his persona. He has had a tragic love affair when young or is a Holocaust survivor. Many operators have spent time in concentration camps, and after a sojourn on Cyprus, arrive in Israel only to spend a lifetime fighting Arabs in every war, after which they are appointed to head up a newly formed anti-terrorist unit. Because they are survivors, they are not only emotionally numb, but have become automatons and workaholics. Sometimes a love interest can repair their damaged psyches, and the heroes fulfill missions and fade off into the sunset, revived and revivified spiritually and emotionally.[30] More often, this background is used to excuse the violent, amoral means authors have their Israeli James Bond imitations use in order to achieve the greater good.

By the late 1970s, Israeli heroes had become as two-dimensional as such American protagonists as Nick Carter or Sam Durell. Drawing on the success of these paperback original series, Adam Hamilton's "Peacemaker" and Stuart Jason's "The Butcher," just to name two short-lived series of avenger novels, authors had their heroes save Israel and smite terrorists who threatened the United States.[31]

As for villains, the Palestinians provided the perfect foils. The decision made in 1968 by Fatah and later the Palestine Liberation Organization to use terrorism either alone or in league with one of their Communist backers across the globe as a political tool to ensure constant visibility of the Palestinian cause created more than a parochial threat to Israel. When bombs began to go off and planes were hijacked—from 1968 to 1976 there were twenty-nine hijackings staged by Palestinian or pro-Palestinian groups[32]— the terrorism war provided unbridled opportunity for fictional improvisation. Once Israeli, British, and American agents began battling not only generic terrorists but Palestinians all over the world who were involved in plane and ship hijacking, hostage taking, and assassinations directed not only at Israelis but anyone who could advance their political agenda, authors had not only an entirely new area to exploit for popular fiction, but other opportunities for creativity that expanded exponentially.

As terrorist incidents filled the front pages of newspapers, interest in Europeans and even the Soviets receded in fiction. There was no equivocation that Arabs were the villains, whether as "generic" Arabs or as Palestinians. Creating plots became easier. Using the news for inspiration, authors crafted scripts based on a modicum of recognizable fact and took them to fanciful horizons. For example, the "Eye of Gaza" terrorists, headquartered in Gaza, plan to drop a nuclear bomb on Jerusalem, but the story is scooped by an American television commentator during the United States elections. Or neo-Nazis and a Palestinian fringe group fire missiles in Geneva, where they are to hit planes transporting Yasir Arafat and the United States president to a peace conference.[33] The popularity of the thriller whose formula required stereotype and an apocalyptic plot encouraged this creativity. Books sold, writers increased output, and publishers were pleased even though the plots were becoming redundant.

By the mid-1980s, so many thrillers with a Middle East plot were appearing that it became possible to chart specific news stories, allow for a time lag for the writing and production of a fictional account, and wait for the familiar event to appear in a printed variation. Plane hijackings from 1968–1970 generated no fewer than seven novels.[34] There were two about the 1972 attack on Israeli athletes at the Munich Olympics.[35] The 1983 bombing of the US Marine headquarters in Beirut was the plot of D. Dye's *Outrage*, published in 1988. With the success of fiction based on fact, it seemed that during the runup to the first Gulf War from 1990 to 1991, publishers and authors were preparing for a readership that would snap up every novel about the war.[36]

Initially, "generic Arabs" became natural foils for Israeli heroes. In the early years, even though villains were typecast as terrorists or masterminds of horrendous conspiracies designed to destroy the West or Israel, authors were loath to have them operate alone, for fear that the characters would be viewed as too intelligent, too capable for those who were out to destroy the West. Much like the patronizing view of Arabs and Muslims that permeated British *jihad* novels before World War II, these secular Middle Eastern *jihadist* villains clearly required European assistance in order to carry out their own conspiracies. A British explosives expert is used to plant the bombs needed to blow up the empty new headquarters of Israeli intelligence, or a British mercenary is teamed with a ruthless former OAS French officer so that a rich Saudi sheikh can plant a nuclear device on a hijacked oil tanker headed for San Francisco.[37] If Israel, which has been attacked by the Arabs, is re-armed by the West, the Saudi can then threaten the United States with destruction.[38] Arabs were also pawns of diabolical anti-Semitic Frenchmen, neo-Nazis, the Chinese Communists and the "military-industrial complex" that uses them even though "both OPEC and the Mother Co. agreed that the Palestinians were a pest out of all proportion to their significance, but the vagaries of history had made them and their petty cause a rallying point for the divergent Arab nations."[39]

As terrorist attacks became more complex and their perpetrators were identified, villains were portrayed in a more realistic fashion, but it seemed obvious to the Western author and the reading public that the malefactors had to be insane to order these acts of destruction. Often such villains as Libya's Colonel Qadaffi were not even named in the novels. His diabolical aura pervades the atmosphere. He may wind up his soldiers and set them moving against Soviet officials who have betrayed him, against British agents, or even against Moshe Dayan. He hires German scientists to infect Israelis with a nerve disease that will transform them into drooling idiots, and in one of his most sensational escapades, Colonel Qaddafi uses a Palestinian scientist to conceal and prime a nuclear bomb in New York City.[40]

When the Israeli/Palestinian terrorist/spy assassination war of the 1970s came to light through the publication of such books as *The Israeli Secret Service, The Hit Team*, and *Spymasters of Israel*, heretofore shadowy personalities, members of the Popular Front for the Liberation of Palestine General Command, and Black September operations agents in Europe received publicity and their backgrounds were fleshed out.[41] Once Palestinian groups began to assassinate Israelis living outside of Israel, and even more so after the Munich Massacre at the 1972 Olympics, Israeli "hit teams" and "vengeance squads" retaliated, killing high-ranking members of the PFLP and Black September, using booby-trapped cars, parcel bombs, tape-recorder bombs, telephone bombs, and straightforward assassination. The most elusive and romantic target, Ali Hassan Salameh, the Black September chief of operations and the planner of Munich, was stalked for six years until he was killed in Beirut in 1979. His character appears in a number of spy novels and thrillers as the handsome Lothario terrorist mastermind who, when plane hijackings were in vogue, plants explosives in electronic devices he hands to his female victims to carry on planes or uses their networking connections in order to enhance his nefarious possibilities. Unaware of the danger, the girls are invariably employees of Western embassies or, conveniently, secretaries to important people.

The character is portrayed as an anti-royalist Moroccan who backs the wrong side in an abortive attempt on the life of King Hassan and then flees to work for Colonel Qaddafi, or a Nasserite Egyptian, out of favor in Sadat's Egypt who works for Arab unity. In Jack Hoffenberg's *17 Ben Gurion*, he is the urbane Egyptian, Hatif Tobari, who is introduced lounging on the balcony of his mistress's plush Mediterranean apartment. A tall, slim man of dark to medium complexion, he is strongly built and "extremely handsome in an Oriental way." His mistress was his opiate, his safety valve, "his release from the tension of intrigue, from the dangers of exposure to the schizophrenia that was so much part and parcel of his maneuverings in the psychotic world of Middle Eastern politics. Always he must live with the possibility of assassination by envious *fedayeen* leaders, whom he despised as disorganized, incompetent, ill-trained rabble, forever engaged in bickering, taking unilateral action without regard for their lives as well as those of others." Unlike them, Tobari, backed by Libya and Iraq, has access to a powerful high explosive that his men will detonate at the appointed time, at specific targets in Israel, effectively destroying the Israeli economy.[42]

Or he is Ahmed Bel Jahra, the villain in Marvin Albert's *The Gargoyle Conspiracy*. A "tall, aristocratic-looking man of thirty-four, with a lean, powerful build, finely chiseled features, and a sardonic mouth" who, having failed at his most recent attempt at terrorism—blowing up a plane at the Rome airport—must achieve a more spectacular success in order to keep his financial backers happy. They might be Gulf oil sheikhs, the Iraqis, or, in this case, Colonel Qaddafi, who underwrites the terrorist's fashionable lifestyle and his dreams of the destruction of Israel. When Bel Jahra was in Europe, "he was dressed with a casual elegance: the sandals handmade of soft, expensive leather, the Levis especially retailored for his small hips, and the blue turtleneck pullover a Cardin." He wanted the plane destroyed both as a symbolic gesture "to punish the airline for flying to Israel," and "to punish the United States for interfering in Arab plans for the Middle East." It is convenient that Iranian officials, who have aided Iraqi Kurds, thus thwarting an Arab power play in the Persian Gulf, are aboard. Although the plan has gone awry, he is soon presented with another opportunity: to kill both King Hussein of Jordan and America's Secretary of State at a party at a renowned French artist's Riviera estate. He enjoys watching the shock of his Libyan backers when he explains how the artist's somewhat plain secretary who, overcome by his charm and good looks, nervously let slip details about the event in an attempt to keep him interested in her. She looked "into his pale gray eyes and saw nothing but eagerness to be with her again." Bel Jahra looks into her eyes and sees nothing but Qaddafi's agent in Geneva, and because of the girl, only he is able to execute the plan.[43]

Most of the villains, however, have no redeeming qualities. Much like the heroes who, with the ever increasing number of spy novels and thrillers produced for the burgeoning market, devolved into automatons, villains also became stick figure caricatures. Harris's Palestinian villain in *Black Sunday* is but one example. Escaping assassination by an Israeli hit team only to work with the inept Michael Lander on the bomb plot directed at the Super Bowl, Muhammad Fusil is the truly negative, totally unsympathetic variation of the Salameh model:

> He had a certain amount of surface passion and a range of visible emotion that was wide and not deep. But he was deep, all right, and cold, and those cold depths held sightless, savage things that brushed and hit one another in the dark. He had learned about himself very early. At the same time he had taught his schoolmates about himself and then he was left alone. Fasil had splendid reflexes and wiry strength. He had no fear and no mercy, but he did have malice. Fusil was living proof that physiognomy is a false science. He was slim and fairly good-looking. He was a monster.[44]

And like many of his counterparts in similar novels, he abuses women who, more often than not, are presented as objects, merely to be used by the men who mastermind and implement the conspiracies. They tend to be weak, subservient types despite the emergence of such real role models as Popular Front for the Liberation of Palestine member Leila Khalid who hijacked an El Al plane in London in 1970.[45] Although women are portrayed as emancipated—they remove the veil, are politically educated, and sexually liberated—these westernized characters are provided for the benefit of the male who is using them. Angela, a.k.a. Nerida, in Arthur Mather's *The Mind Breaker* (1980), grew up in a refugee camp and was recruited to the cause because of her potential as a sexual object. She, like many of her Israeli counterparts, is trained and used to seduce and then kill enemy agents. Where the Arab woman seems to lead is in her cruelty. She may order an assault on the Monastery of St. Catherine at Mt. Sinai and the execution of the monks, or as a lesbian, rejected by a female Israeli captive, turn the prisoner over to eager male subordinates. Unlike women detectives or agents in the Modesty Blaise or Emily Pollifax model, female villains are rarely trusted by their controls to act independently.[46]

While Americans lauded the Israeli victory in 1967 and terrorism struck a responsive chord in American readers, direct attacks on the American economy posed a more powerful existential threat that affected everyone.

More than the 1967 war, the oil boycott and the gasoline lines of the early 1970s brought events in the Middle East directly into the American consciousness.

The United States had stayed out of the Middle East political quagmire during the 1956 Suez War and the Middle East crisis in 1967 and worked with oil companies to keep oil flowing so that by 1972, America was importing nearly one-third of its annual oil consumption from the Middle East. At the OPEC meeting in 1968, the Iraqis and the Saudis secured the passage of a resolution that declared that within five years they, the producing countries, not the United States, the United Kingdom or the multinationals, would set pricing. Soon after in Beirut, OAPEC (Organization of Arab Petroleum Exporting Countries) was formed and its first director, Saudi Ahmed Zaki Yamani became a familiar figure on American television screens.[47] The following year, the king of Libya was overthrown by Muammar Qaddafi, who insisted that oil companies raise the price of crude. When Qaddafi succeeded in forcing up the price of Libyan crude, the Iranians followed suit.

When OAPEC imposed the oil boycott against the United States during the Arab-Israeli war of 1973, with its accompanying scarcity and the resultant sky-rocketing price of fuel accompanied by the accumulation of vast wealth by oil rich states at the expense of Western consumers, Arabs and Muslims were perceived by Americans to be direct threats to Western economies not only with respect to resources abroad but political stability at home. Consumers faced long lines at the gas pump and were asked to lower thermostats and wear sweaters. At the same time, they saw conspicuous consumption by oil-rich Arabs: new model sports cars in showrooms and discarded older Mercedes abandoned on the sides of the desert-bordered, recently macadamized-paved roads. Political cartoons depicted Arabs with noses shaped as oil nozzles and news stories abounded about the potential Arab/Muslim ownership of America. The boycott generated an anti-Arab bias that was mirrored in the portrayal of Middle Easterners in crime fiction. Former confederates became villains; unsavory Levantines and Turks, heretofore vilified, were portrayed as Western allies; and Arabs, whom the British had earlier romanticized as "noble savages," reverted to their historic well-known stereotype as decadent Bedouin bent on destroying the West.

Paul Erdman's novel, *The Crash of '79*, published in 1976, only reinforced the view that the Middle Eastern petro-sheikhs—it did not matter whether they were Persian or Arab because most readers did not know the difference—were out to destroy America through economic *jihad*. The best seller, which remained on *The New York Times* list for more than seven months, treated readers to a primer on international finance laced with Iranian villainy. The Shah, who controlled Iran's oil, wanted more: As prices rose, American banks were going broke and the stock market plummeted, but the Shah wanted to control the entire Persian Gulf oil supply. An American financial wizard is summoned to save the US and the West, but the Shah of Iran also has the bomb, and with it, he seeks to manipulate control of the Persian Gulf. In consultation with his astrologers and court historian, he plans a short "Four Day War" to make his move on Saudi Arabia. Victory would mean the control of oil resources and also the revival of the "Sassanid Empire, an empire that included all the lands bordering on the Persian Gulf on the east, west, and north, and one which had lasted for more than four centuries. It was the reestablishment of the glory of ancient Persia that was the goal of the King of Kings in 1979. For he was fifty-nine, and time was running out."[48] Despite the portentous omens, as luck would have it, the invasion is doomed: Not all of the planes take off, so that while The King of Kings has won his empire, "now it lay under a cloud of lethal radioactivity; its people were either dead or dying, or fleeing for their lives. And nothing remained of the Shah of Iran. His command bunker—and he—had been vaporized"[49] Had it been successful, the Shah's "Four Day War" would have achieved Iranian control of petroleum sources, sparked a financial panic, and brought about the collapse of the US economy, all in one fell swoop.

The impact of Erdman's novel was readily apparent. Successfully combining the news with information not easily accessible to the average person, thrillers like *The Crash of '79* easily engaged a large readership. At the time, there was no cable television news broadcasting continuous global coverage accompanied by the commentary of instant experts summoned to interpret the events. Readers wanted to know how the financial markets worked, what drove OPEC, and how the Iranians could construct a nuclear bomb. The views of the handsome Saudi oil minister Ahmad Zaki Yamani, who during the early 1970s was interviewed countless times on American television, rang true in the novel: "Look out that that window," the Yamani character in the novel demands. "From here to the top of the Persian Gulf is about three hundred miles. Our major oil fields, those of Kuwait, of Iraq, of Iran, are all within a few dozen miles of that coastline. You control that coast and you control half—*half*—the petroleum on earth. If a dictator like Pahlavi would take such control—and make no mistake, he intends to—then your capitalism will be dead very soon!"[50] Despite the fact that the Shah had been America's ally for decades and during the 1970s was designated by Secretary of State Henry Kissinger and President Richard Nixon as the protector of America's interests in the Persian Gulf, not all Americans, especially thriller readers, were so sure of his loyalty.

Erdman's book immediately spawned a plethora of novels about financial markets, the Arabs, and a new economic war against the West that integrated the Arab-Israeli conflict, terrorism, and economic *jihad* novels. The potential for the actual conquest of the West by the East was projected in a number of ways: directly by military or economic means, either linked to the Arab-Israeli conflict or merely a simple matter of personal pique or vengeance. Readers saw a megalomaniacal Shah of Iran, creeping Arab influence in the United States and the manipulation of ordinary Americans by the newly independent oil producers. Their presence could be noted daily at the gas pumps, with increases in the price of gasoline, and by the steadily increasing financial encroachments on the American economy and foreign policy.

Thrillers exploiting this theme, therefore, struck a familiar chord. It was believable that an Arab, educated at Harvard Business School or the London School of Economics could manipulate Wall Street or the commodities and currency markets, wreaking havoc on Western economies with or without the assistance of a Western expatriate.[51] Arabs and Iranians could connive not only to drive up the price of oil, but to wrest control of American finance, education, and the media by purchasing banks, universities, and newspapers, while the Saudis, through the assistance of a Lebanese-American who had been slighted by a New York advertising company, could buy General Motors and the advertising company that had originally employed him.[52] Middle Easterners could work with regimes in North Africa and the international oil companies to control the United States economy or swamp the world with counterfeit dollars intended to disrupt the financial markets. From the American side, fictional revenge came soon enough: Middle Eastern oil fields came into the gun sights of American agents, and plans were concocted to blow them up. By the time Wilbur Smith's *The Delta Decision* appeared in 1979, it did not matter that the real villain, called Caliph, was a multinational corporation; the subliminal association with the Middle East was clearly apparent.[53]

With this new attack on the West, authors modified their stereotypes and caricatures of Middle Easterners as hundreds of books poured into the marketplace. What is interesting here is not so much how the villains were portrayed—obviously with all of the odious characteristics authors could contrive—but who the miscreants were. Allies became enemies, and groups that had formerly been vilified before the 1960s were suddenly seen in a positive light.

The fictional fortunes of the Shah of Iran took a negative turn when he was suddenly transformed from victim to villain. For a good part of the twentieth century, neither British nor American authors gave much thought to Iran or the Shah until Muhamad Reza Pahlavi came to power.[54] Placed on the throne by the Allies during World War II, the Shah was beset by political crises early in his reign. An attempt on his life was followed soon after by the Mossadegh crisis and the accompanying CIA coup (Operation Ajax). Acceding to popular demand, in 1951 the Shah had appointed Mohammad Mosaddegh, scion of an important landed Iranian family but an avowed liberal democrat and Iranian nationalist as prime minister. He was *Time* magazine's "Man of the Year for 1951." Nevertheless, Mossadegh proceeded to nationalize the Anglo-Iranian Oil Company, in which the British held fifty per cent of the stock. The British took the case to the World Court and applied economic sanctions against Iran; the Iranians took control of the refineries at Abadan and received moral support from their people and those of the Third World undergoing decolonization. When the British plan to overthrow Mossadegh failed and American assistance was requested, the United States sent the CIA to engineer regime change. Despite reluctantly agreeing to the plan because of promises of American support for the lifestyle to which he had become accustomed, the Iranian ruler fled the country even before the operation began. After Mossadegh's ouster in 1953, the Shah acknowledged the services of CIA agent Kermit Roosevelt: "I owe my throne to God, my people, my army—and to you," he said.[55]

In American fiction, the Shah was initially portrayed sympathetically, even as rebellions against his regime were underreported in the press, because he was an ally of the United States, and his modernization programs were in sync with American policy.[56] With his increase in international stature because of American support and Iran's increasing oil wealth, spy novel authors began to set their plots in Iran.[57] For British authors, Iran was a setting for peripatetic heroic dentists sent on secret missions, while European playboys went to Iran to protect the ruler from the Soviets, Iranian generals, or even the CIA.[58]

The positive characterization of the ruler of Iran changed dramatically when, in the mid-1970s, not only did his role in the oil boycott become clear, as noted in *The Crash of '79*, but his posturing on television resounded negatively with American audiences. From then until his downfall in 1979, the Shah personified for Americans the megalomaniacal mastermind who, despite being an American ally, would destroy the American economy if it suited him. The Shah, Iran, and the Islamic Republic that followed became a magnet for authors writing of war against the West. Noting the popularity of Erdman's book, other authors capitalized on the Shah's notoriety. In Peter Ritner's *Red Carpet for the Shah* (1975), the villainous shah attacks the Soviet Union. In other novels, he supervises assassination attempts against himself, drives up the price of silver and bankrupts the West, and contrives a major oil spill that will cause irreparable ecological damage.[59]

The Persian extravaganza that the Shah hosted in 1971 to commemorate the 2,500th anniversary of the Persian Empire provided authors with a capstone event they could use to illustrate his caricatured villainy. As he stood near the ruins of the ancient Persian capital at Persepolis, the Shah addressed his putative ancestor Cyrus the Great, creator of the Persian Empire: "Rest in peace," he said. "The Iranian flag is flying today as triumphantly as ever in the past."[60] The display of arrogance, wealth, and power, that included catering from Maxim's of Paris, instead of local Persian delicacies, and parades by soldiers in uniforms of the past Persian dynasties, was reported by the media in stark contrast to the poverty of most of the Shah's subjects, and was used by *New York Times* journalist Eric Pace as a backdrop for his jewel caper *Nightingale*.[61] Only the onset of the Iranian Revolution and the Shah's death from cancer saved him from total ignominy.

The Shah of Iran was not the only character whose depiction was transformed during the economic war against the West. Thriller writers caricatured Arabs, whom nineteenth century British travelers had either romanticized as noble savages or demonized as camel-riding tribesmen, as primitives with a technological upgrade. During the 1970s they were oil entrepreneurs, owners of disposable Cadillacs, and profligate masters of petrodollars put to use against the West.

As is well known, studies about Western views of the Other have a long academic provenance. Scholars of Middle Eastern history and culture have charted how perceptions of the Arab relate to European images of non-Europeans. From rapacious bandit, treacherous enemy, noble adversary, cultural equal (or even nominal superior), to noble savage and religious fanatic, the perennial European view of the Orient has existed over time on two levels. On the conscious, pragmatic everyday level of trade, diplomacy, peace, and even war, as Henri Baudet tells us, life proceeds at its normal pace: people buy, sell, live, and die as human beings. At the same time, in the psychological, unconscious realm, wherein reside myth and imagination, groups become caricatured.[62]

From the time of Muhammad, as Edward Said and others have noted, the Arab/Muslim was viewed as the enemy of Europe/Christendom. He was the treacherous scoundrel whose armies penetrated to the boundaries of civilized Christianity. Yet, despite this reputation, there was a perceptible shift when during the Crusades the Muslim commander, Saladin, emerged as the paragon of chivalry. To this day in the Western mind, Saladin, who defeated the flower of European medieval chivalry, Richard the Lionheart, has come to symbolize for the Westerner all that is heroic. His noble dealings with the enemy Franks exemplified for the Europeans a humanity that they never expected of the infidel. For a time, the Muslim's popularity in Europe outshone that of his contemporaries, Philip Augustus and Frederick I Barbarossa. Dante placed him in the circle for heroic heathens; he became the central character for many a romance; and, legend has it, at one point the Muslim hero traveled to Europe incognito, convinced of the truth of Christianity: he would be a Christian in spite of himself.[63]

With the eighteenth century and the Enlightenment, Europeans became fascinated by the exotic externals, by the foreign dress and furnishings of the Chinese, the Persians, and the Ottoman Turks, even though only a short time before, the Ottomans had brought their armies to the gates of Vienna. Attracted to a variety of civilizations, perhaps because of a free-thinking reaction to a stringent Catholicism (when *Thousand and One Nights* was translated into European languages, it was an instant success) or a wistful hankering for a pristine Golden Age of antiquity, with European penetration of the East, romanticism took over. Where the Ottoman/Islamic civilization had been only shortly before viewed by the secularists as equal to or even superior to the West, with the noble Turk wagging his finger at the lapsed Christian, European victories over the Ottomans gave way to Englishmen sallying forth to the clean, innocent, uncivilized, unpolluted desert. More cosmopolitan in their Istanbul urban setting, the Ottomans, much like the Levantines, came to symbolize the corrupt and the lascivious, while the desert Arab or Bedouin emerged as pure and incorruptible. He was the noble savage of the European Enlightenment, the primitive who, uncontaminated by Europe or Christianity, was innately good, even superior to the average European who was cluttered by religious, social, and industrial baggage. The Arab was seen as proud, free, hospitable, and distinctive, much like Edgar Rice Burroughs's Tarzan—untainted by Western civilization.

This romantic image was pursued by T. E. Lawrence whose publicist Lowell Thomas, sent by John Buchan to Arabia, spread Lawrence's fame throughout the United States. Lawrence's real or imagined exploits in Arabia during World War I sparked the admiration of millions of people who identified with British imperialism. He was depicted in the silken white robes of an emir, accompanied by a large retinue of dagger-bedecked bodyguards. Sallying forth to lead the Arabs in revolt against the Ottomans, Lawrence's image remains unforgettable, not only in *The Seven Pillars of Wisdom*, Lawrence's own account of the mission, but in biography and later, in the film *Lawrence of Arabia*, starring Peter O'Toole. In the book, there is a description of the march that combines the splendid with the barbaric:

> First rode Feisal in white, then Sharraf at his right in red headcloth and henna-dyed tunic and cloak, myself on his left in white and scarlet, behind us three banners of faded crimson silk with gilt spikes, behind them the drummers playing a march, and behind them again the wild mass of twelve hundred bouncing camels of the bodyguard, packed as closely as they could move, the men in every variety of coloured cloths and the camels nearly as brilliant in their trappings. We filled the valley to its banks with our flashing stream.[64]

It is an image pressed into Western imagination that has endured to some degree despite the intrusion of politics and the twentieth century. In some spy novels the Arab appears as an amalgam: a noble, modern version of Saladin—generally a secular military officer.

We meet him in British author Charlotte Jay's *Arms for Adonis* (1960) as a Syrian officer who is a combination of Arab nobility and the pre-Islamic Middle Eastern myth. Here, Saladin is superimposed on the Greek myth of Adonis, a Semitic tale of death and resurrection where the handsome warrior, in love with the beautiful maiden, dies a horrible death only to be reborn every year. There was a temple to Adonis located in Lebanon, where mountain streams wash the red earth to the sea, and the short-lived red anemone, his flower, bloomed among the cedars.[65] In the novel, the hero appears as a Syrian officer who tries to bring about Syrian-Lebanese rapprochement at a time when Egypt and Syria are competing for Lebanese attentions in their attempt to form a Syrian-Egyptian union. Colonel Raschid Ahmed is handsome, slim, straightforward, honest, masculine, and gallant: He wins the heart of an unemployed British heroine, who inadvertently gets caught up in a plot to kill him. To Sarah, he is both the Adonis of the Greek myth and the heroic Arab juxtaposed against the "sleazy" Levantine—Greek or Armenian. When Raschid's brother, who has become a Lebanese businessman, tells the wounded colonel that there will always be room for him in the family business, the Syrian shakes his head. "Can you see me selling suit lengths to fat Armenians and Maronites?" While despairing of the Arab political condition, he is undaunted, pressing on honorably, pursuing his sense of duty. "We are bungling and ineffectual people, Tawfik," he tells his brother. "Even our assassinations misfire; and we are so divided that even as I point a gun at our deadliest enemy, the friend at my side jolts my elbow in case too much credit falls to me. I will change that. I will work for my country, and if I cannot bring it prosperity and raise the dignity of its life, at least I will see that its guns fire straight. That would be a beginning and perhaps it is all we can hope for at the moment."[66]

Another military officer, this time an Egyptian, appears in Lawrence Bachman's *The Bitter Lake* as Major Saladin, a disguised Egyptian general, who swims across the Suez Canal during the June 1967 war and later rows a boat back and forth during the battle, bringing many of his troops to safety. Unlike the Israelis, who are not very personable in their brief contact with the ship's passengers, Major Saladin is cheered on by the Western passengers aboard a nearby ship that is stuck in the Bitter Lake.[67] In another novel, the character is a retired businessman, code named "Saladin," who has returned to the Middle East after making his fortune and decides to work for peace between Arab and Jew, but from a position of strength. By hiring a team to perpetrate a "nonviolent" terrorist act as a sign—in this case, the destruction of a still-empty new headquarters for Israeli intelligence—he hopes to push for a solution to the conflict. Although dying of a terminal disease, he is ultimately murdered by an extremist, whose identity remains unclear.[68]

Arab characters as quasi-heroes also appear in the Nick Carter novels that were published in the United States to provide an American counterpart to James Bond. In some, indigenous Arabs appear as assistants to the hero or facilitators in the local milieu. After all, although presented as an omniscient, multi-cultural agent, from time to time Carter, whose exploits encompass more than two hundred global escapades, uses local expertise. In the 1970s, however, publishers were reluctant to present a fully positive Arab character, so the Egyptian Hakim Sadek, who appears in three Carter novels, is depicted with a marred physiognomy and an appearance that simultaneously shocks and repels Carter's Washington colleague Dan Eiger: "The figure that came toward him was tall and slightly hunched, and the face that seemed to hover suspiciously above it would have made an Arab slave-trader look benign by comparison. The flickering, unmatched eyes, the pockmarked skin, the cruelly curved thin lips, the sidling walk, all added up to a picture of unbelievable depravity." After the two speak, however, and identities are exchanged, a profound transformation ensues. Despite his ugliness, Eiger now saw in Hakim "a man who stood upright and four-square, a man of culture and breeding and intelligence and . . . *wholesomeness* . . . not quite on the same playing field as the Americans perhaps, but okay, nonetheless." Eiger notes to Hakim, his new found colleague, "Maybe it was a trick of lighting or something, but you did look a bit more villainous than I'd expected."[69] Almost, but not completely of the West, the secular Arab would slowly evolve into a hero to appear in that short window during the afterglow of Oslo in the 1990s.[70]

Obviously, more spy novels and thrillers reflected the negative, not only because the genre required clearly identifiable Others, but because in the political climate of terrorism and economic threat, Arab or Muslims as heroes were not believable to American readers. Drawing from his own service in Arabia during World War II, Stuart Jackman, writing at a time when Arabs were busily purchasing western assets and presents a scene similar to the one T. E. Lawrence described and provides a counter-image that exemplifies the negative:

> Abu Marak sat on his camel in the fading light with his rifle across his thighs and watched bin Hafid die. Behind him, mounted and ready to ride, his wolf pack waited in silence, sated with killing, the pouches of their tasseled saddle cloths stuffed with loot. Big, lean men they were, straggle-bearded, hard-eyed, with the high cheekbones and the great hooked nose of the Bedu. They wore white, ankle-length robes, streaked now with blood, and carried the tools of their trade: rifles, shotguns, knives and curved, two-edged swords thrust through the bandoliers around their waists. Eyes slitted against the setting sun, crawling with lice and flies, they sat like hawks in the saddle, the fingers of their left hands hooked into the reins, and waited for Marak to give the word to move out.[71]

Revulsion at the primitive merged with the hedonism that had once caricatured the Ottoman Turks, but was now transferred to the sheikhs whose appearances on television brought familiarity. Instead of quaint natives, however, Americans saw "ragheads," "aliens in beds sheets," and "irrational religious fanatics who wave Kalashnikovs instead of swords" and undertake suicide missions in place of cavalry charges. These hedonistic predators in the guise of the modern petro-sheikhs were oriented to opulence rather than plunder, rode in Cadillacs instead of camels, and lived a belief based on hedonism, a conglomeration of Hindu eroticism and the Western perception of Muslim sexual mores: large harems and many concubines. Instead of engaging in hand-to-hand physical violence, today's Bedouin petro-sheikh can hire financial wizards to purchase giant corporations or terrorists to threaten the very Westerners who have provided him with his powerful new image.[72] No longer to be controlled, Middle Easterners became a direct threat to the West. The noble Bedouin became the sybaritic sheikh, who might mastermind a plot but could also be victimized by a colonel, a Communist agent, or a drug dealer. But whether perpetrator or victim, in fiction he perpetuated negative stereotypes.

Fiction writers also turned to new allies. Non-Muslims—Copts, Armenians, and even Kurds—are brought into plots and given new incarnations. The once evil "Levantines" are transformed, first into local, ethnic nonparticipants in the region's political struggles, and then into anti-Arab foils in the British and later the American struggle against pan-Arabism and Communism. In this capacity, they remain outside of Egyptian, Iraqi, or even Israeli political machinations and have become more closely associated with the West, not only during the Cold War but later as representative secularists allied with the West against Islamic fanaticism. The character could be a British agent disguised as a Levantine businessman in a loud suit and yellow shoes working with resident Greek friends to thwart attempts by Egyptian nationalists to blow up the Aswan Dam, or he may be a policeman who is a Coptic Christian.[73] Eric Ambler's use of the Levantine hero in *The Levanter* also reflects a shift in Western attitudes towards Middle Eastern nationalism. Before the post-colonial era, authors admired the "pure Arab" and reserved racist contempt for minorities who had a Western veneer. By the 1970s, these minorities represented Western values in a genre that was increasingly becoming dominated by American authors.

By the end of the twentieth century, more American authors were writing spy novels and thrillers, as events in the Middle East touched the lives of an ever-expanding reading market. A fictional plot by an American-educated Arab sheikh to nuke Washington as in *Cobalt 60* was a believable threat, and Middle Eastern villains, no longer the pawns of others, were fully capable of war against the West on their own. With the return of American heroes in the spy novels and thrillers published during the post-Vietnam era, changes occurred as the thriller genre metamorphosed yet again and Americans engaged in the terrorist war with a vengeance.

SIX

The American Crusade
Against Terror

In 1975, just before the fall of Saigon, the magazine Soldier of Fortune: The Journal of Professional Adventurers (SOF) appeared on the newsstands. Founded by a former captain in the United States Army Special Forces at a time when many of America's Vietnam veterans, depressed at the defeat, were returning to an unsympathetic America, *Soldier of Fortune* marked a shift in masculine thinking. Discharged soldiers were demoralized: they had fought the war and performed well, but the government had betrayed them. To more than a few veterans, Vietnam was lost by a faulty command structure and a government that did not allow the full military power of the United States to be unleashed against the enemy.

By the mid-1980s there were 35,000 subscribers to *SOF*, and its newsstand readership of 150,000 cut across generational and educational lines.[1] Sales of paramilitary weapons increased in the United States, and in 1981, the National Survival Game was introduced, with the "paintball" version soon to follow. If Americans did not have a real war to fight just then, the era of Presidents Ronald Reagan and George H. W. Bush provided opportunities for paramilitary missions in Central America and Afghanistan, intervention in Lebanon, the Gulf War, and a policy of isolating Libya, Iraq, and Iran as terrorist states.[2] Americans also began to fight back in popular culture which was undergoing changes in the crime fiction genre and in the publishing industry.

Four years before the appearance of *SOF*, Clint Eastwood made the film *Dirty Harry* (1971), and a year after, Charles Bronson starred in *Death Wish*, a tale of vengeance perpetrated by a mild-mannered American citizen who acts because the American justice system was ineffectual and could not rid the streets of crime. There was a malaise in the country; the drug culture pervaded the cities; and the government, unable to cope with its failure in Vietnam, seemed inept in the domestic war against crime. The hard-boiled detective who operated at the fault lines of justice and criminality and the lone individual avenging a society incapable of restoring order from barbarism reflected these sentiments with their return to fiction. John Wayne may have died in 1979, but the hero of *The Green Berets* remained America's number one actor hero as late as 1995.[3]

On the popular culture front, film and fiction provided plenty of vicarious action. On September 20, 1981, Ray Walters in his "Paperback Talk" column in *The New York Times Book Review*, noted the return of virile mass-market paperbacks after a hiatus of more than a decade. The energetic marketing of these "men's action series," with titles like *The Executioner* and *The Destroyer*, at a time when paperbacks were moving from drugstore racks to the chain bookstore, pointed to a resurgence of the James Bond type of hero with a difference. Representing a convergence of thrillers and adventure books with an emphasis on technology and weaponry, and the physical as opposed to the cerebral, Warren Murphy and Richard Sapir's *The Destroyer* and Don Pendleton's *The Executioner* were very successful. From 1968, when the first title, *The Executioner: The War Against the Mafia* appeared, until the end of 2000, Pendleton's hero Mack Bolan had engaged in more than 270 operations. Some 200 million copies of *The Executioner* books are in print;[4] early titles are read and transmitted to new devotees through used bookstores; and many are being reprinted for new audiences. Readers express their admiration for the series through reviews on *Amazon.com* and web pages devoted to the "cult" of Mack Bolan. Characterized by critic Dilys Winn as the "vicious" offshoots of the "paranoid" thrillers, the books went virtually unnoticed by the critics because they were mass-market paperbacks that never appeared in hardcover like the James Bond novels or conventional thrillers and were not represented on *The New York Times* Best Seller list. Like conventional spy novels, books of this subgenre of the spy novel are tales of good overcoming evil through the agency of individuals operating independently of the official law enforcement apparatus. Their illustrious provenance stems from the American Western, the hard-boiled detective novel, and comic books.

These popular fiction novels that combined mystery, the ethos of individualism, and vigilantism mutated into a new subgenre of crime fiction that emerged in the 1970s and 1980s. With roots going back to the origins of America, the first western fictional hero is acknowledged to be James Fenimore Cooper's Natty Bumpo who was a stoic and a killer, the man who walked alone "down those mean forest paths."[5] He became a model for the evolving literary form that followed. From Zane Grey to Louis L'Amour, authors of Westerns who glorified individuality and the frontier told tales of black-clad villains or white-hatted gunslingers, appearing in the nick of time to save the family homestead, restore the widow's inheritance from the evil machinations of greedy, powerful neighbors, or impose stability in towns taken over by outlaws.[6] By the turn of the twentieth century, these frontier tales and detective novels published both in serial and book form, and often written by the same authors under different pseudonyms paralleled developing genres that embodied the ideals of chivalry and justice.

Magazines, such as *The Black Mask* and *Dime Detective*, began to appear during World War I and became popular in the 1920s. Plots focused on corruption, and the hero/detective was a hardened professional, a cynic, and a loner operating against foreigners and the dregs of society, avenging wrongs done against the average person. Dashiell Hammett's cynical, streetwise "hardboiled detective" provided inspiration for American and European writers. Where American authors had once looked to Europe for inspiration, Europeans were now reading American crime novels. The tales were simple: stories of good against evil, cowboys against Indians in the American tradition, much like Mickey Spillane's popular Mike Hammer series, which exemplifies this "sex and guts" approach to the American detective. The hero later emerged as an avenger, one who deviates from accepted social norms, and is not incorruptible.[7]

For new immigrants and factory workers, the magazines not only provided escapist literature but also included advertising that provided an imaginary escape from the boring drudgery of factory work: "Tired of being a 'cog in a machine?'" they were asked. Learn English, and such new skills as the "ins-and-outs of electricity." The magazines, and later the comic books, were reminiscent of British "boys" literature, targeting adolescent boys with physical fitness ads[8] and echoing Richard Hannay in *Greenmantle*, claiming that the individual can make a difference.

During the late 1920s and early 1930s, looming international crises in Europe required more than domestic crime solving. Immigrant Jewish activists who were frozen out of American advertising began drawing comic strips to express their fear of the coming political crisis in Europe in a different way. Drawing upon the concept of vigilantism both in the American western and the Jewish legend of the Golem, a robotic creature whose mission was to combat Jewish victimization,[9] immigrants and children of immigrant artists used the comic book format to develop the concept of a superhero who could single-handedly destroy evil and redeem the world.[10] In 1938, *Superman's* first exploits appeared and sold 900,000 copies. *Batman* followed in 1939. Even before the United States entered World War II, Superman began fighting Nazis, and later, *Superman* comics were sold to American GIs who identified with the fight for "truth, justice, and the American way." As publishers noted the popularity of comic books, more and more superheroes entered the fray, representing the selfless power to save the earth from the demonic villain.[11] Joe Simon and Jack Kirby's Captain America illustrates the iconic template. When scientist Professor Reinstein proffers a "strange, seething liquid" to scrawny, 4F Steve Rogers, the lad turns into a superhero, the "first of a corps of super-agents whose mental ability will make them a terror to spies and saboteurs." "We shall call you Captain America," Rogers is told, "because, like you, America shall gain the strength and the will to safeguard our shores."[12]

These comic books were, in essence, an expression of Wilsonian idealism in foreign policy that, in Henry Kissinger's words, "marched since his watershed presidency, and continues to march to this day."[13] Personally averse to militarism and killing, President Wilson nevertheless led the United States to battle in World War I, the war to end all wars, and "to make the world safe for democracy" because he believed that his actions were consonant with the country's destiny, that America's mission was providential, and it was duty-bound to right every wrong. "The world must be made safe for democracy," he wrote. "Its peace must be planted upon the tested foundation of political liberty. We have no selfish ends to serve. We desire no conquest, no dominion . . . . We are but one of the champions of the right of mankind. We shall be satisfied when those rights have been made as secure as the faith and the freedom of nations can make them."[14]

Comparable to the British boys books of the turn of the twentieth century that imparted an imperialist ethos encouraging young Britons to go off and serve the Empire, comics invited Americans to join the fight for freedom as "Captain America's Sentinels of Liberty" and for a dime, they received a badge recognizing their role in the war "against the spies and enemies in our midst who threaten our very independence." Using restraint instead of force, Captain America was another incarnation of the American cowboy, the hero who draws second in the gun-battle, but shoots faster and straighter. Acting as detective, judge, and jury, he is able to thwart the villains despite the ineptitude of the American legal system.[15]

Comic books were popular escapist literature throughout the 1940s and into the early 1950s, replacing the pulp magazines whose publishers, much like those of the traditional spy novels, were looking for new marketing venues. With the eclipse of graphically violent comics during the early 1950s as a result of the United States Congressional hearings linking comic books to juvenile delinquency, much as they had for James Bond novels, paperbacks became the vehicle for a new type of thriller epitomized in the work of Mickey Spillane, who had written for Marvel Comics before World War II. When Franklin Michael "Mickey" Spillane's comic strip idea about a violent private eye named Mike Danger was rejected, Spillane was advised to take the story to the paperback market. He changed the name of the hero to Mike Hammer. When *I, the Jury* was published in 1947, it was panned by the critics and sold fewer than 4,000 copies. Returning GI's bought it, however, and when Signet published it as a paperback original, more than two million copies were sold. Spillane and later Ian Fleming proved that "men who read the grimiest comic books and men's magazines could be reached through the novel."[16]

Then and now, Spillane's novels expose the internal subversion committed by drug traffickers, the Mafia, and Communist agents, and Mike Hammer is more than a detective. His views mirror those of the average "provincial" American; some call Spillane's creations the logical outcome of the McCarthy era. As in *I, the Jury*, Spillane's most constantly reprinted best seller since it first appeared in 1947, the detective-hero is the police, judge, and jury, pronouncing and violently executing sentences according to how he interprets justice, but without due process. Operating outside the law, he is a vigilante who seems to become more violent as the violence in society increases. We see this American xenophobia and provincialism in *The Body Lovers* (1967), where Mike Hammer uncovers a ring of wealthy foreign sadists, primarily of Middle Eastern extraction, who have diplomatic immunity. The plot provides him with the opportunity to lash out against such international organizations as the United Nations, here described as an agency that protects the corrupters of an innocent America.[17]

In these books, heroes are direct and take a no-nonsense, physical approach toward fighting crime. Both Spillane and Mario Puzo, author of *The Godfather*, had a direct influence on Don Pendleton, whose protagonist,

Mack Bolan, began his war against organized crime and later against international subversion. A natural successor to Nick Carter who operated during the Cold War, Bolan is an updated version for the post-Vietnam era: a James Bond with a difference, whose war was Vietnam, not the Cold War. Returning home from combat, Bolan finds that his family has been done in by organized crime. His father, severely beaten by the Mafia from whom he has borrowed money because he lost his job and his health insurance, dies of a heart attack after shooting Mack's sister, who has become a prostitute to help repay the debt. Having lost everything dear to him, Mack undertakes a one-man war against the mob because the system and his government have failed him.[18] He is a loner who needs no one, not even a girlfriend, except to use sexually when required or to appear at a key moment to save him from the villain's evil clutches. He is worldly, has diverse but specialized expertise, and has a passion for excitement. He is self-reliant, proud, inherently private, honest, candid, loyal, and a man of honor. In sum, Bolan is the unusual common man who plays the game for its own sake and not for money. Society not only accepts but condones his individualism because, like all detectives and spies, he is needed to preserve the social order. All of the responsible institutions have either bungled the job or become totally scrambled in the bureaucratic broken eggs. The use of violence and murder are also acceptable if those are the means required to fill the void left by inept legal and judicial authorities.[19]

Like Rambo in the film *Rambo: First Blood* (1982) the "Executioner" wants to be sure that "we win this time." And, like Rambo, the hero evolves from victim to hero enduring a purification by fire through which he reasserts his masculinity.[20] Until 1978, we see Bolan as a "single-minded man on a mission" focused on the task at hand. Compelled by vengeance and vigilantism, he fights alone with few digressions from the action, even for sex. Traveling from city to city, he is a "one dimensional automaton, a killing machine" who takes the law into his own hands, until after thirty-two episodes he is pardoned and invited to head a White House counter-terrorism organization.[21] Declaring victory over the Mafia—that is, his publishers sensing that the original plot had run dry—Bolan is officially charged with the fight against international terrorism and inaugurates a new career that brings him into contact with Middle Eastern villains.

In 1981, with episode #39: *The New War*, Bolan began a struggle that would occupy the series for the next two decades and beyond. Instead of the mafia and domestic criminals or the ever-present Communists that accounted for most of the villains in thriller literature during the second half of the twentieth century, Pendleton had his protagonist, Bolan, turn to the struggle against international terrorism in a new career that pitted him against a variety of villains. A plot set in the jungles of South America has the hero encounter "bloodthirsty Arabs, slinky femmes fatales, money-grubbing entrepreneurs, troubled agents, and even a hurricane."[22] In the series where new titles appeared monthly, at least one novel a year concerns the Middle East or residents of the region.

The early popularity of *The Executioner*, with its emphasis on weapons and violence, enticed a number of imitators who also combated crime and international terrorism; but few sustained the popularity of the original. Adam Hamilton's *The Peacemaker* relies on intrigue to solve problems, perhaps accounting for the short life of the series, which appeared during the mid-1970s.[23] Joseph Rosenberger's *The Death Merchant* mercilessly mowed down villains—weapons are assiduously catalogued for the reader—as did Andrew Sugar's *The Enforcer*. Sugar's *Israeli Commandos*, published in the wake of the 1967 Arab-Israeli war when the United States was mired in Vietnam, presented a "Rambowitz"-type hero who accelerated the violent action to thwart attempts by Arab terrorists to blow up the American oil refineries in Galveston, Texas, or to destroy an Arab secret weapon hidden in the Alps.[24] The appearance of these "Tough Jews," who emerged from the Six-Day War as Superman unmasked—Western heroes who can fend for themselves and no longer require the Golem's protection—embarrassed more than one liberal Jewish critic.[25]

Plots in these novels are apocalyptic and the issues are clear-cut. The hero not only prevents the nefarious earth-shattering conspiracy, but through superior force and weaponry completely annihilates the stereotypical villain. The prose is almost comic-book style and uses a basic minimalist dialogue which provides a reader's version of an action film.

A number of elements differentiate these new-style "avenger" books from the earlier spy novel/thriller like the Nick Carter series. Unlike James Bond or even early Nick Carter books, often the hero in the Bolan mold is not a real government agent or even one acting *ex officio*. He is not summoned by his Control to complete a mission.[26] Nick Carter, on the other hand, originally an action-adventure series published in the 1920s as *Nick Carter, Detective,* and later revived in the 1960s in the wake of the Bond craze as Nick Carter, "Killmaster," worked for the American government. Also known as N3, Carter is a Killmaster for AXE, the US Special Espionage Agency, "the smallest and most deadly arm of American global intelligences." Carter may lack most of Bond's gadgetry and elitist pretensions, but he is supposed to personify the quintessential American as strong, brave, and intelligent. He is the "paramount spy." As expressed in the "Guidelines for Prospective Nick Carter Writers," "He kills efficiently and without hesitation when necessary"; "he is a powerful virile man with exceptionally keen senses and quick reflexes"; and he is irresistible to women. Nick is a master of weaponry and the accouterments of armed combat surveillance and espionage. His assignments take him to all parts of the world, and he knows the geography, culture, and languages of innumerable countries. Throughout his adventures, however, Carter retains his faith in the government.

Published in the wake of the James Bond hysteria, Carter plots are more fanciful than the standard hardcover spy novel fare. Reflecting an earlier era, villains include mad scientists, Communists, Japanese masterminds, ex-Nazis, and Arabs. In the Middle East venue, Chinese attempt to take over North Africa; there are drugs in Istanbul; ex-Nazis and Arabs plot to destroy Israel; and Berbers, assisted by the Chinese, invade France by tunneling under Gibraltar. There is an Arab version of the Mafia that steals microfilm to sell to the Communists and an Arab sheikh who uses a group of Bahamians in his attempt to take over the world.[27]

By contrast, plots in The Executioner series have superseded the Arab-Israeli conflict and the Cold War and reflect the breakup of the Soviet Union and the onset of international terrorism. They incorporate the conflict in the Balkans, civil war in Algeria, and terrorism, and also provide a similar variety of villains as the Carter series that are mixed and matched with plots and locales that could be realistic, but often are improbable. In the 1980s, villains portrayed in the novels include the usual Arabs, Turks, Armenians, Iranians, and Iraqis, but also Germans, Japanese, women, Asians, Communists, Japanese Yakuza operating in Japan and in Las Vegas, Bulgarians, various Latin Americans, renegade CIA agents, US Weathermen Underground, white Aryans, and Satanic cultists. Their villainy includes kidnappings, drug deals, pornography, imprisonment and torture of missing pilots and MIAs in Vietnam, the destruction of Israel, thefts of radioactive material, serial murder, white slavery, and the destabilization of the American nuclear program. There are also assassination attempts against the king of Saudi Arabia and conspiracies by Iranian exiles.

During the 1990s, plots and villains are representative of the new multicultural and globalized world. Jewish terrorists appear as Israeli traitors in the Mossad, Africans, Bulgarians, and the Soviets in Afghanistan. Plots occur in Hawaii, Florida, South Africa, Mexico, Bolivia, Bosnia, Boston, and Sri Lanka. Books published in 1997 describe designs against America by a Serbian warlord in Bosnia, general nuclear terrorism, Islamic fanatics in Egypt, terrorists in Sri Lanka, and narcotics in Jamaica. Four other novels concern right-wing terrorism in the United States, urban war in Boston, Spetsnaz terrorists fought by a coalition of the United States and Russia, and foreign terrorists in Washington, DC.

Although Bolan, like Carter, works alone, each hero is provided with either assistance on location or is accompanied by a team of experts. Bolan fights in the "New War" with his hand-picked, multicultural commando team composed of Asians, Hispanics, and Jews—but no Muslims. He is assisted on location when necessary by local Arabs or Muslims. In *Vengeance* (1999), for example, which takes place primarily in Libya and Algeria, Bolan, unlike the multilingual Nick Carter, needs an Arabic-speaking contact who works closely with the hero. Gholomreza Kordiyeh, an Algerian moderate of indeterminate background, participates in all of the action together with Bolan. His English is perfect, and he is an exact counterpart to Bolan as they blow away leaders of Islamic groups backed by Libya's Muammar Quaddafi, who tries to unite the terrorists under his leadership, all the while competing with the ambitions of an African-American Muslim convert who tries to use the groups in his attack on the United States.

Like James Bond, Nick Carter, the product of an earlier age, is larger than life. He is conversant in all languages. In *The Casbah Killers* (1962), he speaks French, some Arabic, and understands Berber. In *Thunderstrike in Syria* (1979), he is fluent enough in Arabic and Hebrew to try psychological tricks in those languages. After all, he has had training in anthropology and psychology. They are part of his arsenal of unimaginable weapons and technical expertise. Thus, in a Syrian terrorists' prison, when Carter wishes to identify his fellow inmates, he lets go with a particularly vile curse in Arabic in order to shock the men to reveal their true identities. *Sotto voce*, our hero explains the reasons to the reader: "Very often cultural instinct forces one to react faster than conscious, controlled thought. If the men were Moslem, rage should flicker briefly in their eyes before they caught themselves in realization of how I had tricked them with the filthy insult." Undaunted, Carter tries again after one of the men, speaking in Hebrew, accuses him of being a terrorist plant: "Rapidly, losing my patience, I said in Hebrew, if you're Israelis, how did you get here . . . ?"[28] Even if Turkish, Urdu, Pushtu, or Farsi were required, Carter's linguistic skills would be appropriate for the job. If he has local assistance, it is from Westernized characters.

In contrast to the Nick Carter novels, exotic, picturesque locales, gourmet food, cigars, wine, luxury cars, and haute couture are out of place in Bolan's life; for his conflict, threatening as it does all civilization on the planet, requires constant vigilance and total physical and mental concentration. Heroes and villains act on a level playing field. Intelligent, technologically sophisticated villains operate in the United States or in an international venue. Despite the varying ethnic identities, they must still be stereotyped to ensure reader identification. What sets apart the hero and his commando team—usually multicultural, including Asian experts in the martial arts—is the total commitment to fighting America's enemy, even outside the system if need be, because societal institutions, just like the military command in Vietnam that did not allow valiant American soldiers to win, have let people down. The heroes, always alert to danger and bereft of a normal life, combat the terrorists who may be in league with organized crime, as in *The Iranian Hit* (1982), to avenge, albeit in fiction, the deaths of the 241 United States Marine peacekeepers who died as a result of a suicide bombing of their barracks in Beirut. Published in 1984, *Beirut Payback* is preceded by a note of appreciation: "To the US Marines in Beirut seen wearing 'The Executioner' headband on their helmet. An appropriate banner of courage. Live large!" Bolan notes the similarity of Beirut to Vietnam and insists that this time, Americans will prevail.

Attitudes toward women have also changed and have become more negative in this male-dominated genre. With the exception of the female detective, and the infrequent female operative such as Modesty Blaise, whose exploits were conceived more as a counterpart to James Bond, as Wonder Woman was to Superman, women do not appear in heroic roles. In the Bond novels, chivalric courtship rituals still exist and the art of seduction is still detailed—the exotic locale, fine food and wine, and a sexy car are integral components of the script. By the 1990s, these niceties have given way to situations of mutual need and propinquity that propel the operative and assistant towards each other, especially if they are opposites. Otherwise, the hero's woman is the good wife whose death by brutal attack or accidental bombing is the event that compels him to undertake the mission, and thereby, restore the moral order.[29]

The female as villain is either a member of the commando team or the actual villain. She is often used as a throwaway sex object by the male villain, whose own true love may have been killed in an Israeli bomb attack against his village, an event which acts as the catalyst for his vengeance against the Zionists. Also portrayed as the "temptress," the woman may be sent to seduce the hero. The hero of the James Bond era might have fallen for her wiles, but today's Mack Bolan is not only not tempted, but repelled.[30] Often, women he grows close to are killed off.

Unlike their predecessor James Bond, most of the more recent avenger heroes use violence, not sex, to heighten the tension. In fact, violence is stressed. The stable of Nick Carter authors, who range from high school dropouts to serious stylists, but all of whom follow plot guidelines handed out by the publisher, are advised to set their books in a foreign locale and to use graphic violence. In *Thunderstrike in Syria*, Nick tells us:

> I still had five cartridges left in Wilhelmina and put one of them into a Syrian's face at pointblank range. I then tossed the Luger to my left hand, after dropping the Stechkin, and gave a half-twist to my right arm. Hugo jumped from his case and his handle slid into my hand. I jumped to one side to avoid a string of 7.62mm bullets at about the same time that Risenberg slammed a Syrian across the face with the side of a Stechkin machine pistol. Risenberg didn't slow down. With a short burst he sprayed the two men who rushed him, then spun and fired the AKM at two more SLA's, one of whom was a woman, the flat-nosed projectiles punching the two in the stomach. The man fell back and died without a murmur, but the woman let out a high-pitched scream.[31]

By the mid-1980s, the violence is gorier: "He dived into that gun nest, yanking out his combat knife and whittling away at the three men. Blood spurted everywhere as the flashing blade bit deep into the flesh, slicing into vital organs, leaving the surprised trio sprawled around The Executioner."[32] Online reviewers evaluate the books in terms of how they depict violence and describe weaponry.

The link between violence and eroticism is more explicit in the Nick Carter series. More erotic attention is paid to Carter's anthropomorphic "companions" than to the females he lackadaisically seduces. There is Wilhelmina, his 9mm Luger; Pierre, a tiny gas bomb; and Hugo, his pencil-thin stiletto sheathed in a chamois case. Pierre is attached to his upper thigh, like a "third testicle." In *Thunderstrike in Syria* (1979), Carter bemoans the loss of Hugo and Wilhelmina: "Without him and Wilhelmina, I felt almost naked. But not quite, I still had Pierre, my gas bomb." Despite mortal danger and the plethora of miscellaneous weaponry lying about, he returns to Syrian headquarters to rescue, like the damsel in distress, his lost "friends." In fact, most any page in *Thunderstrike in Syria* produces an international arsenal straight from the pages of *Jane's* Weapons Systems. In use, just to name a few at random, are a military Mauser, Spanish Mauser, Glisenti automatic, Soviet 9mm Stechkin machine pistol, Belgian CAL submachine gun, West German Sturn Gewehr, Czech light machine gun, SFR Israeli Galil assault rifle, Uzi machine gun, and assorted tanks, armored vehicles, and helicopter gun ships. All of this is in 184 pages, most taken up with violence.

In the Bolan series, weapons are not only listed, but their specifications are described. As Bolan and Kordiyeh approach the office building, both were dressed in business suits despite the heat, and they carried imitation leather attaché cases in their left hands, "leaving the right free to reach for armpit-holstered hardware if they were accosted on the street. Each briefcase contained a Spanish-made Z-84 submachine gun, strongly resembling the venerable Uzi, except that its metal stock folded over the top of the weapon's receiver, instead of collapsing accordion-style. The Z-84 has a cyclic rate identical to the Uzi, at 600 rounds per minute, feeding on a 36-round box magazine inserted through the pistol grip."[33] Don Pendleton was known to test out weapons before writing about them and provided illustrations and descriptions in special editions to the series.

These low-end paperbacks were soon to receive a boost with the success of spy novels that used American military technology as the heroic vehicle to thwart American enemies in the post-Cold War era. To the surprise of many in the publishing industry, Tom Clancy's *The Hunt for Red October*, written by a Maryland insurance agent and United States Navy buff and published in 1984 by the Naval Institute Press, soon became a runaway hardcover best seller.[34] Lauded by both President Reagan and Secretary of the Navy John Lehman, Clancy's non-action techno-thriller reads like a combination chess game and hi-tech manual. Originally based on a computer game,[35] Clancy's novel injected military technology into the spy novel genre, to spotlight American technological excellence and weapons superiority, and revivify the American hero who could successfully vanquish the enemy on his own without the assistance of others.[36] Still a loner, he is an individual, often touched by tragedy during the Vietnam era or by personal loss because of terrorist attack, but he is now erudite, technologically invincible, and does not necessarily have to engage in bloody hand-to-hand combat to be believable. He could fly a jet or a stealth bomber, command a ship, design a missile, and direct SMART bombs exactly to target, thus eliminating the blood and gore that characterized his paperback counterpart.

The new "techno-thriller" appeared at a time when President Ronald Reagan talked of renewing America's faith in its ideals and recommitted America to a responsible world role.[37] Reflecting the end of the Vietnam syndrome, the "Reagan revolution" was not only economic: his supporters maintained that the recovery of morale after Vietnam and the Iranian hostage crisis restored American standing in a world that looked to the United States for leadership. America is "still a land of heroes and all the courage and love of freedom that ever was before," said the president. The role of the United States military was to bring peace and light to the world rather than to build an American empire. Reagan doubled the Pentagon's budget, re-activated mothballed World War II era battleships reminiscent of World War II heroism, and had a positive attitude toward the military. America was again "standing tall," and soldiers became the icon of the Reagan recovery. "Who else but an idealist would choose to become a member of the Armed Forces and put himself or herself in harm's way for the rest of us?" he asked.

An iconic military was apparent almost immediately after Reagan's election, when he presented a Vietnam veteran with the Medal of Honor and initiated a reinterpretation of the Vietnam war: "Several years ago we brought home a group of American fighting men who had obeyed their country's call and who fought bravely and as well as any in our history. They came home without a victory not because they'd been defeated, but because they'd been denied permission to win." Counter-narrative films appeared that provided a revisionist view that did not necessarily reflect those prevailing in Hollywood, but drew huge audiences. *An Officer and a Gentleman* projected manhood and true love, and *Top Gun* highlighted military technology. Both were productions that would have been unthinkable in the immediate aftermath of the Vietnam War. Rambo's question, "Do we get to win this time?" in *First Blood Part II*, became a rallying cry for the reassertion of American manhood,[38] not only in popular culture but also in the American national identity. After all, the Reagan presidency was to be perceived as masculine as opposed to that of Jimmy Carter's feminine, inept administration in office during the Iranian hostage crisis and the abortive rescue of Americans in Iran. The 1990s "saw a reevaluation of that hard body, not for a return to the Jimmy Carter soft body but for a re-articulation of masculine strength and power through internal, personal, and family-oriented values."[39]

In this patriotic atmosphere, Clancy's book sold three million copies within two years of its appearance, establishing a template for financial success[40] and attracting a new category of authors to the genre. Individuals with military hi-tech experience began to write thrillers that starred American military technology operated by American flyers, former astronauts, and ship commanders as heroes.[41] In both *The Med* (1988) and *The Gulf* (1990) by David Poyer, a graduate of the US Naval Academy who served on destroyers, the plots concern the movement and machinations of the US Sixth Fleet, which maneuver to send Marines to rescue hostages in Syria and to defeat the Iranian navy. Often there are no villainous characters. The books, like their prototype, *The Hunt for Red October*, focus on the detailed operations of reconnaissance aircraft, jet fighters, stealth bombers, cruise missiles, and target bombing confirmed by sophisticated camera and satellite photos that provided the "clean" violence that typifies these novels.[42] The bombing of Libya during the Reagan presidency provided good plot opportunity that has endured,[43] as have threats to the Saudi oil fields that required US tactical fighters to be prepared for an Iranian threat.[44]

Unlike their paperback originals, whose readership was largely critically ignored except for the sales figures they generated, these books appeared in hardcover, were promoted by mainstream trade publishers, and proliferated—in a sense legitimizing Mack Bolan and his colleagues. The military-tech experts added the standard conspiratorial plot, but there was a perceptible shift in characterization when villains were added. By the 1980s and 1990s, Arab and Muslim villains had evolved: no longer two-dimensional caricatures of ineptitude, they had to be intelligent and well educated in order to be a credible match for the American flyers in novels that featured one-on-one air-to-air combat, and they had to be able to fly MIGs well, so that a comparative analysis of the competing planes could be described.[45] Both the hero and the villain in R. J. Pineiro's *Ultimatum* (1994) are loners who, although they are members of their respective countries' military establishment, often take matters into their own hands, earning each other's begrudging respect by the end of the novel. The handsome Iraqi Colonel Abunnasr Manesh hated Americans because of the death of his parents in Operation Desert Storm, but disliked his President Saddam Hussein even more because of the Iraqi leader's brutalization of the competent members of the Iraqi officer corps. Successful at luring American pilots into the no-fly zone, early in the novel he shoots down Navy Lieutenant Kevin "Crackers" Dalton and the conflict between the two pilots becomes more personal than political. Saved by an Israeli female Mossad agent and a Kurdish operative after the American's plane is shot down in southern Iraq, Dalton discovers a secret Iraqi nuclear installation, is rescued, and lives to fly again against the now General Manesh. A mid-air collision and a nuclear blast obliterate both. Here there is respect for the opposing military—members of the same corps of brother officers who are often nonpolitical and just caught up in defending their countries.

PLOTS 1980–1999		
	1980–1989	1990–1999
Murder Mysteries	23	37
World War I	1	
Jihad	11	7
World War II	5	4
Cold War	1	1
Coups	14	3
Arab-Israeli Conflict	46	14
Crime	4	3
Oil	3	
Economic Threat	7	
Terrorism	28	28
Nuclear Threat	4	8
Lebanon	4	2
Iran	7	1
Afghanistan	5	
Libya		1
Iraq		5
Military Tech	7	19
Gulf War		13
World War III / Apocalypse	1	5
Other	6	6
TOTAL	177	157

With terrorism becoming the plot device of the 1990s, and with Iran, Iraq, and Libya seen as states sponsoring terrorism, authors had ample opportunity to broaden the conspiratorial field beyond the Arab-Israeli conflict. The more than twenty-five military hi-tech novels[46] published during the last twelve years of the twentieth century using the Middle East for plot and setting really focused on Iran, Iraq, and Libya with five novels appearing just in 1990. As the number of thrillers about the Middle East increased at the end of the 1980s, it was to be expected that the Gulf War in 1990–1991, would generate even more military tech novels. Not only did authors have the lead time of Desert Shield in which to prepare, but there was publishing momentum, and it seemed that the readership was eagerly awaiting product. Although more than eight novels were published about the war, the surprise was that none of them made the *New York Times* hardcover best seller list. Was it because of a lack of interest in fictional accounts of the war or cable news overkill? After all, on CNN one could watch the war in real time and detailed feature articles appeared in the press. This perhaps obviated, it seemed, the need for fiction.

Nonetheless, a sample of the books that did appear reflects a number of plot shifts. As in the real world, the fictional Vietnam Syndrome was reversed. Not only are the heroes American pilots and American and British agents and commandos, but Israelis, when they do appear, are depicted in a role subordinate to Americans—a reversal of the Israeli superhero character of the 1970s. By the 1990s, just as the Israeli role was minimal in the war, in fiction the Israeli role is similarly diminished: Israel requests American assistance and is seen as little more than a provider of useful intelligence. Unlike the 1970s, when Israeli heroes played starring roles in spy novels and thrillers, Americans are the acknowledged heroes and Israel is more likely to request assistance from Americans in preventing an Iraqi military attack on Israel than to take the lead in any operation.[47]

Times had changed. The Persian Gulf War vindicated both the Americans and the British, and the shame of Vietnam and Suez was erased. With the fall of the Soviet Union and the end of the Cold War threat, the United States and its coalition partners, especially Great Britain, reasserted themselves as bona fide Western heroes of the 1990s. Fiction writers responded with US Navy SEALs and Air Force commandos destroying weapons of mass destruction[48] and creating new paperback series. Based on actual events of the Gulf War, James Ferro's *Going Deep* (1999) is advertised as "the final word in air-to-ground combat. Ripping the desert dunes apart with brutal efficiency, the only thing harder than the machines are the men and women who fly them." The novels are dedicated to the brave pilots who flew the A-10 Warthogs over the Persian Gulf.[49] Whether stealing a MIG, battling in the desert, finding toxic chemicals or targeting the Iraqi leader while he is en route from town to town, the pilots perform admirably against whatever tactics the Iraqis use against them. The books have been heavily marketed online: *Amazon.com* provides sample pages, the front cover and back, and reviews of the books that have appeared to date.[50] Other military-tech novels covered incidents in the no-fly zones, Iraqi pilots buzzing the borders, which pilots need to judge intently to determine whether to shoot the planes down.[51]

Novels about the Gulf War also incorporate themes of terrorism, finance, and the nuclear threat. They present detailed accounts of the secret construction of the Iraqi military machine and the sophisticated financial machinations required to fund Saddam Hussein's weapons program. The war, fought in detail, spotlights the American air power used to destroy Iraqi weapons, nuclear capabilities, and biological agents. Other plots include the destruction of Iraqi programs to rebuild its nuclear capability, Saddam's attempts to avenge his defeat, by holding hostage the original American Declaration of Independence, and an Iranian Islamist assassination coup against Saddam.[52] Even after the Gulf War, however, Saddam was portrayed more like a battlefield foe than a terrorist villain, especially after the "no-fly" zones were established in Iraq. More than twenty novels have had him threaten his neighbors with weapons of mass destruction and plot assassinations, but by and large his villainy is limited.

This is not the case with Libya's Muammar Qaddafi, who before his recent recantation of terrorism, was characterized in fiction as villainy personified, much like the Shah of Iran in the 1970s, whose diabolical schemes included controlling oil and the economic destiny of the West. In the late 1970s, authors portrayed Qaddafi as the *éminence grise* behind Palestinian terrorist plots for the destruction of Israel, planting nuclear devices in New York City, and destroying the West's financial system.[53] In the 1980s, threats of international terrorism revived after Americans were killed by Libyan agents in a German discotheque and the US retaliated by bombing Libya in 1986. The subsequent explosion of Pan Am Flight 103 over Lockerbie, Scotland heightened the threat. The fictional Qaddafi was the villain behind the kidnapping of scientists and the assassinations of American and British government officials.[54]

As the mid-1990s approached, it looked as if thriller writers were running out of steam. With the Oslo talks and the Arab-Israeli détente, that conflict did not engender the readership that it once commanded. Fear of the future abated with the fall of the Soviet Union at the "end of history." There was no paranoia like that which occurred at the turn of the twentieth century or at the end of the 1960s to drive the sales of spy novels and thrillers. Some best-selling authors set their novels in the past. Mysteries about pharaonic Egypt suddenly appeared along with the detective novels by Elizabeth Peters and Michael Pearce that revived interest in pre-World War I British-occupied Egypt.[55] Courtroom dramas and legal thrillers were on best seller lists as readers seemed to lose interest in the genre that had spanned the century. Also, with the turn of the twenty-first century, authors and even readers of *Soldier of Fortune* magazine began to flirt with books about the imminent millennium and the apocalypse.[56]

Religion combined with crime once again hit the bookstores after September 11, 2001, when radical Islamists became central to the American war on terrorism and Islamic *jihad* returned to American fiction with a vengeance.

SEVEN

Jihad, the Apocalypse,
and Back Again

The Iranian Islamic Revolution in 1979 sparked a resurgence of novels about religious *jihad* against the West. By the mid-1980s, authors were once again writing about trouble emanating from Iran and spreading throughout the entire Islamic world. The fear that something "ugly and unprecedented was threatening civilization, democracy and the entire Western liberal tradition" kept CIA agent Peter Randall up at night, "much as the rising terror of Nazism had troubled his father's dreams in the mid-thirties." Randall, the protagonist in Daniel Easterman's novel *The Last Assassin*, was worried about "militant Islam."[1]

By the last third of the twentieth century, literary references had certainly moved away from the "Great Game" or plots designed to bring down the British Empire to an Islamic fanaticism that threatened America and the entire world. During the runup to the twenty-first century, plots drew on themes of *jihad* against the West, *jihad* against the Arab-Israeli peace process, and a fictional flirtation with the millennium, eschatology, and the apocalypse—the Battle at Armageddon— after all, is to occur in the Middle East.

Agent Randall confronts all of these demons in a novel that incorporates all types of villainy under the aegis of Islamic fanaticism. Religious zealots are groomed by an evil mastermind to assassinate seven world leaders in order to set in motion the sequence of events that will ultimately bring about a new world order dominated by the black-robed mullahs. Equating militant Islam with the Nazi threat of forty years earlier, Easterman contrives a massive Shiite conspiracy against the West, combining real events of the late 1970s–early 1980s that metastasize into a fictional world-shaking crisis. The return to Iran of the Ayatollah Khomeini and the ouster of the Shah, the American embassy takeover by Iranian students, plots against the pope and President Sadat of Egypt, an abortive assassination attempt against President Jimmy Carter, the failed attempt to rescue the American hostages, and the siege at the mosque in Mecca held by a Shiite "mahdi" and his followers all lead to the coup de grace—the explosion of a nuclear device detonated from Iran—the catalyst for an East-West conflict that would end with the apocalypse and a new Islamic order. Age-old villains are revived and new ones added: the descendants of Hasan-i Sabah's Assassins are at work again, organizing their minions from all over the world—merchants from Hong Kong and the United States, a professor from Columbia University in New York, and scores of impressionable poverty-stricken young men with religious fanaticism in their eyes are manipulated by the one-handed mullah dressed in black who has joined forces with the Nazi German scientist to destroy Western civilization.

Although a thematic hodgepodge, Easterman's novel provides a useful introduction to this chapter because it incorporates what will become significant tropes by the turn of the twenty-first century, when the United States, not unlike Britain at the beginning of this story, becomes the target of religious fanaticism. Under the broad conspiratorial umbrella of *jihad*, novels published during the last two decades of the twentieth century reflect concerns with *jihad* and religious extremism as the enemy of the Arab-Israeli peace process. Authors flirted with the apocalypse as the millennium approached, and returned to *jihad*ist attacks against the West after 9/11.

While Americans were reading *Soldier of Fortune* magazine, Iran became an Islamic republic in 1979, a pivotal year in Middle East politics although few realized it at the time. In February, the secular regime of the Shah was overthrown and replaced by a Shiite regime; in March, President Anwar Sadat and Prime Minister Menachem Begin signed the Egyptian-Israeli peace agreement in Washington; and in December, the Soviet Union invaded Afghanistan.[2] A year later, Islamic extremists assassinated Anwar Sadat and Iranians held Americans hostage in the United States Embassy in Tehran. The government of Prime Minister Begin took on religious nationalist overtones, and the United States began to arm Islamic religious militants in their struggle against the Soviets in Afghanistan.

The Iranian Revolution of 1979—the reality of an Islamic takeover of an ostensibly Westernized country, Iran—augured a new era. With Nasser's death (1970) and the Egyptian-Israeli peace treaty (1979) a reality, terrorism sponsored by religion became the most visible threat emanating from the region, seemingly with another cast of characters. Islamic fanaticism or Islamism once again spilled over into fiction, only this time, the West was not able to manage "Islam" by subverting the allegiance of the natives or controlling the otherwise uncontrollable Muslims. By the early 1980s, it was obvious not only that "Islam" could not be controlled by outside forces, but that it was perfectly capable of perpetrating villainy on its own. The Ayatollah Khomeini's return to Iran, the American hostage crisis, the success of the Islamic revolution, and the subsequent emergence of Islamist political parties and regimes throughout the Middle East were proof that "Islam" was back, resuscitating the fear of a direct attack by the irrational East upon the secular, enlightened West.

Themes from novels of the 1920s were revived. Dennis Wheatley had written earlier of turning back the clock to the Ottoman-Islamic days of the Old Regime where his villains inspired a religious reaction against the institution of Ataturk's secular Turkish republic.[3] Thirty years later, author Edward Aarons introduced Selim Raschid, the villain in his *Assignment: The Cairo Dancers*, a somewhat appealing mullah rogue who speaks in rationally mellifluous Oxfordian tones: "I see you think I am a madman touched by pseudo-divine mission," he confesses to the nearly taken-in hero from Yale, Sam Durell, who must foil his efforts at world domination.[4] But it was not until the last two decades of the twentieth century, however, that books took Islamic fanaticism to new horizons.

By the 1970s, America, like Britain, was in the gun sights of a fictionalized Islam. Richard Graves's *Cobalt 60*, the novel that introduces this book, is a good example. Despite its fanciful plot—the attempted assassination of members of the United States Congress by a disgruntled Arab sheikh—the novel presages Arab anti-Western sentiments that for American readers evoked plots of *jihad*, revenge, terrorism, and the conquest of the West by Islam, this time not by hordes of sword-wielding Muslim fanatics, but by a Western-educated (graduate degree in physics) religious zealot who uses methods of the nuclear age financed by modern banking techniques. Typical of thrillers and spy novels published after the 1970s, it draws on the American penchant for belief in religious conspiracy. Whereas *jihad*ist conspiracies against Britain were viewed from the perspective of the imperial matrix, *jihad* against America had religious overtones that had come to the New World with the Mayflower.

There has always been a tendency in American politics to examine issues through the prism of a fundamentally religious view of the world, historian Richard Hofstadter noted more than half a century ago in his classic essay "The Paranoid Style in American Politics." Politics is often described with Christian imagery based on fundamentalist dualism of good versus evil, the old Manichaean view wherein all social, economic, and political ills can be traced to a single source: the Devil. If the causes of impending doom are destroyed, the theory goes, good will prevail and the Apocalypse will be averted. This paranoia expresses itself in the almost constant fear of some huge irrational plot or conspiracy of international proportions, a plan to perpetrate evil deeds of unimaginable fiendish horror on the unsuspecting American public. The plots, occurring during times of stress, have included fear of such threats to American life as the "abolition of slavery," "Roosevelt's declaration of war against Nazi Germany," the real-life assassinations of public figures (John and Robert Kennedy and Martin Luther King, Jr.), the oil shortage conspiracy of the 1970s, or more recently in 2001, the attacks on the World Trade Center in New York and the Pentagon in Washington.[5]

Different ages produced different crises and different culprits. In the Revolutionary era, it was the Bavarian Illuminati who were thought to subvert religion and the existing order. They were said to be in league with the Jesuits, who were suspected later for their alleged infiltration of a primarily Protestant America, despite the fact that the former were anti-clerical. In the 1790s, the established clergy in New England warned their flocks against the organization, seemingly oblivious to the fact that ten years earlier it had officially been disbanded on the grounds that it was a cabal that included the most active leaders of the French Revolution. It had become "one great and wicked project fermenting and working all over Europe," people read from an analysis of the group written by a Scottish mathematician, John Robison, in his *Proofs of a Conspiracy Against All Religions and Governments of Europe Carried on in the Secret Meetings of the Freemasons, Illuminati, and Reading Societies.* Writing in 1798, Robison saw the group as a "libertine, anti-Christian movement, given to the corruption of women, the cultivation of sensual pleasures, and the violation of property rights. Its members had plans for making a tea that caused abortion, a secret substance that 'blinds and kills when spurted in the face,' and a device that sounds like a stench bomb—a method for filling a bedchamber with pestilential vapours."[6]

It hardly matters that the views of the Illuminati, based on ideas stemming from Enlightenment rationalism, were mildly anti-clerical and naively utopian in their hopes of bringing all men under the rule of reason.

The president of Yale University scathingly attacked the group, associating its members with the Antichrist that was attempting to subvert American religion via an Illuminati-inspired Jacobin plot to implement Jeffersonian democracy in America, even though it seems that no Illuminati ever set foot on American shores.

During the nineteenth century, the Freemasons were designated conspirators, even though they had many American members, including not only a number of the Founding Fathers, but also Aaron Burr and Andrew Jackson, both of whom were depicted as villains—Burr for treason and Jackson for attempts to subvert the free enterprise system. Descended from the medieval English stonemason guild, the Freemasons developed international cellular organizations during the eighteenth century, drawing members from all over the Western world by their esoteric rituals, ancient religious trappings, and chivalric code. Their secrecy inspired paranoia from both sides of the political spectrum. The Catholic Church opposed the movement because the Masons were supranational and extra-organizational and their loyalty was suspect. They threatened the established order and were alleged perpetrators of numerous plots and revolutions. They were perceived to be as much of a threat then as international Communism was during most of the twentieth century.

To the stereotypes of religious and racial prejudice against blacks and Asians, add Catholics and Jews, the international Jewish conspiracy, munitions czars, the Mafia, multinational corporations, international Communism, (and petro-sheikhs); then throw in some mysteriously tightly-knit command post installed somewhere in the hidden recesses of the Vatican, under the subway systems of Europe, in the banking houses of London or New York, in small restaurants in New York City's Little Italy, in the secret confines of the Kremlin, or the opulent harems of Gulf sheikhdoms, and you have the late twentieth-century conspirator. Before World War II, novels depicting the threat of the world Jewish conspiracy were rife, inspired no doubt by the infamous Russian forgery *The Protocols of the Elders of Zion*, published in the United States by Henry Ford as *The International Jew: The World's Foremost Problem*. After the war, the popular conspirators in spy novels and thrillers were Communists (Russian, Chinese, and Cuban), the Mafia, Nazis and Neo-Nazis, and Arabs in the guise of petro-sheikhs, terrorists, and Muslim fanatics.[7]

By the 1980s, as the mullahs replaced the Shah and the Arab oil sheikhs as the megalomaniacal villains who dominated fiction after the 1973 Arab-Israeli war, not only was the West threatened by control of the oil spigot by these same religious fanatics, who also managed to acquire nuclear weapons,[8] but "Islamic" conspiracies mirrored the terrorist plots of the 1970s, providing authors with conspiratorial alternatives for the Palestinians, who by the 1990s were engaged in a peace process with Israel and were slowly being replaced by Islamic "fanatics."

Moreover, the lingering effect of the Iran hostage crisis (1979–1980), which in part dictated United States foreign policy for more than the next two decades, legitimized Iran as a designated foe, and fanatical Muslims became villains by extension. They could be Palestinian terrorists who worked for an Islamic regime that controlled them, Lebanese Shiʿite terrorists who attacked American interests, or even generic Muslim Arabs who wished to avenge the slights and insults perpetrated by the West against their co-religionists over the centuries. Just as in the terrorism plots, authors were never at a loss for material and could have their villains bring on World War III, a nuclear holocaust, Armageddon, and the usual bacterial, chemical, and biological warfare against the West. During the 1980s no fewer than fourteen novels with Islamic fanatic villains appeared; there would be at least twelve more during the next decade.[9]

Islamic fanaticism also became a subtext in novels about the Arab-Israeli conflict itself, which was gradually evolving into a religious rather than political dispute, a *kulturkampf* that pitted an irrational East bent on destroying the West. In this paradigm, the heroes are not only secular but are indigenous to the region, projecting their Western authors' antipathy towards religious and nationalist extremism of any kind.[10] The return of Saladin, the eponymous chivalrous Arab of the Crusades is symbolic. Counterpoised against a growing Islamic threat after the 1979 Islamic Revolution in Iran, secular Israelis and Arabs become the key combatants set to rescue the Middle East from those who would hijack the region from rightful leaders.

Anwar Sadat, although an observant Muslim, was also an urbane, Westernized Arab with whom American television personalities Barbara Walters and Walter Cronkite felt comfortable. They praised his visit to Jerusalem (1977), his pursuit of peace, and his advocacy of an open economy. But most of all, he opposed religious fanaticism so that with Camp David and the inauguration of the peace process, anyone, and especially Egyptians[11] who worked for a peaceful solution to the Arab-Israeli conflict embodied heroic attributes. Villains, by definition, became either Muslims engaged in holy war or Jewish religious extremists who opposed peace and also indulged in holy war.[12] Authors also provided scenarios wherein not only moderate Palestinians and Israelis work together, but they even included

Syrians in the struggle against the common threat of religious fanaticism of whatever stripe, against Holocaust denial, against Saddam Hussein, and for human rights, justice, and Western values.[13]

Gordon Pape and Tony Aspler's novel *The Scorpion Sanction* (1980) is a good example. An assassination attempt using nuclear weapons against the Egyptian and American presidents who are to sign an aid agreement in Cairo is the plot; the heroes are Egyptian and Israeli secular military men who begrudgingly work together to foil the nefarious threat; and the villain is an Egyptian religious leader who heads a team of fanatical acolytes.

Egyptian Colonel Ahmed Rahman embodies all of the qualities we have come to associate with the West. He is handsome, dashing, with a "large leonine head, white teeth and a bushy mustache, a good sense of humor, his physique marred only by a crooked left elbow, the result of a boyhood accident that the village doctor had set improperly" and which took all the arts of his expensive Greek tailor to conceal it. He is humane, a man of humble origins who became a superb military officer who has saved more than one Egyptian president from assassination or coup. An Egyptian patriot, he has no love for Israelis and is furious when the Egyptian president informs him that the government has called in the Israeli Mossad to assist in the investigation of the possible nuclear plot.

"Have you so little faith in our own security service that you would bring in outsiders?" he asks his boss.

> Bar-Zeev would be more of a hindrance than a help. How could this man know more about the PLO than we do? Is he an Arab? No, he's a Jew. An immigrant at that. He wasn't even born in Israel.[14]

Over Rahman's protest, the Israeli is brought in, reluctantly on his part as well, and is lectured on Arab professionalism, Arab honor, and adherence to the Palestinian cause, despite the treaty with Israel.

To both men, the common enemy is religious fanaticism, a threat that will force these secular operatives to put their political differences aside for the moment, and even agree to combat it together—"I understand that you will not require kosher food," Rahman notes as he accompanies Bar-Zeev from the airport to Cairo. "I am not an observant man," replied Bar-Zeev quietly. "In the religious sense." "Of course," responded Rahman.

Their nemesis is Sheikh Rashad Munir, a professor of Islamic studies at al-Azhar University in Cairo, who heads up a sect of religious fanatics called the Wind of the Desert. His followers, recruits from his classes and a ragtag group of Palestinian terrorists, are branded on the foot with the sign of the scorpion, iconic of the professor's sojourn in the desert when, removing his sandals, he was stung in the foot by the deadly nocturnal arachnid and lay in a coma.

> In my delirium during the night, when my fever was at its height, I had a vision of the Prophet Muhammad. He came close to me, he wiped my forehead with his cloak, and he commanded me to become well and to devote my life to Allah. In the morning I awoke and the fever was gone.[15]

Vowing to return Israel to the Arabs and, as the Mahdi, to return the Arab world to Islam, the sheikh threatens Cairo with nuclear attack so that he can become the instrument for the Muslim return to the purity of early Islam. He uses Western technology to destroy the West he despises and re-appears *in fact* in the personalities of the Islamist theoretician Sayyid Qutb and his acolytes Ayman al-Zawahiri and Osama bin-Ladin. After the be-ginning of America's War on Terror, fictional enemies modeled on them require no explanation.

By the end of *The Scorpion Sanction*, there is mutual respect, but appre-hension about the future. "When we signed the peace treaty, Uri, I thought there would be no more of this." Bar-Zeev sighed and replied. "You can call me a cynic, Ahmed, but ink on a piece of paper doesn't change human nature. History is a prophet no one listens to. There'll always be men who will act their sick dreams in the name of religion."[16]

A decade after the publication of Pape and Aspler's novel, with the onset of the Oslo peace talks, authors go a step further. Some warn outright against religious obstructionists to the peace process from both the Muslim and Jewish sides. Robert Rosenberg, for example, whose hero Avram Cohen is a Dachau survivor and a man of humanistic values, the tough but vulner-able epitome of American perception of Israeli hero, solves crimes both in Jerusalem and in Los Angeles, notes in the introduction to *House of Guilt*:

> *House of Guilt* was written between the Hebron massacre and Yitzhak Rabin's assassination. So although this is a work of fiction, its roots are in reality of life in Israel during that period. Therefore, it is also about the gap between Jerusalem and Tel Aviv.
>
> That struggle is Israel's own inner conflict, one that seems to stretch around the world—between those who look to the past for their inspi-ration, and insist they have an absolute knowledge, and those who can

see that if indeed this is a messianic age, it is a result of the confluence of knowledge, the recognition of information as the only inexhaustible resource human beings possess on this planet.

He introduces the novel with a warning that "religiosity does not insure innocence, just as liberation does not guarantee wisdom."[17] Cohen is worried about the role of Jewish religious fundamentalism in his beautiful Jerusalem. In the novel, the crime is committed by Jewish and Christian apocalyptic fanatics.

Other writers introduce liberal Israelis and import Arab-American protagonists to assist the peace process along.[18] Jon Land's series of novels that partners the iconoclastic Israeli female operative Daniella Barnea with Palestinian-American ex-Detroit policeman Ben (Bayan) Kamal presents the team as the hope for future Israeli-Palestinian relations. They foil plots by religious fanatics of all stripes: rabbis, Islamic clerics, Vatican Swiss Guards, and assorted terrorists.[19]

But by the end of the 1990s, with the outbreak of the second Intifada and the end of the halcyon days of Oslo, Land, like other thriller writers, looked to the end of the century and began to flirt with the Apocalypse. With the runup to the millennium, more and more thrillers took on an apocalyptic tinge, which dovetailed with the publication of books that dealt increasingly with the occult, conspiracy, the "End of Days," and a decidedly Christian approach to issues of *jihad* and the Apocalypse.[20]

These books had already begun to appear during the 1970s and the 1980s, which ushered in a new era of American interest in the occult, UFOs, mysticism, and ESP. Hal Lindsey's *The Late Great Planet Earth*, suggesting that the countdown to Armageddon was already in process, was the bestselling nonfiction book of a decade during which biblical prophecy was big business and was followed in the 1990s by Tim LaHaye and Jerry B. Jenkins' *Left Behind* series of blockbuster novels that explicated the concept of "rapturing" saved Christians. Writing and preaching about the end times in the newly developing mega-churches and on Cable TV, Bible teachers were also watching the growth of political Islam as the Ayatollah Khomeini took power in Iran and as the *jihad* in Afghanistan proved instrumental in the fall of the Soviet Union. It would not be long until the shift from Russia as the "Evil Empire" to Islam as a member of the "Axis of Evil" when extremists declared war on the West.[21] At the same time that "Islam" entered the American consciousness as a political threat, the run-up to the millennium produced a religious revivalism with an apocalyptical belief that united the

Israeli Right with the American Christian Right that had become politicized during the presidency of Ronald Reagan and took power during the administration of George W. Bush. Secular and religious conspiracy plots that had developed on separate tracks in fiction now converged and were packaged in spy novel and thriller format.

Just as conspiracy theories were rife in the new American republic, so, too, was apocalyptical millennialism, the view that the return of Jews to Jerusalem was also a part of the tradition of the "kingdom on the hill." Taking a page from seventeenth century British Puritanism, perhaps one quarter of today's American Evangelical Christians also subscribe to "dispensational pre-millennialism," a theology enunciated by the nineteenth century British Protestant, John Nelson Darby (1800–1882), who traveled extensively and began preaching in America in the early 1860s. His belief, based on the biblical Book of Revelation, was that after a series of epochs or "dispensations," history as we know it will end, to be followed by the establishment of a divine kingdom that will last for a thousand years. But before the millennium can come about, many Evangelical Christians believe, an apocalypse in which this world is destroyed will occur. Before that can happen, however, a number of conditions must be fulfilled: the Jews must return to Israel; the Jewish Temple must be rebuilt; and the Jews must be given the opportunity to consider the error of their ways, recant, and accept Jesus in order to be saved before the cosmic battle between good and evil that will consume the world occurs. Advocates, attuned to the politics of the day, pored over texts, seeking the particular date that would initiate the timetable, the countdown to the end of time.[22] When, at the end of World War I, the Balfour Declaration was issued, it was seen as a sign that cosmic events were unfolding.

While it is true that evangelicals were more concerned with the Scopes Trial and battles over evolution during the period between the two world wars, James J. Hunter published two unusual novels for the Evangelical Press that could be characterized as "apocalyptic" spy novels combining religion and politics. Set in the Palestine Mandate, during World War II, *The Mystery of Mar Saba* (1940) illustrates the notion that "the descendants of Ishmael were usurpers who were being controlled by communist, Nazi, or even satanic influences," in order to deny the British role in facilitating the Jewish return to the Holy Land, thus paving the way for the Second Coming. The heroes are a British police official and his born-again American assistant.[23] Hunter's second novel, *Banners of Blood* (1947), was published after World War II just before the United Nations' vote on the partition of

Palestine. Although the villains are different, they, too, threaten not only British imperial interests but also the unfolding of the divine plan. The Jewish atheistic Canaanite fanatics who acknowledge the pagan god Moloch and practice sacrifices, and whose goal is to rebuild Zion with "fire and blood," presage the novels of the 1990s in which Christian conservative writers warn Jews to return to the true religion of their fathers before the last battle between Gog and Magog.[24]

Events unfolding on the ground—the establishment of the State of Israel in 1948, the return of Jerusalem to Jewish rule in the 1967 Arab-Israeli war, and the end of the Cold War in 1989—were all seen as prophetic indicators both to messianic Jews and to millennial Christians. The Reverend Billy Graham's father-in-law, L. Nelson Bell, wrote in *Christianity Today* "that for the first time in more than 2000 years Jerusalem is now completely in the hands of Jews gives the student of the Bible a thrill and a renewed faith in the accuracy and validity of the Bible."[25] Viewed as aggressors who lived in continual warfare with the rest of the world, the Arabs, more than ever, were seen "as foils to God's plans in the Middle East and on the side of Satan and the Antichrist."[26]

When, three years after Menachem Begin became Israeli prime minister, President Ronald Reagan was elected as president of the United States, an unlikely alliance was formed. To Christian believers, Begin was neither the godless terrorist of Hunter's *Banners of Blood* nor the antithesis of the liberal Jewish heroic ideal; rather, to them, he was the embodiment of the religious nationalist who walked and talked the Bible—using the biblical names Judea and Samaria, to justify in biblical terms the retention of the West Bank. For his part, Reagan was a believer who had close ties with Jerry Falwell and the Moral Majority, authors Hal Lindsey and Tim LaHaye, and Colonel Oliver North. At one point, the American president told Jewish supporters: "You know, I turn back to your ancient prophets in the Old Testament and the signs foretelling Armageddon, and I find myself wondering if—if we're the generation that is going to see that come about. I don't know if you've noted any of these prophecies lately, but believe me, they certainly describe the times we're going through."[27]

Looking towards the millennium, some Christian conservative writers who published books focusing on prophecy and millennial themes, packaged their ideology in spy novel and thriller format. As the Soviet threat receded, writers at the turn of the twenty-first century increasingly worried about the onset of the End of Days. Conflating the villainy of Muslim terrorists and the Antichrist, they also warned Jews to return to the faith before Armageddon.

In one reading of the biblical prophet Ezekiel, America became the new Israel; other exegetes concluded that the satanic forces remained at war with Israel. "Were all the Jews left on earth restored to the small territory of Palestine," the pastor from Tennessee told Congress in Joel C. Rosenberg's thriller, *The Ezekiel Option* (2005), "what temptation or provocation could they offer to arouse the allied armies of earth to invade them? No, my countrymen, it is not ancient Jewry that will witness this invasion. There is another Israel, the Israel of America." But Undersecretary of State for Political Affairs Ken Costello was not so sure. He had uncovered clues from the Dead Sea Scrolls and memoirs of President Ronald Reagan. "A modern, resurrected State of Israel *was* in the Russian crosshairs, precisely as Ezekiel had predicted. He picked up his cell phone and dialed the West Wing."[28]

By this, his third novel, *The Ezekiel Option*, Rosenberg was riding a bestseller wave. A born-again Christian who has had extensive political and research experience in his work at think tanks and for political candidates and pundits, Rosenberg explicitly uses the thriller to disseminate his belief in Evangelical Christianity; but, unlike the "Left Behind" series, which although written as a thriller is more evocative of "science fiction," he interprets current politics biblically. In books that predicted the war with Iraq over Saddam's acquisition of nuclear weapons and even the death of Yasir Arafat, novels which drew him accolades and advertising from conservative television pundits who touted his prescience as the American invasion plans for Iraq unfolded in 2002/2003,[29] Rosenberg's *The Ezekiel Option* has Israel go nuclear when threatened by an alliance between Russia and Iran that emerges as the new international threat after the fall of Saddam and the death of Arafat. The author's interpretation of the Biblical Moshekh and Elam as Russia and Iran comes from the Book of Ezekiel, the prophecy purported to be President Ronald Reagan's favorite—"Was it really possible that the man who had rightly designated the Soviet Union as the Evil Empire had been basing his conclusions on biblical prophecies?" asks Rosenberg's character Costello, as he devours books on the Bible, Jewish history, and a biography of Ronald Reagan, in preparation for warning the American president that Israel, not the United States, was the target. In the last conflict, Israel would be saved by divine intervention. Finally, Iran's assertion that "Allah is not on the side of the Jews," would be proved false when earthquakes and fiery projectiles engulfed the villainous regimes, many of whose people were already converting to Christianity. Clearly, some fictional battle lines for the twenty-first century had been drawn. Holy war was practiced by both sides—a *jihad*ist conspiracy from the Muslims, a crusade by evangelical Christians.[30]

Rosenberg surprised his readers when he switched publishers. Unlike LaHaye, who had begun publishing in 1995 with an evangelical Christian publishing house only to sign a multi-million dollar contract with trade press Bantam, Rosenberg achieved immediate acclaim through publishing with a mainstream trade press, but then, deciding that his true public was more religious than secular, he chose to have his third novel published by Tyndale House, whose market is decidedly Christian. As Rosenberg told an interviewer:

> Tyndale, of course, has the most-successful fiction series in American publishing history. They've done an astounding job with the Left Behind series, but I told my agent they wouldn't be interested in *The Ezekiel Option*. I figured they get thousands of proposals for end-times fiction and wouldn't want to see another one. But my agent insisted we at least give it a try, and were overwhelmed by how positive their response was . . . . They were excited about *The Ezekiel Option* story and said they were looking for a new series of books that would lead up to the Rapture . . . . Perhaps *The Ezekiel Option* will get people reading the Scriptures and looking at the news in a different way than they ever had before. Perhaps it will get people thinking and talking about a 2,500 year old prophecy that may be as real as tomorrow's headlines.[31]

More novels that depicted the progressive denouement of apocalyptic eschatology followed.[32]

LaHaye and Jenkins, on the other hand, whose fictional battle of Armageddon and Jesus' triumphant return had already taken place some twelve years after the appearance of the first in the Left Behind series, wrote prequels to satisfy popular demand and initiated a new thriller series featuring a biblical scholar/archaeologist, his publisher no doubt having in mind the success of Dan Brown's *The Da Vinci Code*. Still in the throes of the millennium, and for a while uncertain how to proceed in the wake of 9/11, publishers drew on a readership purchasing millennial thrillers at the turn of the twenty-first century, a period not unlike the turn of the twentieth century, which spawned the spy novels and created the thrillers that dominated crime fiction about the Middle East for a hundred years.

Authors and publishers had learned much during the twentieth century and the thriller of the early twenty-first century illustrated that fact. Cover art evolved from pictures of men in turbans with knives at the throats of innocent Western women to the ubiquitous scene of a mushroom cloud above Washington, DC. After 9/11, to be sure, men in turbans still appeared, but the weapons were more deadly now and the villains, infinitely more intelligent, are less grotesquely stereotyped. A look at two novels written two decades apart by Nelson DeMille—a best-selling practitioner of the art of the thriller, will illustrate the point.

By the Rivers of Babylon (1978) is typical of the post-1967 thrillers of the day. The terrorists who plant the explosive devices in the Concorde planes while they are under construction in France before delivery to Israel have managed a superb coup, outfoxing Israeli security. Instead of one hijacked Concorde, they blow up one and force the second, whose passengers are Israeli officials on their way to a peace conference, to set down near the ancient city of Babylon, where the Jews were exiled in ancient times and sat and wept during the period of the prophet Jeremiah. Clearly the plot is a sadistic attempt by the sexually deviant Palestinian villains assisted by an anti-Semitic American military officer outraged at being stationed in the Jewish state, to disrupt the peace process. But their leader is not Palestinian; he is an Iraqi who joined forces with a Palestinian who "began culling both male and female orphans from various camps. About twenty of the Tiger Cubs are tigresses . . . . [who] trained for years in the Shamiyah Desert for special assignments that never seemed to come off."[33] Needless to say, this group of well-armed Palestinian youth trainees who just happen to be in the neighborhood meet the same fate. On the Israeli side, it just so happens that the general on board is an archaeology buff who knows the ins and outs of the ruins of Babylon and the few relatively unarmed Israelis are Holocaust survivors and Sabras who defend themselves until rescued by the Israeli "cavalry."

More than twenty years later, De Mille wrote again about international terrorism in *The Lion's Game*. This novel also features a plane hijacking, only this time the scene is not the Middle East, but New York's John F. Kennedy International Airport. The hero is not Israeli, but a New York wiseguy policeman who holds a begrudging admiration for the villain, whose intelligence and planning have stymied the Americans. Asad Khalil, a serial assassin whose family was killed when America bombed Libya, though a man of rage, has been well trained by both the KGB and Libyan intelligence. He tracks the Americans on the Libyan bombing mission sent to kill Qaddafi and kills them one by one, leaving the ill, aging former US president as his last target. Asad [Lion] Khalil considers himself to be an "Islamic freedom fighter." The Arab-American on the New York Police force explains: "There's a long tradition of the lone Arab horseman, like in the American West—mean and lean . . . . who rides alone and will take on an army."[34] Indeed, Khalil has only contempt for the American soldier who relies on high-tech instead of personal heroics.

> The Americans never go into battle unless they've done all they can to assure victory before the first shot is fired. This is like shooting a lion from a vehicle with a telescopic sight. It is not victory at all—only slaughter . . . . What good is a physical victory without a spiritual or moral victory? I have not made the odds go against me—I have simply made the odds even, so that no matter who wins the game, I am the winner.[35]

During the final duel between Khalil and John Corey on the president's ranch in California, the denouement is not entirely clear: the president is alive; Corey is spared; and Khalil disappears, perhaps to continue the fight another day, or to take out his rage on Colonel Quaddafi who has betrayed him.

While temporarily confused about who wears the white hat and who the villains are, Corey notes that "the world was changing, the country was changing. America was not and had never been a country of one race, one religion, one culture. The glue that held us together was to some extent language, but even that was a little shaky. Also, we shared a central belief in law and justice, political freedom and religious tolerance. Someone like Abbah Ibin Abdellah [the pompous consultant for the FBI] was either a loyal and patriotic American and valuable special agent, or he was a security risk. He was almost undoubtedly the former. . . ."[36] During the 1990s, multiculturalism and anti-heroics, character development, and generic book jacket art marked changes in the genre that had evolved since mid-century.

The events of 9/11 and the war in Iraq changed all that. Despite a temporary hiatus in publishing while authors flirted with the apocalypse and wrote detective novels set in pre-World War I Cairo or Istanbul, publishers and authors seemed unsure where the genre was going.[37] The trends that converged accidentally at the end of the 1960s to create the publishing phenomenon that became the Middle East thriller would continue. Instead of the on-going Arab-Israeli conflict and Palestinian terrorism, global terrorism and the ramifications of the Gulf War have combined with religious fanaticism, the possibility of economic instability, and advances in military technology proven in Afghanistan, Iraq, and Lebanon to provide the themes that would occupy thriller readers through the first decade of the twenty-first century.

By the end of 2002, terrorism was back in fiction and tried-and-true authors returned to the genre. Writers new to spy novels and thrillers were also picking up the slack. Osama Bin Laden had already appeared in David Hagberg's *Joshua's Hammer* (2000); Jack Higgins turned to the Gulf, and Daniel Silva's sensitive Israeli killer was tracking terrorists all over Europe.[38] British and American operatives starred in novels published both in Britain and the United States as their intelligence services cooperated and worked together to thwart international terrorism.

"During his time in the Middle East," we read in Frederick Forsyth's *The Afghan* (2006), the CIA officer "had had much to do with the British, and, unlike some of his fellow countrymen who had been trying to cope with the hellhole of Iraq for three years, he was not too proud to admit that the CIA's closest allies in what Kipling once called 'the Great Game,' were a repository of much arcane knowledge about the badlands between the Jordan River and the Hindu Kush." British soldiers, administrators, operatives, and "eccentric explorers" . . . "had been trudging over desert, mountain range and goat pen in the zone that had now become the intelligence time bomb of the world." The British code-named the CIA "the Cousins" or "the Company," and the Americans called the London-based Secret Intelligence Service, "the Friends" or "the Firm."[39] They would work together.

After an innocuous cell phone call leads British and Pakistani intelligence agents to an apartment in Peshawar where they intercept some important members of al-Qaeda who are planning an attack against the United States, they find a computer, and sending the data to Washington for decipherment, set in motion an Anglo-American spy operation to foil an imminent attack. But, what was the target? The clues were elusive.

"Was it fiercely guarded?" asked Harrison.

"Two men died trying to prevent us seeing it."

"Ah, well, yes. Understandable . . . I fear it can be nothing but a reference to some kind of project, some operation. And not a small one."

"Something big?" asked the man from Homeland Security.

"Gentlemen," a member of the Quran-expert Arabist advisory group that US intelligence has put together replied, "devout Muslims—not to say fanatical ones—do not regard al-Isra lightly. For them it was something that changed the world. If they have a code-named something al-Isra, they intend that it should be huge . . . I think I can speak for us all in suggesting you find out what it refers to. Whatever else, they would never give the title al-Isra to a mere satchel bomb, a devastated nightclub, a wrecked commuter bus."[40]

Clearly, the only way to stop the plan was to find an individual to infiltrate al-Qaeda and prevent the cataclysm from the inside.

They would require a Sandy Arbuthnot/Richard Hannay for the twenty-first century. A Brit raised in the Middle East who knew the culture—someone like "the older boy in his white Iraqi dishdasha, racing about the lawn of the house in the Saadun suburb of Baghdad," to the delight of his father's guests, laughing with pleasure and shouting, "but Nigel, he's more like one of us"—would be required.[41] And he would have to be fluent not only in Arabic but Afghan dialects as well and be a professional soldier trained in covert operations to boot. They find their ideal candidate in Mike Martin, a member of the British SAS, the corps "formed in the Western Desert in 1941, and its empathy with the sands of Arabia has never left it." He is a professional who served in covert operations; he had slipped into Afghanistan and fought with the Afghans against the Russians.[42]

At his home in rural England, he sees the cars coming, and when the mission is presented to him, Mike Martin responds in typical Hannay fashion: his "thoughts flitted to a scene in his all-time favorite film. T.E. Lawrence has offered Auda abu Tayi money to join him in the attack on Aqaba. He recalled the great reply: Auda will not ride to Aqaba for the British gold, he will ride to Aqaba because it pleases him." Martin stood up, agreed and went to get his kit. "There's not much of it. Enough to fill the boot, no more," he said. And, later, when it was all over, a memorial service was held. But "only those grouped around the Clock Tower knew that Mike Martin, Parachute Regiment and SAS colonel, retired, had done this for four thousand complete strangers, none of whom ever knew he existed."[43]

Events in the Middle East had come full circle: In 1916, John Buchan wrote about a young British officer who, working between Mosul and the Persian frontier as a muleteer . . . south into the Bakhtiari Hills, found out about the *jihad* to bring down the British Empire. Discovered and shot just before the battle at Kut, he staggered into the British camp "with ten bullet holes in him and a knife slash on his forehead," and set in motion the plots that would engage the modern spy novel set in the Middle East during the twentieth century, a genre that evolved from spy novel to thriller using plots of British heroics to save the Empire and Anglo-American cooperation to save Western civilization from *jihad* and global terrorism.

Notes

A *Note regarding citations*: Complete citations of novels (city, publisher, date of publication) will be included in the notes only when quotations are used from specific volumes. Otherwise, only the initial date of publication will be provided.

Chapter 1

1. This definition comes from Caroline Reitz, *Detecting the Nation: Fictions of Detection and the Imperial Venture* (Columbus: Ohio State University Press, 2004). Popular culture theorists note that fiction for popular consumption emerged in Britain with the Industrial Revolution and urbanization. Whether popular culture was a capitalist imposed device to maintain control, a product of the people or an interactive process is a continuing debate (John Storey, *Cultural Theory and Popular Culture: An Introduction*, 5th ed. (New York: Pearson, 2009).

2. It is understood that today, Muslims use the term *jihad* to mean "to exert an effort" both in a moral sense and also in defense of the Islamic community. In this book, *jihad* connotes the Western perception of "holy war" as it has been used in the crime fiction books under study.

3. John Sutherland, *Bestsellers: Popular Fiction of the 1970s* (London: Routledge and Kegan Paul, 1981), 18–23.

4. Janice Radway, *Reading the Romance: Women, Patriarchy, and Popular Literature* (Chapel Hill: University of North Carolina Press, 1984).

5. Michael Denning, *Cover Stories: Narrative Ideology in the British Spy Thriller* (London, 1987), 18–20.

6. Conversation by author with acquisitions librarian at the Long Beach Public Library, Long Beach, New York, May 18, 2009.

7. John M. Reilly, "Publishing, History of the Book," in Rosemary Herbert, ed., *The Oxford Companion to Crime and Mystery Writing* (New York: Oxford University Press, 1999), 360; George Kelley, "Paperbacks," Herbert, 323.

8. Lars Ole Sauerberg, "Literature in Figures: An Essay on the Popularity of Thrillers," *Orbis Litterarum* 38(1983), 98.

9. Jerry Palmer, *Potboilers: Methods, Concepts and Case Studies in Popular Fiction* (London: Routledge, 1991), 38–40.

10. Judith Rosen, "Sleuthing in the Stores," *Publishers Weekly* (April 22, 2002), 5; Albert Greco, *The Book Publishing Industry*, 2nd ed. (Lawrence Erlbaum, 2004).

11. Profitability in the book industry is much like the film industry, which was inherently anti-war in the immediate aftermath of Vietnam but, despite the Hollywood political climate began to produce such pro-military films as the Rambo series, *Top Gun* and *An Officer and a Gentleman*, because of their profitability. Publishers publish books that are deemed marketable.

12. The traditional set of rules for mystery writers is found in Father Ronald Knox's introduction to *The Best English Detective Stories of 1928*. Edited by Knox and Harrington (New York, 1928).

13. Heta Pyrhonen, *Murder from an Academic Angle: An Introduction to the Study of the Detective Narrative* (Columbia, South Carolina: Camden House, 1994); John Ball, ed., *The Mystery Story* (New York: Penguin, 1978); Julian Symonds, *Mortal Consequences: A History from the Detective Story to the Crime Novel* (New York: Schocken Books, 1973).

14. Examples: Archaeological digs in Egypt: John Hymers, *Utter Death* (1952); Frank Gruber, *Bridge of Sand* (1963); Elizabeth Peters, *The Curse of the Pharaohs* (1981); Robin Cook, *Sphinx* (1979). Turkey: Sylvia Angus, *Death of a Hittite* (1969); Israel: Margot Arnold, *Zadok's Treasure* (1980). Iraq: Agatha Christie, *Murder in Mesopotamia* (1936). Cruise ships on the Nile: Francis McKinley, *Death Sails the Nile* (1933); Agatha Christie, *Death on the Nile* (1937); Jessica Mann, *Death Beyond the Nile* (1988).

15. This example comes from Safia El Wakil, "Egypt in American and British Popular Fiction," *Images of Egypt in Twentieth Century Literature* [Proceedings—International Symposium on Comparative Literature, 1989] (Cairo, 1991), 392.

16. Manning O'Brine, *Corpse to Cairo* (1952).

17. Phyllis A. Whitney, "Gothic Mysteries," in John Ball, ed., *The Mystery Story* (New York: Penguin, 1976), 223–232

18. Anne Eliot, *Incident at Villa Rahmana* (New York: Hawthorne Books, 1972), 12.

19. Anne Maybury, *The Midnight Dancers* (New York: Random House, 1973), 4.

20. Zeynep Çelik, *Empire, Architecture, and the City: French-Ottoman Encounters, 1830–1914* (Seattle: University of Washington Press, 2008); see also the work of Susan Ossman, *Picturing Casablanca: Portraits of Power in a Modern City* (Berkeley: University of California Press, 1994).

21. Phyllis Whitney, *Black Amber*(New York: Appleton Century Crofts, 1964), 13–14.

22. Jerry Palmer, *Thrillers: Genesis and Structure of a Popular Genre* (London: Edward Arnold, 1978). In this case, thrillers are not unlike the police procedural where readers follow the ratiocinations of the detective as he proceeds to solve the crime.

23. Raphael Rothstein, *The Hand of Fatima* (New York: Manor, 1979), back flap.

24. Bruce Merry, *Anatomy of the Spy Thriller* (Montreal: McGill Queens University Press, 1977), 134.

25. Paul Henissart, "Of Spies and Stories," *The Writer* 91(1978), 16.

26. Examples: Journalists: Marvin Kalb and Ted Koppel, *In the National Interest* (1977); David Ignatius, *Agents of Innocence* (1987); Eric Pace, *Any War Will Do* (1973); *Nightingale* (1979). Academics: Richard Bulliet, *The Tomb of the Twelfth Imam* (1979) and *The Gulf Scenario* (1984); Howard M. Sachar, *Man on the Camel*(1981). Politicians: Spiro Agnew, *The Canfield Decision* (1976); William S. Cohen, *One-Eyed Kings* (1991).

27. Daniel Silva, *The Mark of the Assassin* (1998); Nelson DeMille, *Night Fall* (2004).

28. Ken Follett, "The Spy as Hero and Villain," in Lucy Freeman, ed., *The Murder Mystique: Crime Writers on Their Art* (New York: Frederick Ungar, 1982), 81.

29. Richard Gid Powers, "J. Edgar Hoover and the Detective Hero," *Journal of Popular Culture* 9(1975), 257–278.

30. Amy Johnson Frykholm, *Rapture Culture: Left Behind in Evangelical America*. (New York: Oxford University Press, 2004), 3. See also Melani McAlister, "Prophecy, Politics, and the Popular: The Left Behind Series and Christian Fundamentalism's New World Order," *The South Atlantic Quarterly* 102 (2003), 773–798.

31. Gershom Gorenberg, "Book Review: *The Remnant*," *The American Prospect* 13(September 23, 2002).

32. *New York Times*, February 11, 2002. This has been borne out by Frykholm's study cited above.

33. Robin Winks, "The Genre of Mystery and Spy Fiction Should Get Serious Study but It Must be for the Right Reasons," *The Chronicle of Higher Education* (August 2, 1989) and his *The Historian as Detective* (New York: Harper, 1968); Steven M. Neuse, "Teaching Political Science with Chillers and Thrillers," *Teaching Political Science* 7(1980), 153–167.

34. Richard Slotkin, *Gunfighter Nation: The Myth of the Frontier in Twentieth Century America* (New York: Atheneum, 1992), 356, 626.

35. LeRoy Panek, *The Special Branch: The British Spy Novel, 1890–1980* (Bowling Green: Bowling Green University Popular Press, 1981), 287–288; Merry, 4; Robert Jewett and John Shelton Lawrence, *Captain America and the Crusade*

Against Evil: The Dilemma of Zealous Nationalism (Grand Rapids, MI: William B. Eerdmans Publishing Company, 2003), 28.

36. Norman Daniel, *Islam and the West: The Making of an Image*(Edinburgh: Edinburgh University Press, 1960) and *Islam, Europe and Empire* (Edinburgh: Edinburgh University Press, 1966).

37. On Foucault, note James D. Faubion, ed., *Michel Foucault Essential Works: Power* (Hammondsworth: Penguin, 2002). See also studies by John M. MacKenzie, *Orientalism: History, Theory and the Arts* (Manchester: Manchester University Press, 1995) and *Propaganda and Empire: The Manipulation of British Public Opinion 1880–1960* (Manchester: Manchester University Press, 1984).

38. Edward Said, *Orientalism* (New York: Pantheon, 1978). See also Storey cited above.

39. Note the book by Jon Thompson, *Fiction, Crime, and Empire: Clues to Modernity and Postmodernism* (Urbana: University of Illinois Press, 1993).

Chapter 2

1. John Buchan, *Greenmantle* (London: Penguin Books, 1956), 17–19.

2. Buchan considered that the alliance of America and Britain would be the greatest safeguard for peace. Wherever an American appears in a Buchan novel, he is a sympathetic character. Like Ian Fleming during World War II, Buchan worked with the American secret service (David Stafford, *The Silent Game: The Real World of Imaginary Spies* (Athens, GA: University of Georgia Press, 1991), 69–70, 164–165).

3. Martin Green, "John Buchan," in Rosemary Herbert, ed., *The Oxford Companion to Crime and Mystery Writing* (New York: Oxford University Press, 1999), 49.

4. On Buchan see David Daniell, *The Interpreter's House: A Critical Assessment of John Buchan* (London: Thomas Nelson and Sons, Ltd., 1975); Andrew Lownie, *John Buchan: The Presbyterian Cavalier*, Rev. ed. (Boston: David R. Godine, 2003).

5. Keith Grieves, "*Nelson's History of the War*: John Buchan as a Contemporary Military Historian 1915–22," *Journal of Contemporary History* 28(1993), 533–551.

6. On the early history of the genre, see Eric Ambler, "Introduction," in Eric Ambler, ed., *To Catch a Spy: An Anthology of Favorite Spy Stories* (New York: Atheneum, 1965), 7–22; Michael Gilbert, "The Spy in Fact and Fiction," in John Ball, ed., *The Mystery Story* (New York: Penguin, 1978); David Skene Melvin, "The Secret Eye: The Spy in Literature; the Evolution of Espionage Literature—A Survey of the History and Development of the Spy and Espionage Novel," *Pacific Quarterly* 3(1978), 11–26; LeRoy L. Panek, *The Special Branch 1890–1980: The British Spy Novel, 1890–1980* (Bowling Green: Bowling Green University Popular Press, 1981); David A.T. Stafford, "Spies and Gentlemen: The Birth of the British Spy Novel, 1893–1914," *Victorian Studies* 24(1981), 491–509.

7. David Trotter, "The Politics of Adventure in the Early British Spy Novel," in

Wesley K. Wark, ed., *Spy Fiction, Spy Films and Real Intelligence* (London: Frank Cass, 1991), 33.

8. Ibid., 31.

9. The story of the Dreyfus case was just about paraphrased in William Le Queux's, *Behind the Throne* (1905) (Panek, 10).

10. Stafford, "Spies and Gentlemen," 499–501; Ambler, 14–15.

11. Trotter, 38.

12. Ibid., 36–37.

13. Ibid., 39.

14. Ibid., 32, 38.

15. H.V.F. Winstone, *The Illicit Adventure* (London: Jonathan Cape, 1982), 6–7.

16. Trotter, 30.

17. Ibid.

18. Buchan *Greenmantle*, 21.

19. Peter Hopkirk, *Like Hidden Fire: The Plot to Bring Down the British Empire* (New York: Kodansha International, 1994), 18–24; see also Reeva Spector Simon, *Iraq Between the Two World Wars: The Militarist Origins of Tyranny* (New York: Columbia University Press, 2004), chapter 2: "The Officers, Germany and Nationalism." On the German agents, see R. L. Melka, "Max Frieherr von Oppenheim: Sixty Years of Scholarship and Political Intrigue in the Middle East," *Middle Eastern Studies* (1973), 81–93; Benjamin Schwarz, "Divided Attention: Britain's Perception of a German Threat to Her Eastern Position in 1918," *Journal of Contemporary History* 28(1993), 103–122; Fritz Fischer, *Germany's Aims in the First World War* (New York: W.W. Norton, 1967); Gottfried Hagen, "German Heralds of Holy War: Orientalists and Applied Oriental Studies," *Comparative Studies of South Asia, Africa and the Middle East* 24(2004), 145–162.

20. Ibid., 31.

21. Winstone, 17.

22. Ibid., 80.

23. U.S. Ambassador to Turkey, Henry Morgenthau had discussions about German *jihad* plans with his German counterpart in Istanbul (Henry Morgenthau, *Secrets of the Bosphorus*, 2nd edition [London: Hutchinson and Company, 1918], 105).

24. Wassmuss as the subject of a British novel: Rex Adams, *The Star of Persia* (1942). Later German agents in the area appear in Robert Mason, *The Arab Agent* (1944).

25. Henri Baudet, *Paradise on Earth: Some Thoughts on European Images of Non-European Man* (New Haven: Yale University Press, 1965), 1–2.

26. Buchan, *Greenmantle*, 19.

27. The concept of a "mahdi," a charismatic leader chosen by God at the end of time to bring truth and justice to the world and, to overthrow, if necessary, the temporal order is not only a belief integral both to Sunni and Shia Islam, but

there are many examples of religious leaders who have declared *jihad* against the existing government in order to return to what they believe are the original tenets of Islam and reform society.

28. Quoted in Brian V. Street, *The Savage in Literature: Representations of 'Primitive' Society in English Fiction 1858–1920* (London: Routledge and Kegan Paul, 1975), 141. See also David B. Edwards, "Mad Mullahs and Englishmen: Discourse in the Colonial Encounter," *Comparative Studies in Society and History* 31 (1989), 649–670.

29. Roger T. Stearn, "War Correspondents and Colonial War, c. 1870–1900," in John M. MacKenzie, ed., *Popular Imperialism and the Military 1850–1950* (Manchester: Manchester University Press, 1992), 150.

30. Buchan, *Greenmantle*, 17.

31. Ibid., 18. Note the Ottoman declaration of *jihad* on November 11, 1914 (Rudolph Peters, *Jihad in Classical and Modern Islam: A Reader* [Princeton: Marcus Wiener, 1996], 55–57).

32. Quoted in Gilbert, 208.

33. Buchan, *Greenmantle*, 15.

34. Ibid., 21.

35. J.A. Mangan, "'The Grit of Our Forefathers': Invented Traditions, Propaganda and Imperialism" in John M. MacKenzie, ed., *Imperialism and Popular Culture* (Manchester: Manchester University Press, 1986), 120.

36. Jeffrey Richards, "Popular Imperialism and the Image of the Army in Juvenile Literature," in John M. Mackenzie, ed., *Popular Imperialism and the Military*; Joseph Bristow, *Empire Boys: Adventures in a Man's World* (London: Harper Collins Academic, 1991).

37. Panek, 44.

38. Alan Sandison, *The Wheel of Empire: A Study of the Imperial Idea in Some Late 19th Century and Early 20th Century Fiction* (New York: St. Martin's Press, 1967).

39. Richards, 87–88; Panek, 54–56. On Baden-Powell, see Michael Rosenthal, *The Character Factory: Baden-Powell and the Origins of the Boy Scout Movement* (New York: Pantheon Books, 1984).

40. Quoted in Panek, 53.

41. Ibid., 54–56; Richards, 87–88.

42. Eric Ambler derides this as a temper tantrum (Ambler, 17–18).

43. J. Railton Holden, *Suez Side Ace* (London: Newnes, 1938), 254; 256.

44. Rex Adams, *The Star of Persia* (1942), 112.

45. Buchan, *Greenmantle*, 22.

46. Ibid., 29.

47. Note Frederick Forsyth's, *The Afghan* (2006) for a twentieth century version. Here, only the British are capable of placing a mole in al-Qaeda. See also Edward Said's introduction to Rudyard Kipling's *Kim* (New York: Penguin, 1987).

48. John M. MacKenzie, "T. E. Lawrence: The Myth and the Message," in Robert Giddings, ed., *Literature and Imperialism* (London: Macmillan, 1991); 156, 161.

49. Curzon's *Oxford Lecture 1907* quoted in Trotter, 46–47.

50. Buchan, *Greenmantle*, 31. Note Buchan's factual account in his *Nelson's History of the War. Vol. XIII: The Position at Sea, the Fall of Erzerum, and the First Battle of Verdun* (London: Thomas Nelson and Sons, Ltd., 1916), 82–98.

51. Buchan, *Greenmantle*, 257. Note the German female villain in Rex Adams's *The Star of Persia* (1942), a novel that is partly set during World War I.

52. Buchan, *Greenmantle*, 271.

53. Ibid.

54. Lownie, 141.

55. Examples: Charles Cooper, *The Turkish Spy* (1932); Rex Adams, *The Star of Persia* (1942).

56. F. McKinley, *Death Sails the Nile* (Boston: The Stratford Company, 1933), 3.

Chapter 3

1. Operator 1384, *The Catacombs of Death* (London: Hutchinson, 1936), 53.

2. Operator 1384, *The Son of Allah* (London: Rich and Cowan, 1937, 86–87. See also Operator 1384, *The Black Arab* (1939) about a Mahdi plot in Palestine; Otwell Binns, *The Three Black Dots* (1929).

3. Graham Seton, *Colonel Grant's Tomorrow* (London: Thornton Butterworth, 1931), 123.

4. Examples: Talbot Mundy, *The Lion of Petra* (1932); *Jimgrim and Allah's Peace* (1933); *Affair in Araby* (1934).

5. Sax Rohmer, *The Mask of Fu Manchu* (New York: Pyramid Books, 1932), 21. The historical "Masked Prophet" was active during the period of the Abbasid dynasty. Rohmer may have been inspired by a nineteenth-century Romantic poem, "Lalla Rookh, an Oriental Romance." In the poem, Thomas Moore, the Irish "National Poet" depicts a "monstrous embodiment of French Jacobinism in the form of the eighth century false prophet Mokanna (Jeffrey W. Vail, "The Standard of Revolt: Revolution and National Independence in Moore's *Lalla Rookh*," *Romanticism on the Net* 40(2005). I thank Richard Bulliet for the information about Moore's poem.

6. Ibid., 60.

7. Ibid., 99–100.

8. *The Mask of Fu Manchu* was made into a film by MGM in 1932 and starred Boris Karloff, Lewis Smith, and Myrna Loy (Jack G. Shaheen, *Reel Bad Arabs: How Hollywood Villifies a People* (New York: Olive Branch Press, 2001), 323.

9. Julian Symons, *Mortal Consequences: A History from the Detective Story to the Crime Novel* (New York: Schocken Books, 1973), 225–226. Symons cites Ellery Queen in noting the origin of Sax Rohmer: Sax = a sharp blade, and Rohmer = wanderer or "Freelance."

10. Robert Briney, "Death Rays, Demons, and Worms Unknown to Science," in John Ball, ed., *The Mystery Story* (New York: Penguin, 1976), 235–289.

11. Christopher Frayling, "Sax Rohmer and the Devil Doctor." *London Magazine* 13(1973), 65–80.

12. Cay Van Ash and Elizabeth Sax Rohmer, *Master of Villainy: A Biography of Sax Rohmer* (Bowling Green: Bowling Green University Popular Press, 1972), 18–19. These books include *Brood of the Witch Queen* (1918); *Tales of Secret Egypt* (1920); *She Who Sleeps* (1929); *Tales of East and West* (1929); *Daughter of Fu Manchu* (1931); *The Mask of Fu Manchu* (1933); *The Bat Flies Low* (1935); *White Velvet* (1936).

13. Ibid., 26.

14. Devendra P. Varma, *The Gothic Flame: Being a History of the Gothic Novel in England: Its Origins, Efflorescence, Disintegration, and Residuary Influence* (New York: Russell and Russell, 1966), 237. See also Sprague De Camp, *Literary Swordsmen Sorcerers: The Masters of Heroic Fantasy* (Sauk City, WI: Arkham House, 1976), 5; On Orientalism in Romance novels see Jessica Taylor, "And You Can Be My Sheikh: Gender, Race, and Orientalism in Contemporary Romance Novels," *The Journal of Popular Culture* 40(2007), 1032–1051.

15. L. David Allen, "Sax Rohmer," in E.F. Bleiler, ed., *Supernatural Fiction Writers: Fantasy and Horror* (New York: Charles Scribner's Sons, 1985), 555. Before the first Dr Fu Manchu book, Rohmer provided music and lyrics for *The Camel's Parade, A Desert Arabesque* (1910)—"Show'r thy blessings Allah: then shall each heart be glad// Be ye, Lord, with our Caravan, bound for Old Baghdad" (Frayling, 66).

16. Clive Bloom, *Cult Fiction: Popular Reading and Pulp Theory* (New York: St. Martin's Press, 1996), 185.

17. Van Ash, 278.

18. Ibid., 10–12; see also Robin W. Winks, "Sinister Orientals: Everybody's Favorite Villains," in Dilys Winn, ed., *Murder Ink: The Mystery Reader's Companion.* (New York: Workman Publishing, 1977), 491–493; Robert G. Lee, *Orientals: Asian Americans in Popular Culture* (Philadelphia: Temple University Press, 1999).

19. Quoted in Harold R. Isaacs, *Scratches on Our Minds: American Views of China and India* (Armonk, New York: Sharpe Inc., 1980), 116.

20. The quote comes from *The Insidious Fu Manchu* in William F. Wu, *The Yellow Peril: Chinese Americans in American Fiction 1850–1940* (Hamden, CT: Archon Books, 1982), 165.

21. Ibid., 116–117.

22. Robert E. Briney, "Sax Rohmer: An Informal Survey," in Francis M. Nevins, Jr., ed., *The Mystery Writer's Art* (Bowling Green, OH: Bowling Green University Popular Press, 1970), 47–49.

23. Ibid., 62.

24. Van Ash, 278.

25. Bruce Kneale, *Appointment in Cairo* (London: Evans Brothers, Ltd., 1950), 25–26.

26. Sax Rohmer, *Daughter of Fu Manchu* (New York: Pyramid Books, 1964), 54.

27. See Timothy Mitchell, *Colonizing Egypt* (Berkeley: University of California Press, 1991); Michael J. Reimer, "Colonial Bridgehead: Social and Spatial Change in Alexandria 1850–1882," *International Journal of Middle East Studies* 20(1988), 531–553; Hossam M. Mahdy, "Travelers, Colonisers and Conservationists," in Paul Starkey and Janet Starkey,eds., *Travellers in Egypt* (London: I.B. Tauris, 1998).

28. Sax Rohmer, *She Who Sleeps* (New York: Collier, 1928), 84.

29. Max Rodenbeck, *Cairo: The City Victorious* (New York: Knopf, 1999), 137.

30. "In Egypt Rohmer had seen whirling dervishes hypnotize themselves into an ecstatic condition" (Van Ash, 212).

31. William Morton Fullerton, *In Cairo* (1891) quoted in Rodenbeck, 136.

32. Percy White, *Cairo* (London: Constable, 1914), 41.

33. Ibid., 82–83.

34. Quoted in Rodenbeck, 140.

35. White, 131.

36. Homi K. Bhabha, *The Location of Culture* (London: Routledge, 1994), 86–90.

37. Selwyn Jepson, *The Death Gong* (New York: Howard Watt, 1927), 174.

38. Derek Hopwood, Derek and Diana Grimwood Jones. "Servants of the Empire: Sidelights on the British in Egypt," in B.C. Bloomfield, ed., *Middle East Studies and Libraries: A Felicitation Volume For Professor J.D. Pearson* (London: Mansell, 1980), 70.

39. White, 97.

40. Ibid., 173.

41. Ibid., 78.

42. Jean-Marc Ran Oppenheim, "The Twilight of a Colonial Ethos: The Alexandria Sporting Club, 1890–1956" (PhD Dissertation, Columbia University, 1991), 27–34.

43. Arthur Weigall, *The King Who Preferred Moonlight* (London: Hutchinson and Company, 1928), 8, 39. See also Roger Bax, *Death Beneath Jerusalem* (1938).

44. Rohmer, *The Mask of Fu Manchu*, 98, 102.

45. "Tales of Abû Tabâh" in *Tales of Secret Egypt* (1920).

46. Sax Rohmer, "Yashmak of Pearls," *Tales of Secret Egypt* (London: Methuen, 1920), 6.

47. Sax Rohmer, "Breath of Allah," *Tales of Secret Egypt* (London: Methuen, 1920), 142.

48. Ibid., 136.

49. Sax Rohmer, "The Death Ring of Sneferu," *Tales of Secret Egypt* (London: Methuen, 1920), 35.

50. Rohmer, *She Who Sleeps* (New York: Collier, 1928), 87. Rohmer used Hassan es-Sugra earlier in *Tales of Secret Egypt* where his character is questionable. There,

he was for many years a trusted employee of the British Historical Society who tells Kernaby that his archaeologist employer has abandoned the excavation of the Pyramid of Meydum which contains extraordinary jewelry, since the workers refused to enter because of a curse. Finding himself in debt, es-Sugra offers Kernaby the opportunity to accompany him to the tomb to find the ring, but runs away. The character is more positive in *She Who Sleeps*.

51. Ibid., 95.

52. Sax Rohmer, *Bimbashi Baruk of Egypt* (New York: Robert McBride, 1944), 22–23.

53. Ibid., 228.

54. Sax Rohmer, *Daughter of Fu Manchu* (New York: Pyramid Books, 1932), 53.

55. Rohmer, *The Mask of Fu Manchu*, 127–128.

56. Ibid., 292–293.

57. For an example of an Israeli mole, see Peter Abrahams, *Tongues of Fire* (1982);

58. A.J. Quinnell, *The Mahdi* (New York: William Morrow, 1982), 19.

59. Ibid., 25–26.

60. Ibid., 297.

61. John M. MacKenzie, "The Popular Culture of Empire in Britain," in Judith M. Brown and Wm Roger Louis, eds., *Oxford History of the British Empire: The Twentieth Century* (Oxford: Oxford University Press, 1999), 222–223; John G. Cawelti, *Adventure, Mystery and Romance: Formula Stories as Art and Popular Culture* (Chicago: University of Chicago Press, 1976), 31.

62. LeRoy L. Panek, *The Special Branch: The British Spy Novel, 1890–1980* (Bowling Green: Bowling Green University Popular Press, 1981), 68–83. See also John M. Mackenzie, *Propaganda and Empire: The Manipulation of British Public Opinion 1880–1960* (Manchester: Manchester University Press, 1984).

Chapter 4

1. Examples: *jihad*—Francis Gerard, *The Prince of Paradise* (1938); Charles L. Leonard, *Expert in Murder* (1945); military coups and mandate politics—Glyn Griffith, *Fire over Baghdad* (1939); Desmond Stewart, *Leopard in the Grass* (1951); George Young, *The Man Called Lenz* (1954); World War II—Eric Ambler, *Journey into Fear* (1940); Roland Daniel, *The Death House* (1941); Michael Home, *The House of Shade* (1942); Robert Mason, *Cairo Communiqué* (1942); Charles L. Leonard, *Fanatic of Fez* (1943); Sax Rohmer, *Egyptian Nights* (1944)—includes the adventures of Bimbashi Baruk of Egypt; Clement Wood, *Death in Ankara* (1944); Robert Mason, *Arab Agent* (1944).

2. Examples: Bruce Munslow, *Deep Sand* (1955); Peter Saxon, *The Violent Hours* (1957).

3. Examples: John Hymers, *Utter Death* (1952); Anthony Parsons, *Death by the Nile* (1955).

4. Allan MacKinnon, *Assignment in Iraq* (1960).

5. Examples: Bruce Munslow, *No Safe Road* (1959); Anthony Heckstall-Smith, *The Man with Yellow Shoes* (1957); Ann Bridge, *The Lighthearted Quest* (1956).

6. John Sherwood, *Undiplomatic Exit* (New York: Doubleday, 1958), 49–50.

7. Ruth Wadham, *Weekend in Baghdad* (London: Gollanz, 1958), 71.

8. Examples: Graham Seton, *Colonel Grant's Tomorrow* (1931); Geoffrey Household, *The High Place* (1950); George Goodchild, *The Last Secret* (1956); Hammond Innes, *The Doomed Oasis* (1960); Warren Tute, *The Cairo Sleeper* (1977).

9. Simon Harvester, *A Breastplate for Aaron* (1949).

10. Michael Hastings, *The Sands of Khali* (London: MacDonald, 1964), 190–191. On orientalism and travel literature see Rana Kabbani, *Europe's Myths of Orient* (Bloomington: Indiana University Press, 1986).

11. John Atkins, *The British Spy Novel: Styles in Treachery* (London: John Calder, 1984), 257–260.

12. *The Powder Barrel* (1965); *Visa to Limbo* (1978); *The Median Line* (1979).

13. William Haggard, *The Median Line* (New York: Walker and Company, 1979), 3–4.

14. Example: Paul Henissart, *Narrow Exit* (1974).

15. Example: Hammond Innes, *The Black Tide* (1983).

16. Joel Hopkins, "An Interview with Eric Ambler," *Journal of Popular Culture* 9(1975), 286. On Ambler see Herbert Mitgang, "The Thrilling Eric Ambler," *The New York Times Book Review* (September 13, 1981); Ambler's "Introduction" in *To Catch a Spy: An Anthology of Favorite Spy Stories* (New York: Atheneum, 1965).

17. David Stafford, *The Silent Game: The Real World of Imaginary Spies* (Athens, GA: University of Georgia Press, 1991), 183; Myron J. Aronoff, *The Spy Novels of John le Carré: Balancing Ethics and Politics* (New York: St. Martin's Press, 1999); Melvyn Bragg, "*The Little Drummer Girl*: An Interview with John le Carré," in Matthew J. Bruccoli and Judith S. Baughman, eds., *Conversations with John le Carré* (Jackson: University of Mississippi, 2004), 72–85; see also Melanie McAlister's assertion that the novel is a "hostage" novel(Melanie McAlister, *Epic Encounters: Culture, Media, and U.S. Interests in the Middle East, 1945–2000* [Berkeley: University of California Press, 2001]).

18. "Gerald Seymour," in "Craft Notes," in Myron J. Smith, Jr. and Terry White, eds., *Cloak and Dagger Fiction: An Annotated Guide to Spy Thrillers*, 3rd edition (Westport: Greenwood Press, 1995), 669.

19. Gerald Seymour, *The Glory Boys* (New York: Random House, 1976).

20. Ibid., 67–68.

21. Ibid., 117.

22. Ibid., 273.

23. Note Raymond Chandler's explication of the masculine hard-boiled novel as opposed to the feminine detective story in his article "The Simple Art of Murder," *The Atlantic Monthly* (December, 1944); on his impact see David Glover

and Cora Kaplan, "Guns in the House of Culture: Crime Fiction and the Politics of the Popular," in Lawrence Grossberg, Cary Nelson, and Paula Treichler, eds., *Cultural Studies* (New York: Routledge, 1992), 213–216.

24. Tony Bennett and Janet Woollacott. *Bond and Beyond: The Political Career of a Popular Hero* (London: Macmillan Education, Ltd., 1987), 23.

25. Jerry Palmer, *Thrillers: Genesis and Structure of a Popular Genre* (London: Edward Arnold, 1978), 98–100.

26. David Cannadine, "Fantasy, Ian Fleming and the Realities of Escapism," in his *In Churchill's Shadow: Confronting the Past in Modern Britain* (New York: Oxford University Press, 2003), 280–281. Note that Fleming, like Buchan, may be patronizing, but takes the time to explain the political realities of the day to the Americans (301). On Buchan and America, see Stafford, 69.

27. David Cannadine, "James Bond and the Decline of England," *Encounter* 53(1979), 46–55.

28. Graham Dawson, *Soldier Heroes: British Adventure, Empire and the Imaginings of Masculinities* (London: Routledge, 1994), 179; John Atkins, *The British Spy Novel: Styles in Treachery* (London: John Calder, 1984), 105. The appearance of William Haggard's Colonel Russell, an urbane throwback to the Hannay school should be noted. For example, see his *Visa to Limbo* (1978) or *The Powder Barrel* (1965).

29. Ibid., 306; and James Chapman, *License to Thrill* (New York: Columbia University Press, 2000), 38–39.

30. Cannadine, "James Bond and the Decline of England, 46–55.

31. Cannadine, "Fantasy: Ian Fleming and the Realities of Escapism," 290.

32. Orrin Klapp, *Heroes, Villains and Fools: The Changing American Character* (Englewood Cliffs: Prentice Hall, 1962), 50–64. For a prosopography of Middle Eastern villainy see Reeva S. Simon, *The Middle East in Crime Fiction—Mysteries, Spy Novels and Thrillers from 1916 to the 1980s* (New York: Lilian Barber Press, 1989), chapter 6.

33. Dilys Winn, "From Poe to the Present," in *Murder Ink: The Mystery Reader's Companion* (New York: Workman Publishing, 1977), 4.

34. Graham Lancaster, *The Nuclear Letters* (New York: Atheneum, 1979).

35. George H. Lewis, "Spy Fiction American Style," *Journal of Communication* 25(1975), 132–137.

36. Andy East, "The Spy in the Dark: A History of Espionage Fiction," *The Armchair Detective* 19(Winter 1986), 23–40.

37. Edward Aarons, *Assignment: The Cairo Dancers* (New York: Fawcett, 1965), 18, 19.

38. Edward Aarons, *Assignment: Zoraya* (New York: Fawcett, 1960), 30.

39. East, 23–40.

40. Will Murray, "The Saga of Nick Carter, Killmaster," *The Armchair Detective* 15 (1982), 316–317.

41. Her adventures take her to Kuwait in *Sabre Tooth*(1966) and Algeria in *A Taste*

for Death (1969). See Peter O'Donnell, "Becoming Modesty," in Dilys Winn, ed. *Murder Ink: The Mystery Reader's Companion* (New York: Workman Publishing, 1977), 158–160; Robbie B.H. Goh, "Peter O'Donnell, Race Relations and National Identity: The Dynamics of Representation in 1960s and 1970s Britain," *Journal of Popular Culture* 32(Spring 1999), 29–43, and Bernard A. Drew, " Adventurer and Adventuress," in Rosemary Herbert, ed., *The Oxford Companion to Crime and Mystery Writing* (New York: Oxford University Press, 1999), 7.

42. Due to her popularity, the publisher reprinted the material from the first novel in the series, *The Unexpected Mrs. Pollifax* (1966) at the end of the paperback edition of *Mrs. Pollifax, Innocent Tourist* (New York: Fawcett, 1997).

43. Bennett and Woolacott, 82–83. Bond was updated in the 1980s. In the books by John Gardner, Bond drinks moderately, smokes low tar cigarettes, and drives a fuel efficient Saab 900 Turbo instead of a Bentley (Edwin McDowell, "James Bond Making 'Wild Comeback'" *The New York Times* (June 5, 1982).

44. East, 25. It seems that Kennedy later regretted the admission. (Arthur Schlesinger, Jr., "He Won't Tell, Should We Care?" *The New York Times* (January 9, 2000); Oreste del Buono and Umberto Eco, *The Bond Affair* (London: Macdonald, 1966); Kenneth J. Van Dover, *Murder in the Millions: Erle Stanley Gardner, Mickey Spillane, Ian Fleming* (New York: 1984); Michael Denning, *Cover Stories: Narrative Ideology in the British Spy Thriller* (London: Routledge and Kegan Paul, 1987).

45. Del Buono and Eco, 22.

46. Jacques Barzun, "Meditations on the Literature of Spying," *American Scholar* 34 (1965), 167–178; Edmund Wilson, "Who Cares Who Killed Roger Akroyd," as cited in Thomas Chastain, "Q. Who Cares Who Killed Roger Ackroyd? A. Millions of Readers Do," *Publishers Weekly* 213(March 13, 1978), 58.

47. Bennett and Woollacott, 12, 24–27.

48. There were 11 about the Middle East published in 1964.

Chapter 5

1. G. Jay Rausch, "Developments in Espionage Fiction," *Kansas Quarterly* 10(1978), 75. See F. Van Wyck Mason, *The Cairo Garter Murders* (1938); *The Dardanelles Derelict* (1949); *Two Tickets for Tangier* (1955).

2. Examples: Edward Aarons, *Assignment: Ankara* (1961); Adam Hall, *The Tango Briefing* (1973); F. Van Wyck Mason, *Two Tickets for Tangier* (1955).

3. Edward Aarons, *Assignment: Zoraya* (New York: Fawcett, 1960), 53.

4. Quoted in Douglas Little, *American Orientalism: The United States and the Middle East since 1945* (Chapel Hill: The University of North Carolina Press, 2002), 14.

5. Ibid., 44.

6. Ian Fleming came to Washington to assist (Thomas J. Price, "Spy Stories, Espionage and the Public in the Twentieth Century," *Journal of Popular Culture* 30 [1996], 84–89).

7. "Office of Strategic Services," Norman Polmar and Thomas B. Allen, *Spy Book: The Encyclopedia of Espionage* (New York: Random House, 1997), 408–410; "CIA," Ibid., 115–121; see also David F. Rudgers, "The Origins of Covert Action," *Journal of Contemporary History* 35 (2000), 249–262—Special Ops were also authorized under Truman.

8. Jane Smith, *Islam in America* (New York: Columbia University Press, 1999).

9. Michael J. Cohen, "The Strategic Role of the Middle East after the War," in Michael J. Cohen and Martin Kolinsky, eds., *Demise of the British Empire in the Middle East: Britain's Responses to Nationalist Movements 1943–55* (London: Frank Cass, 1998).

10. Jeffrety T. Richelson, *A Century of Spies: Intelligence in the Twentieth Century* (New York: Oxford University Press, 1995).

11. Donald McCormick and Katy Fletcher, *Spy Fiction: A Connoisseur's Guide* (New York: Facts on File, 1990), 269.

12. Stephen Kinzer, *All the Shah's Men: An American Coup and the Roots of Middle East Terror* (Hoboken: John Wiley and Sons, Inc., 2003), 4–5.

13. For the literary collaboration between the FBI and crime stories in pulp fiction magazines see Richard Gid Powers, "J. Edgar Hoover and the Detective Hero," *Journal of Popular Culture* 9(1975), 257–258.

14. Katy Fletcher, "Evolution of the Modern American Spy Novel," *Journal of Contemporary History* 22(1987), 329. Charles McCarry joined the CIA in 1958 after a career as a journalist and speechwriter for Eisenhower (Ibid., 325).

15. Myron J. Smith, Jr., *Cloak and Dagger Bibliography: An Annotated Guide to Spy Fiction 1937–1975* (Netuchen, N.J.: Scarecrow Press, 1976), 197; Polmar and Allen, 274–275; Fletcher, 319–331.

16. Turks had already become Westernized as the Ottoman Empire was transformed into Turkey through the medium of officer camaraderie and secularism. By the end of World War II, eunuchs and other Oriental vestiges of the Ottoman regime disappeared in fiction as Istanbul and Ankara became centers of international intrigue populated with White Russians, Hungarian countesses, Communists, and Balkan fellow travelers, Nazis, French and British agents. This is the setting of Eric Ambler's *Journey into Fear*, where the red-light district in Istanbul could be run-down Berlin, and where the Turkish secret agent who helps the British armaments engineer escape the Nazis is intelligent, Western, and wears his hair cut short. By the 1960s, officials have become Westernized, the police are efficient, and Turks could be from any European country.

17. Examples: Richard Starnes, *The Flypaper War* (1969); Thomas R. Roberts, *The Heart of the Dog* (1972); William F. Brown, *Thursday at Noon* (1987). See also David Ignatius, *Agents of Innocence* (1987) on US policy during the Lebanese civil war.

18. Melani McAlister, *Epic Encounters: Culture, Media, and U.S. Interests in the Middle East, 1945–2000* (Berkeley: University of California Press, 2001), 156–157.

19. On Israeli intelligence coups see Ian Black and Benny Morris, *Israel's Secret Wars: A History of Israel's Intelligence Services* (New York: Grove and Weidenfeld, 1991); on British and American concern about moles see Richelson.

20. Jonathan D. Sarna, *American Judaism: A History* (New Haven: Yale University Press, 2004), 204–205; and his "A Projection of America as It Ought to Be: Zion in the Mind's Eye of American Jews," in Allon Gal, ed., *Envisioning Israel: The Changing Ideals and Images of North American Jews* (Jerusalem: Magnes Press, 1996).

21. Quoted in Gershom Gorenberg, *The Accidental Empire: Israel and the Birth of the Settlements 1967–1977* (New York: Times Books, 2006), 48.

22. Mason, *The Cairo Garter Murders* (New York: Doubleday, 1938), 119.

23. Michelle Mart, "Tough Guys and American Cold War Policy: Images of Israel 1948–1960," *Diplomatic History* 20(1996), 357–380; see also Deborah Dash Moore, "From David to Goliath: American Representations of Jews around the Six Day War," in Eli Lederhendler, ed., *The Six Day War and World Jewry* (University Press of Maryland, 2000); Paul Breines, *Tough Jews: Political Fantasies and the Moral Dilemma of American Jewry* (New York: Basic Books, 1990); Karen Brodkin, *How Jews Became White Folks and What That Says about Race in America* (New Brunswick: Rutgers University Press, 1999).

24. Leonard Harris, *The Masada Plan* (New York: Popular Library, 1976), 45–46. See also Michael Barak, *The Secret List of Heinrich Roehm* (1976); Jack Hoffenberg, *17 Ben Gurion* (1977).

25. On the impact of the Vietnam War on US-Israeli relations and on American Jews, see Judith A. Klinghoffer, *Vietnam, Jews and the Middle East: Unintended Consequences* (New York: St. Martin's Press, 1998).

26. Thomas Harris, *Black Sunday* (New York: G.P. Putnam's Sons, 1975), 171.

27. For an analysis of the film version see McAlister, 187–192.

28. Examples: Barry Weil, *Dossier IX* (London: Hamilton, 1969); Sandor Frankel and Webster Mews, *The Aleph Solution* (New York: Stein and Day, 1978); Matti Golan, *The Geneva Crisis* (1981).

29. Examples: Barry Weil, *Dossier X* (1969); Anthony Price, *The Alamut Ambush* (1972); David Benedictus, *The Rabbi's Wife* (1976); Michael Barak, *The Secret Life of Heinrich Roehm* (1976); Uri Dan and Peter Manor, *Ultimatum PU94* (1977); Howard Kaplan, *The Damascus Cover* (1977); Amos Aricha and Eli Landau, *Phoenix* (1979).

30. Examples: Ken Follet, *Triple* (1979); Morris Farhi, *The Last of Days* (1983).

31. Examples: Harry Arvey, *Eleven Bullets for Mohammed* (1975); *Operation Kuwait* (1975) both published by Bantam Books; Andrew Sugar's "Israeli Commandos": #1 *The Aswan Assignment* (1974); #2 *The Fireball Assignment* (1974); #3 *The Kamikazee Assignment* (1975); #4 *The Alps Assignment* (1975) published by Manor Books. The glorification of violence as the antithesis of the traditional stereotype of the Jewish male weakling that these fictional heroes embodied,

however, frightened liberal American Jews. These were neither the values of American Jewish liberalism nor of the Labor Zionism of Israel as the "Light unto the Nations." This dissonance would be exacerbated after the Likud came to power in 1977.

32. McAlister, 182.

33. Examples: Charles McCarry, *The Better Angels* (1979); Charles Robertson, *The Elijah Conspiracy* (1980).

34. Examples: Alfred Coppel, *Thirty-Four East* (1974); John Crosby, *An Affair of Strangers* (1975); Sheila Lawrence, *A Million Tears* (1977); Nelson DeMille, *By the Rivers of Babylon* (1978); William Wingate, *Bloodbath* (1978); Raphael Rothstein, *The Hand of Fatima* (1979); Barry Schiff and H. Fishman, *The Vatican Target* (1979).

35. Examples: Harry Arvay, *Eleven Bullets for Muhammad* (1975), James Patterson, *The Jericho Commandment* (1979).

36. Examples: John Nance, *Scorpion Strike* (1992); Julian Rathbone, *Sand Blind* (1993); Harold Livingston, *To Die in Babylon* (1993); David Mason, *Shadow over Babylon* (1993).

37. Andrew Osmond, *Saladin* (1975).

38. Colin Forbes, *The Year of the Golden Ape* (1974).

39. Trevenian, *Shibumi* (New York: Ballantine, 1979), 136. Other examples: Sally M. Singer, *For Dying You Always Have Time* (1971); Gerald A. Browne, *Hazard* (1973); W.J. Weatherby, *Goliath* (1981); Nick Carter, *The Casbah Killers* (1969); Ian St. James, *The Balfour Conspiracy* (1981); Charles Robertson, *The Elijah Conspiracy* (1980).

40. Larry Collins and Dominique Lapierre, *The Fifth Horseman* (1980).

41. Richard Deacon, *The Israeli Secret Service* (New York: Taplinger, 1977); David B. Tinnin, *The Hit Team* (Boston: Little, Brown, 1976); Stewart Steven, *The Spymasters of Israel* (New York: Macmillan, 1980).

42. Jack Hoffenberg, *17 Ben Gurion* (G.P. Putnam's Sons, 1977), 118–121.

43. Marvin Albert, *The Gargoyle Conspiracy* (1975).

44. Harris, *Black Sunday*, 175.

45. Claire Sterling, *The Terror Network* (New York: Holt, Rinehart, and Winston, 1981), 122–123.

46. Examples: Arthur Mather, *The Mind Breaker* (1980); Alfred Coppel, *Thirty-Four East* (1974); Barry Schiff and H. Fishman, *The Vatican Target* (1979).

47. Little, 65.

48. Paul Erdman, *The Crash of '79* (New York: Pocket Books, 1976), 385.

49. Ibid., 423–424.

50. Ibid., 156–157.

51. Examples: Stein and Stein, *On the Brink* (1977); Nick Carter, *The Green Wolf Connection* (1979). The Nick Carter book, *Deadly Doubles* (1978) includes Nazis and Japanese for good measure.

52. Peter Tannous and Paul Rubinstein, *The Petrodollar Takeover* (1975).

53. During the 1970s some eighteen novels were published that incorporated a plot about Arab/Islamic control of Western economy/control oil.

Examples: David Jordan, *Nile Green* (1973); Kenneth Evans, *A Rich Way to Die* (1973); Paul E. Erdman, *The Silver Bears* (1974); Tannous and Rubinstein, *The Petrodollar Takeover* (1974); Nick Carter, *Trouble in Paradise* (1978); Allan Topol, *The Fourth of July War* (1978); Nick Carter, *Deadly Doubles* (1978); James Leigh, *The Caliph Intrigue* (1979).

54. Reeva Spector Simon, *"The Tomb of the Twelfth Imam* and other Tales of Crime," in Neguin Yavari, Lawrence G. Potter, and Jean-Marc Oppenheim, eds., *Views from the Edge: Essays in Honor of Richard W. Bulliet* (New York: Columbia University Press, 2004).

55. Quoted in Mark J. Gasiorowski, "The 1953 Coup d'Etat in Iran," *International Journal of Middle East Studies* 19(1987), 278.

56. Gary Sick, *All Fall Down: America's Tragic Encounter with Iran* (New York: Random House, 1985) 9.

57. Note Gerard de Villiers's novel *Versus the CIA* (1969) with its hints of Operation Ajax.

58. Examples: James Leasor, *Passport to Oblivion* (1964). Leasor, a dentist by trade, is also a British agent who is sent to Teheran to thwart an assassination plot against the Shah; Simon Harvester, *Unsung Road* (1960). Other novels include Peter Somerville-Large's *Couch of Earth* (1975); John Christian, *The Persian Death Trap* (1976).

59. Peter Ritner, *Red Carpet for the Shah* (1975); In Alan Williams, *Shah-Mak [A Bullet for the Shah]* (1976) the Shah plots assassination attempt against himself; Benjamin Stein with Herbert Stein's *On the Brink* (1977) concerns a conspiracy by Saudi Arabia and Iran to drive up the price of oil that leads to runaway inflation and prospects of economic disaster in the US and the West. Authors also took the Shah to task for the Iranian-American abandonment of the Kurds during the 1970s (Yoram Hamizrahi, *Golden Lion and the Sun* [1982]).

60. Quoted in Sick, 12.

61. When the Shah fell, he reverted to victim.

62. Norman Daniel, *Islam and the West: The Making of an Image* (Edinburgh: Edinburgh University Press, 1960); Henri Baudet, *Paradise on Earth: Some Thoughts on European Images of Non-European Man* (New Haven: Yale University Press, 1965); Edward Said, *Orientalism* (New York: Pantheon, 1978).

63. Baudet, 21–22.

64. T. E. Lawrence, *The Seven Pillars of Wisdom* (New York: Dell, 1926), 143.

65. Mary Stewart uses the story in *The Gabriel Hounds* (1967) for gothic romance flavor.

66. Charlotte Jay, *Arms for Adonis* (London: Collins, 1960), 193.

67. Lawrence P. Bachman, *The Bitter Lake* (1970).

68. Andrew Osmond, *Saladin* (1975).

69. Nick Carter, *Weapon of the Night* (New York: Award, 1978), 44–45.

70. Mysteries by Julian Rathbone or Joan Fleming feature Turkish detectives. The Turkish enlisted man, "Mustafa" or "Abdul," is as slow and plodding as any of his Third World counterparts, and the Turkish peasants are more or less interchangeable with the peasants of southern or central Europe. Once Turkey joins NATO, all sorts of agents appear, retrieving something or other from inaccessible drops along the Soviet frontier, or stopping the drug trade (Julian Rathbone, *Diamonds Bid* [1967], *With My Knives I Know I'm Good* [1969], *Trip Trap* [1972]; Joan Fleming, *When I Grow Rich* [1962]; Phyllis Whitney, *Black Amber* [1965]). Turks had already achieved that status. See James Bond's Turkish ally in Ian Fleming, *From Russia with Love* (1957); also Nick Carter, *Istanbul* (1965), *The Turkish Bloodbath* (1980). During the 1990s, Turkish detectives operate independently in detective novels set in Istanbul and in Germany in the novels of Jakob Arjouni originally published in German: *Happy Birthday, Turk* (1993); *And Still Drink More* (1994); *One Death to Die* (1997).

71. Stuart Jackman, *Sandcatcher* (New York: Atheneum, 1980), 7. In Edward Aarons, *Assignment Zoraya*, published by Fawcett in 1960, the Bedouin tribesmen are likened to "a pack of ragged hunting dogs" (108).

72. Example: Peter Tannous and Paul Rubinstein, *The Petrodollar Takeover* (1975).

73. Examples: Alfred Coppel, *The Apocalypse Brigade* (1981); Desmond Meiring, *A Talk with the Angels* (1985); Daniel Easterman, *Name of the Beast* (1992).

Chapter 6

1. James William Gibson, *Warrior Dreams: Violence and Manhood in Post-Vietnam America* (New York: Hill and Wang, 1994), 7–9; see also Susan Jeffords, *The Remasculinization of America: Gender and the Vietnam War* (Bloomington: University of Indiana Press, 1989).

2. Andrew J. Bacevich, *The New American Militarism: How Americans Are Seduced by War* (New York: Oxford University Press, 2005), 19. Syria and Hafez al-Assad rarely appear as villains whereas since the mid-1980s, Libya and Colonel Qaddafi, Iraq and Saddam Hussein, and Iran and Ayatollah Khomeini or an Iranian/Shi'ite "mullah" have appeared a fictional villains. Novels depicting Col. Qaddafi's plots against the United States and Israel include Richard Cox, *Ground Zero* (1985); J. Case, *Cody's Army: Assault into Libya* (1986); David E. Fisher and Col. Ralph Albertazzie, *Hostage One* (1989); Harold Coyle, *Bright Star* (1990).

3. Gary Wills, "John Wayne's Body," *The New Yorker* (August 19, 1996), 39–49; on the impact of Wayne on American culture and as a commentary on foreign policy, see Richard Slotkin, *Gunfighter Nation: The Myth of the Frontier in Twentieth Century America* (New York: Atheneum, 1992).

4. Robert McG. Thomas, Jr., "Don Pendleton, 67, Writer Who Spawned a Genre," *The New York Times* (October 28, 1995); Will Murray, "The Executioner Phe-

nomenon," in Jon L. Breen and Martin Harry Greenberg, eds., *Murder Off the Rack: Critical Studies of Ten Paperback Masters* (Metuchen: The Scarecrow Press, 1989); William H. Young, *A Study of Action-Adventure Fiction: The Executioner and Mack Bolan* (Lewiston: The Edwin Mellon Press, 1996).

5. Richard Brookhiser, "Deerslayer Helped Define Us All," *Time* (November 9, 1992) quoted in Bill Crider, "The Western," in Rosemary Herbert, ed., *The Oxford Companion to Crime and Mystery Writing* (New York: Oxford University Press, 1999), 493.

6. For this convergence see Slotkin, 194–228.

7. Christopher LaFarge, "Mickey Spillane and His Bloody Hammer," in Bernard Rosenberg and David Manning-White, eds., *Mass Culture, the Popular Arts in America* (Glencoe, Ill.: The Free Press, 1960), 176–186; Charles L. P. Silet, "The First Angry White Male—Mickey Spillane's Mike Hammer," *The Armchair Detective* 29(1996), 195–199; Joseph S. Roucek, "The American Detective, Murder and Violent Novel in its Sociological Aspects," *Indian Journal of Social Research* 2(1964), 178–186; Raymond Chandler, "The Simple Art of Murder," *Atlantic Monthly* (December, 1944).

8. Erin A. Smith, "How the Other Half Read: Advertising, Working-Class Readers, and Pulp Magazines," *Book History* 3(2000), 204–230. On Charles Atlas the 97 pound weakling and comics, see Gerard Jones, *Men of Tomorrow: Geeks, Gangsters and the Birth of the Comic Book* (New York: Basic Books, 2004).

9. The Golem stories became part of popular culture at the beginning of the twentieth century with Gustav Meyrink's *Der Golem* (1915); English translation (1928). The story inspired plays, films, orchestral suites, and ballets.

10. For a fictional account of the development of the comic book, see Michael Chabon's *The Amazing Adventures of Kavalier and Clay* (2000). Studies of the genre include: Bradford W. Wright, *Comic Book Nation: The Transformation of Youth Culture in America* (Baltimore: Johns Hopkins University Press, 2001); Matthew P. McAllister, Edward H. Sewell, Jr., and Ian Gordon, *Comics and Ideology* (New York: Peter Lang, 2001); Arie Kaplan, *From Krakow to Krypton: Jews and Comic Books* (Philadelphia: The Jewish Publication Society of America, 2008); Robert Jewett and John Shelton Lawrence, *Captain America and the Crusade against Evil: The Dilemma of Zealous Nationalism* (Grand Rapids: William B. Eerdmans Publishing Company, 2003); Robert Genter, "With Great Power Comes Great Responsibility": Cold War Culture and the Birth of Marvel Comics," *The Journal of Popular Culture* 40 (2007), 953–978; Mike S. Dubose, "Holding Out for the Heroic: Reaganism, Comic Books Vigilantes, and Captain America," *Journal of Popular Culture* 40 (2007), 915–935.

11. Jewett and Lawrence, 32.

12. Ibid., 26. The quote is from the first episode of *Captain America*.

13. Quoted Bacevich, 10. See also Walter Russell Meade, *Special Providence: American Foreign Policy and How It Changed the World* (New York: Routledge, 2002).

14. Quoted in Jewett and Lawrence, 72.

15. Ibid., 33–35.

16. Jones, 261–262.

17. Mickey Spillane, *The Body Lovers* (New York: Signet, 1967), 137.

18. Gibson, 34–35.

19. Ralph Harper, *The World of the Thriller* (Cleveland: The Press of Case Western Reserve University, 1969).

20. Jeffords, 128–130.

21. Murray, 139–142.

22. Young, 98.

23. Ibid., 449–465.

24. Andrew Sugar, *Israeli Commandos #2: The Fireball Assignment* (1974); *Israeli Commandos #4: The Alps Assignment* (1975).

25. Harry Brod, "Of Mice and Supermen: Images of Jewish Masculinity," in T. M. Rudavsky, ed., *Gender and Judaism: The Transformation of Tradition* (New York: New York University Press, 1995), 283.

26. In the "Malko" series by Gerard de Villiers, the President calls in Malko, a European, for assistance because he does not trust the CIA.

27. Nick Carter, *Safari for Spies* (1964); *Istanbul* (1965); *Assignment Israel* (1967); *Casbah Killers*; *Cairo Mafia* (1972); *Trouble in Paradise* (1978). On Nick Carter see Will Murray, "The Saga of Nick Carter, Killmaster," *The Armchair Detective* 15 (1982), 316–329.

28. Nick Carter, *Thunderstrike in Syria* (New York: Charter, 1979), 94.

29. Example: Tom Clancy, *Patriot Games* (1987).

30. Harriett Hawkins, Classics and Trash: Traditions and Taboos in High Literature and Popular Modern Genres (New York: Harvester, 1990), 19–20.

31. Carter, *Thunderstrike in Syria*, 172.

32. Don Pendleton, *The Executioner Mack Bolan: Beirut Payback* (Toronto: Worldwide, 1984), 175.

33. Don Pendleton, *Mack Bolan: Vengeance* (New York: Worldwide Library, 1999), 65.

34. John Sutherland, *Reading the Decades: Fifty Years of the Nation's Best-Selling Books* (London: BBC Worldwide, 2002), 141.

35. Piotr Siemion, "No More Heroes: The Routinization of the Epic in Techno-Thrillers," in Joseph Tabbi and Michael Wutz, eds. *Reading Matters: Narrative in the New Media Ecology* (Ithaca: Cornell University Press, 1997), 193–223.

36. After his initial success, Clancy would go on to write standard political thrillers.

37. Richard Nixon on Ronald Reagan quoted in Jeffords, 3. In the film "Red Dawn," after the United States is invaded by the Soviet Union and Cuba, American high school students based in Colorado undertake a guerrilla war against the invaders.

38. Bacevich, 98–116.

39. Jeffords, 13.

40. Bacevich, 116. Clancy's books remain on the bestseller list. John le Carré's books on the list are short-lived, and other authors temporarily shifted to the nineteenth century for plots before returning to the Middle East after 9/11.

41. Examples: Timothy Rizzi, *The Strike of the Cobra* (1993); *The Phalanx Dragon* (1994).

42. Jack Merek, *Blackbird* (1990) and *Target Stealth* (1989).

43. Richard Cox, *Ground Zero* (1985); Greg Dinallo, *Purpose of Evasion* (1990)

44. Richard Herman, Jr., *The Warbirds* (1989).

45. Stephen Coonts, *Final Flight* (1988).

46. Examples: Harold Coyle, *Sword Point* (1988), *Bright Star* (1990); G. Dinallo, *Purpose of Evasion* (1990); Jack Merek, *Target of Stealth* (1989), *Blackbird* (1990); David Poyer, *The Gulf* (1990).

47. Rich Herman, *Firebreak* (1991).

48. Orr Kelly, *Seals Eagle Force: Desert Thunder* (1998).

49. James Ferro, *Snake Eaters* (2001).

50. *HOGS #1: Going Deep* (1999); *#2: Hog Down* (1999); *#3: Fort Apache* (2000); *#4: Snake Eaters* (2001); *#5: Target: Saddam* (2001); *Death Wish* (2002).

51. Robert Gandt, *With Hostile Intent* (2001)

52. Julian Rathbone, *Sand Blind* (1993); David Ignatius, *The Bank of Fear* (1994); Frederick Forsyth, *The Fist of God* (1994); P.J. Pineiro, *Ultimatum* (1994); John Nance, *Scorpion Strike* (1992); David Hagberg, *Desert Fire* (1993); Jeffrey Archer, *Honor Among Thieves* (1993); David Mason, *Shadow Over Babylon* (1993).

53. Examples: William Haggard, *The Median Line* (1979); Larry Collins and Dominique Lapierre, *The Fifth Horseman* (1980); Will O'Neill, *The Libyan Kill* (1980); Michael Goodkin, *Paper Gold* (1981); Franklin Allen Leib, *Fire Arrow* (1988).

54. Examples: David E. Fisher and Col. Ralph Albertazzie, *Hostage One* (1989); Frank O'Neill, *Roman Circus* (1990); Harold Coyle, *Bright Star* (1990);

55. Examples: Michael Pearce's series of "Mamur Zapt" novels; Elizabeth Peters's series of Amelia Peabody novels listed in the novels bibliography.

56. On the link between *Soldier of Fortune* magazine and the millennium see Philip Lamy, "Millennialism in the Mass Media: The Case of *Soldier of Fortune* Magazine," *Journal for the Scientific Study of Religion* 31(1992), 408–424. Note also the novels of Oliver North cited in the next chapter.

Chapter 7

1. Daniel Easterman, *The Last Assassin* (Garden City: Doubleday, 1985), 207.

2. See also David W. Lesch, *1979: The Year That Shaped the Modern Middle East* (Boulder: Westview Press, 2001).

3. Dennis Wheatley, *The Eunuch of Stamboul* (1935).

4. Edward Aarons, *Assignment: The Cairo Dancers* (Greenwich, CT: Fawcett, 1965), 61.

5. Richard Hofstadter, *The Paranoid Style in American Politics and Other Essays* (Chicago: University of Chicago Press, 1965), 3–40; see also Eugen Weber, *Apocalypses: Prophecies, Cults and Millennial Beliefs Through the Ages* (Cambridge: Harvard University Press, 1999); Bruce E. Brandt, "Reflections of 'The Paranoid Style' in the Current Suspense Novel," *Clues* 3(1982), 62–69.

6. Ibid., 11.

7. Ethnic Arab stereotypes almost mirror anti-Jewish stereotypes (Ronald Stockton, "Ethnic Stereotypes and the Arab Image," in Ernest McCarus, *The Development of Arab-American Identity* (Ann Arbor: University of Michigan Press, 1994).

8. Timothy Rizzi, *The Phalanx Dragon* (1994).

9. Examples: Alfred Coppel, *The Apocalypse Brigade* (1981); Andrew Kaplan, *Scorpion* (1985); David Brierly, *Skorpion's Death* (1985); William F. Brown, *Thursday at Noon* (1987); Desmond Meiring, *The Wildcatter* (1988); Kent Harrington, *The Gift of the Falcon* (1988); Jack Merek, *Blackbird* (1990); Gordon Thomas, *Deadly Perfume* (1991); Robin White, *The Sword of Orion* (1993); Robert Cullen, *Heirs of the Fire* (1997); John R. Maxim, *Haven* (1997).

10. Note the study by Mark Juergensmeyer, *Terror in the Mind of God: The Global Rise of Religious Violence* (Berkeley: University of California Press, 2000).

11. Note the Copt hero in Daniel Easterman, *Name of the Beast* (1992).

12. Examples: William Bayer, *Pattern Crimes* (1987); Roger L. Simon, *Raising the Dead* (1988). In both books the detectives and the villains are Jews; there are no Arabs in the plots.

13. Examples: Daniel Easterman, *The Final Judgement* (1996); Jon Land, *The Walls of Jericho* (1997); Anthony Price, *The Alamut Ambush*(1972).

14. Gordon Pape and Tony Aspler, *The Scorpion Sanction* (New York: Bantam Books, 1980), 27.

15. Ibid., 127.

16. Ibid., 315.

17. Robert Rosenberg, *House of Guilt: An Avram Cohen Mystery* (New York: Scribner, 1996), 7–8. Recent examples of the apocalyptic plot include Glenn Kleier, *The Last Day* (1997) and the best selling Left Behind series by Tim LaHaye and Jerry B. Jenkins that include *Assignment: Jerusalem, Target Antichrist—ASSASSINS* (Wheaton: Tyndale House, 1999). On the best-seller lists for weeks in 2000, these books combine elements of science fiction, a Rambo-type potboiler with contemporary characters who drive Range Rovers and use the Internet (Dinitia Smith, "Apocalyptic Potboiler is Publisher's Dream," *The New York Times* [June 8, 2000]). See also the chapter "Publishers at the Pulpit: Evangelical Publishing Fiction in the Twentieth Century, in Jan Blodgett, *Protestant Evangelical Literary Culture and Contemporary Society* (Westport: Greenwood Press, 1997).

18. Examples: Barbara Sofer, *The Thirteenth Hour* (1996); Zev Chafets, *Hang Time* (1996). During the Oslo interlude, a number of unlikely detective heroes ap-

peared: the Pakistani who saved the British crown (Payne Harrison, *Black Cipher* [1994]; the Iranian detective in New York (Salar Abdoh, *The Poet Game* [2000]); and the novels by Arjuni already cited.

19. See Jon Land's *The Pillars of Solomon* (1999); *A Walk in the Darkness* (2000); *Keepers of the Gate* (2001); *Blood Diamonds* (2002); *The Blue Widows* (2003).

20. Jon Land, *The Last Prophecy* (2004).

21. Timothy P. Weber, *On the Road to Armageddon: How Evangelicals Became Israel's Best Friend* (Grand Rapids: Baker Academic, 2004), 207–208; see also Michael Barkun, *A Culture of Conspiracy: Apocalyptic Visions in Contemporary America* (Berkeley: University of California Press, 2003).

22. Darby's theology and its impact on American culture is analyzed in Paul Boyer, *When Time Shall Be No More: Prophecy Belief in Modern American Culture* (Cambridge: Harvard University Press, 1992).

23. Weber, 170.

24. Examples: Frank Simon, *Veiled Threats* (1996); *Walled Terror* (1997); Ellen Gunderson Traylor, *The Priest* (1998).

25. Quoted in Donald Wagner, "Reagan and Begin, Bibi and Jerry: The Theopolitical Alliance of the Likud Party with the American Christian "right", *Arab Studies Quarterly* 20 (1998), 33–52.

26. Weber, 186.

27. Wagner, 33–52. Novelist Joel C. Rosenberg also uses the quote in *The Ezekiel Option* (2005).

28. Joel C. Rosenberg, *The Ezekiel Option* (Wheaton: Tyndale House, 2005), 374–376.

29. *The Last Jihad* (2002); *The Last Days* (2003).

30. Oliver North's trilogy that began to appear in 2002 marks a transition to this new trend. Closely mirroring the George W. Bush administration's perceptions of threats to American security, North's hero warns America of the new dangerous world that has emerged with the globalization of terrorism. A Marine combat veteran, coordinator of the US government's counter-terrorism activities during the Reagan administration, and television personality, North not only uses the thriller format to present his interpretation of Middle East politics, but he also advances his own political agenda. By the end of the three novels *Mission Compromised* (2002), *The Jericho Sanction* (2003), and *The Assassins* (2005), fictional hero Marine Major Peter Newman exonerates Oliver North in the Iran-Contra affair and re-affirms his Christian faith. The books made the *New York Times* Best Seller list even though they were not published by a mainstream trade press but by a Tennessee-based Christian publishing company. Combining politics and religion, North's novels were touted and publicized by conservative radio and television talkshow hosts and religious web sites. Combining military expertise and Christian belief, the novels take us from Reagan militarism to the Bush religious crusade, policies that will be reflected in another shift in crime fiction as the thriller returns to the religious war.

31. "LeftBehind:InterviewwithJoelRosenberg," 2–5 (http://www.leftbehind.com). No longer available.

32. *The Copper Scroll* (2006); *Dead Heat* (2008).

33. Nelson DeMille, *By the Rivers of Babylon* (New York: Berkley, 1979), 141.

34. Nelson DeMille, *The Lion's Game* (New York: Warner Books, 2000), 454.

35. Ibid., 423.

36. Ibid., 257.

37. Examples: novels by Barbara Nadel, Michael Pearce, and Elizabeth Peters cited in the bibliography.

38. Titles: Daniel Silva, *The Mark of the Assassin* (1998); *The Kill Artist* (2000); *The English Assassin* (2002); *The Confessor* (2003); *A Death in Vienna* (2004).

39. Frederick Forsyth, *The Afghan* (New York: G. P. Putnam's Sons, 2006), 46–47.

40. Ibid., 36–37.

41. Ibid., 52.

42. Ibid., 75.

43. Ibid., 343.

Fiction Bibliography

The list incorporates the titles on which this study is based. It also includes novels cited in the text, some of which appeared after 2000. It is not a complete list of all of the crime fiction novels that use the Middle East for plot, location, or character, because it is virtually impossible to identify all of the titles. There is no systematic, comprehensive bibliographic control for pulp fiction and paperback originals. Standard bibliographies, while indexed, do not provide enough detail to enable the user to locate all specific titles related to the Middle East. I have relied on Allen J. Hubin's *Crime Fiction 1749–1980* and the supplements and editions of Myron J. Smith, Jr.'s *Cloak and Dagger Fiction* and various internet search engines in addition to my own idiosyncratic perusal of library and bookstore shelves. I have also included only those books that I was able to examine. There are some paperback titles that I identified, but because they were inaccessible, they are not included on this list. The more than 800 crime fiction titles published during the twentieth century is the sample upon which this book is based.

Citations include authors (with pseudonyms where known), titles, publishers, and dates of publication both for British and American imprints.

Aarons, Edward S. *Assignment: Afghan-Dragon*. Greenwich, Conn: Fawcett, 1976; London: Coronet, 1979.

———. *Assignment: Ankara*. Greenwich, Conn.: Fawcett, 1961; London: Muller, 1962.

———. *Assignment: The Cairo Dancers*. Greenwich, Conn.: Fawcett, 1965.

————. *Assignment: Madeleine*. Greenwich, Conn.: Fawcett, 1958; London: Muller, 1960.

————. *Assignment: Moon Girl*. Greenwich, Conn.: Fawcett, 1967.

————. *Assignment: Zoraya*. Greenwich, Conn.: Fawcett, 1960; London: Muller, 1961.

Abbott, John. *Scimitar*. London, William Heinemann, Ltd., 1992; New York: Crown, 1992.

Abdoh, Salar. *The Poet Game*. New York: Picador, 2000.

Abrahams, Peter. *Tongues of Fire*. New York: M. Evans, 1982.

Adams, Rex. *The Star of Persia*. London: George G. Harrap and Co., Ltd., 1942.

Aellen, Richard. *Flash Point*. New York: Donald E. Fine, 1991.

Agnew, Spiro T. *The Canfield Decision*. New York: Playboy, 1976; London: W. H. Allen, 1977.

Alan, Ray [pseud.: Joseph Lawrence Valls-Russell]. *The Beirut Pipeline*. London: Collins, 1980; New York: Farrar, Straus, 1980.

————. *My Bonny Lies Under the Sea*. London: Joseph, 1963.

Albano, Peter. *Assault of the Super Carrier*. New York: Kensington, 1996.

Albert, Marvin H. *The Gargoyle Conspiracy*. Garden City, New York: Doubleday, 1975; London: Deutsch, 1975.

Aldridge, James (Harold Edward). *I Wish He Would Not Die*. London: Bodley, 1957.

————. *Mockery in Arms*. London: Joseph, 1974; Boston: Little, Brown, 1974.

Allen, Eric. *Death on Delivery*. London: Hammond, 1958.

Ambler, Eric. *The Care of Time*. New York: Farrar, Straus, 1981.

————. *Journey into Fear*. London: Hodder, 1940; New York: Knopf, 1940.

————. *A Kind of Anger*. London: Bodley Head, 1964; New York: Atheneum, 1964.

————. *The Levanter*. London: Weidenfeld, 1972; New York: Atheneum, 1972.

————. *The Light of Day*. London: Heinemann, 1962; New York: Knopf, 1963; also published as *Topkapi*. New York: Bantam, 1964.

————. *The Mask of Dimitrios*. London: Hodder, 1939; also published as *A Coffin for Dimitrios*. New York: Knopf, 1939.

Ames, Delano. *They Journey by Night*. London: Hodder and Stoughton, 1932; also published as: *Not in Utter Nakedness*. New York: Dial, 1932.

Anderson, Patrick. *The Pleasure Business*. San Diego/New York: Harcourt Brace Jovanovich, 1989.

Angus, Sylvia. *Death of a Hittite*. New York: Macmillan, 1969.

Anthony, Evelyn [pseud.: Evelyn Bridget Patricia Stephens Ward-Thomas]. *The Persian Price*. New York: Coward, McCann, 1975; also published as *The Persian Ransom*. London: Hutchinson, 1975.

Appleby, John. *Barbary Hoard*. New York: Coward, McCann, 1952; also published as *The Singing Cave*. London: Laurie, 1952.

Arathorn, D. W. *Kemal*. New York: Harper, 1982.

Archer, Jeffrey. *Honor Among Thieves*. New York: HarperCollins, 1993.

Ardman, Harvey. *Endgame*. New York: Avon, 1975.

Aricha, Amos. *The Flying Camel*. New York: Dutton, 1987.

Aricha, Amos, and Eli Landau. *Phoenix*. New York: New American Library, 1979; London: Futura, 1979.

Arjouni, Jacob. *And Still Drink More!: A Kayankaya Mystery*. New York: Fromm International, 1994.

———. *Happy Birthday Turk*. New York: Fromm International, 1993.

———. *One Death to Die*. New York: Fromm International, 1997.

Arnold, Margot [pseud.: Petronelle Marguerite Mary Cook]. *Exit Actors, Dying*. New York: Playboy, 1979.

———. *Sinister Purposes*. New York, Fawcett, 1988.

———. *Zadok's Treasure*. New York: Playboy, 1980; London: Chivers, 1982.

Arvay, Harry. *Eleven Bullets for Mohammad*. London: Corgi, 1975; New York: Bantam, 1975.

———. *Operation Kuwait*. London: Corgi, 1975; New York: Bantam, 1975.

———. *Piraeus Plot*. London: Corgi, 1975; New York: Bantam, 1975.

Atiyah, Edward S. *Donkey from the Mountain*. London: Hale, 1961; also published as *The Cruel Fire*. Garden City, New York: Doubleday, 1962.

Atkinson, Hugh. *The Man in the Middle*. London: Hart-Davis, 1973; New York: Putnam, 1973.

Atlee, Philip [pseud.: James Atlee Phillips]. *The Spice Route Contract*. Greenwich, Conn.: Fawcett, 1973.

———. *The Underground Cities Contract*. Greenwich, Conn.: Fawcett, 1974.

Awni, Margery. *Silence Over Sinai*. New York: Pyramid, 1976.

Bachmann, Lawrence P. *The Bitter Lake*. Boston: Little Brown, 1970.

Bagley, Desmond. *Flyaway*. Garden City: Doubleday, 1979.

———. *The Spoilers*. London: Collins, 1969; Garden City, N.Y.: Doubleday, 1970.

Bailey, Anthony. *Making Progress*. New York: Dial, 1959; London: Joseph, 1959.

Baker, William Arthur Howard. *The Guardians*. London: Mayflower, 1967; also published as *The Dirty Game*. New York: Lancer, 1967.

———. *The Man Who Knew Too Much*. London: Amalgamated, 1955.

Ballard, Robert and Tony Chiu. *Bright Shark*. New York: Delacorte, 1992.

Ballinger, Bill S. *The Source of Fear*. New York: Signet, 1968; London: Hale, 1971.

Bannister, Jo. *Shards*. New York: Doubleday, 1990.

Barak, Michael [pseud.: Michael Bar Zohar]. *Double Cross*. New York: New American Library, 1981.

———. *The Phantom Conspiracy*. New York: Morrow, 1980; London: Weidenfeld, 1981 (as Michael Bar Zohar).

———. *The Secret List of Heinrich Roehm*. New York: William Morrow, 1976; London: Weidenfeld, 1976.

Barber, Noel. *A Woman of Cairo*. London: Hodder, 1984; also published as *Sakkara*. New York: Macmillan, 1984.

Baron, Aileen Garsson. *A Fly Has a Hundred Eyes*. Chicago: Academy Chicago, 2002.

Barron, Donald. *The Man Who Was There*. London: Chatto, 1969; New York: Atheneum, 1969.

Barton, Donald R. *Once in Aleppo*. New York: Scribners, 1955.

Bartram, George. [pseud.: Kenneth M. Cameron] *The Aelian Fragment*. New York: Putnam, 1976.

Bax, Roger [pseud.: Paul Winterton]. *Death Beneath Jerusalem*. London: Nelson, 1938.

Bayer, William. *Pattern Crimes*. New York: William Morrow, 1987.

———. *Tangier*. New York: Dutton, 1978.

Bayne, Spencer. *Agent Extraordinary*. New York: Dutton, 1942. London: Eyre, 1944.

Bearden, Milt. *The Black Tulip*. New York: Random House, 1998.

Beare, George. *The Bee Sting Deal*. London: Longman, 1972; Boston: Houghton Mifflin, 1972.

———. *Bloody Sun at Noon*. Boston: Houghton Mifflin, 1971.

———. *The Very Breath of Hell*. London: Longmans, 1971; Boston: Houghton Mifflin, 1971.

Beecher, William. *Mayday Man*. Washington, DC, Brassey's, 1990.

Benedictus, David. *The Rabbi's Wife*. London: Blond, 1976; New York: M. Evans, 1976.

Bennett, Kem. *The Devil's Current*. London: Collins, 1953; Garden City, N.Y.: Doubleday, 1953.

Benton, Kenneth. *Craig and the Midas Touch*. London: Macmillan, 1975; New York: Walker, 1976.

———. *Craig and the Tunisian Tangle*. London: Macmillan, 1974; New York: Walker, 1975.

Binns, Otwell. *The Three Black Dots*. London: Ward, 1929.

Black, Ian Stuart. *Journey to a Safe Place*. London: Constable, 1979. New York: St. Martin's Press, 1979.

Black, Lionel [pseud.: Dudley Barker]. *Arafat Is Next!* London: Collins, 1975; New York: Stein and Day, 1975.

Blankfort, Michael. *Behold the Fire*. New York: New American Library, 1965; London: Heinemann, 1966.

Block, Lawrence. *The Thief Who Couldn't Sleep*. Greenwich, Conn.: Fawcett, 1966.

Boland, John C. *Death in Jerusalem*. New York: St. Martin's Press, 1994.

Bond, Larry. *Day of Wrath*. New York: Warner Books, 1998.

Boyle, Denis. *Death at Devil-Fish Point*. London, Robert Hale, Ltd., 1961.

Brackett, Leigh. *Silent Partner*. New York: Putnam, 1969.

Bradley. Michael [pseud.: Gary Blumberg]. *Blood Bargain*. New York, Paperback Library, 1974.

Braun, M.G. *That Girl from Istanbul*. New York: Berkley, 1966.

Bridge, Ann [pseud.: Lady Dolling Saunders O'Malley]. *The Dark Moment*. New York: Macmillan, 1952.

———. *The Lighthearted Quest*. London: Chatto, 1956; New York: Macmillan, 1956.

Brierley, David. *Skorpion's Death*. London: William Collins and Sons; New York: Summit Books, 1985.

Briley, John. *The First Stone*. New York: William Morrow, 1997.

Brown, Bruce. *Desert Duel*. Pittsburgh: Sterling House Publishers, 1999.

Brown, Dale. *Shadows of Steel*. New York: Putnam, 1996.

———. *Wings of Fire*. New York: Putnam, 2002.

Brown, William F. *Thursday at Noon*. New York: St. Martin's Press, 1987.

Browne, Gerald A. *Hazard*. New York: Arbor House, 1973; London Hart Davis, 1974.

———. *West 47th*. New York: Warner, 1996.

Brunais, Andrea. *Night of the Litani*. Tampa: Mancorp, 1996.

Buchan, John. *Greenmantle*. London: Hodder, 1916; Doran: 1917.

Bukiet, Melvin Jules. *Strange Fire*. New York: WW Norton, 2001.

Bulliet, Richard. *The Gulf Scenario*. New York: St. Martin's Press, 1984.

———. *The Tomb of the Twelfth Imam*. New York: Harper and Row, 1979.

Burke, Lee John. *The Cairo Counterplot*. London: Hale, 1977.

Bury, Stephen. *The Cobweb*. New York: Bantam, 1996.

Byfield, Barbara N. *A Parcel of Their Fortunes*. Garden City, New York: Doubleday, 1979.

Caidin, Martin. *Cyborg*. New York: Arbor House, 1972; London W.H. Allen, 1973.

Caillou, Alan [pseud.: Alan Lyle-Smythe]. *Afghan Onslaught*. New York: Pinnacle, 1972.

———. *Alien Virus*. London: Davies, 1957; also published as *Cairo Cabal*. New York: Pinnacle, 1974.

———. *Assault on Fellawi*. New York: Avon, 1972.

———. *Dead Sea Submarine*. New York: Pinnacle, 1971.

———. *A Journey to Orassia*. Garden City, N. Y.: Doubleday, 1965; London: W.H. Allen, 1966.

———. *Who'll Buy My Evil?* New York: Pocket Books, 1966.

Callison, Brian. *A Plague of Sailors*. London: Collins, 1971; New York: Putnam, 1971.

Cameron, Lou. *The Empty Quarter*. London, Frederick Muller, 1963.

Canning, Victor. *The Golden Salamander*. New York: Mill Books, 1949.

———. *A Handful of Silver*. New York: Sloane, 1954; also published as *Castle Minerva*. London: Hodder, 1955.

———. *Twist of the Knife*. New York: Sloane, 1955; also published as *His Bones Are Coral*. London: Hodder, 1955.

Carr, John Dickson. *The Arabian Nights Murder*. New York: Harper and Row, 1936; London: H. Hamilton, 1936.

Carstairs, John Paddy. *No Wooden Overcoat*. London: W. H. Allen, 1959.

———. *A Smell of Peardrops*. London: W.H. Allen, 1966.

Carter, Nick [pseud.: John Messmann]. *The Arab Plague*. New York Award, 1970; also published as *The Slavemaster*. London: Tandem, 1970.

———. [pseud.: Manning Lee Stokes]. *Assignment: Israel*. New York Award, 1967; London: Tandem, 1968.

———. [pseud.: Forrest V. Perrin]. *Beirut Incident*. New York Award, 1974.

———. [ ]. *Blood of the Scimitar*. New York: Charter, 1985.

———. [pseud.: Ralph Eugene Hayes]. *The Cairo Mafia*. New York: Award, 1972; London: Tandem, 1972.

———. [pseud.: Jon Messmann]. *The Casbah Killers*. New York: Award, 1969: London: Tandem, 1962.

———. [ ]. *Day of the Mahdi*. New York: Charter, 1984.

———. [pseud.: Lawrence Van Gelden]. *Deadly Doubles*. New York Charter, 1978; London: Star, 1980.

———. [pseud.: Jim Bowser]. *Death of the Falcon*. New York Award, 1974.

———. [pseud.: Craig Nova]. *Dr. Death*. New York: Award, 1975.

———. [pseud.: Saul Wernick]. *The Fanatics of Al Asad*. New York Award, 1976.

———. [pseud: Dennis Lynds]. *The Green Wolf Connection*. New York: Award, 1979.

———. *The Israeli Connection*. New York: Charter, 1982.

———. [pseud.: Manning Lee Stokes]. *Istanbul*. New York: Award, 1965; London: Tandem, 1969.

———. [pseud.: Linda Stewart]. *The Jerusalem File*. New York: Award, 1975; London: Star, 1978.

———. [pseud.: Al Hine]. *Massacre in Milan*. New York: Award, 1974; London: Tandem, 1977.

———. [ ]. *Middle East Massacre*. New York: Jove, 1989.

———. [pseud.: Ralph Eugene Hayes]. *The Omega Terror*. New York Award, 1972; London: Tandem, 1973.

———. [pseud.: Valerie Moolman]. *Safari for Spies*. New York Award, 1964; Digit, 1965.

———. [pseud.: DeWitt S. Copp]. *Six Bloody Summer Days*. New York Award, 1975; London: Tandem, 1978.

———. [pseud.: Ralph Eugene Hayes]. *Strike Force Terror*. New York: Award, 1973.

———. [pseud.: Joseph Rosenberger]. *Thunderstrike in Syria*. New York: Ace-Charter, 1979.

———. [pseud.: Robert Derek Steeley]. *Trouble in Paradise*. New York: Charter, 1978; London: Star, 1980.

———. [pseud.: Jerry Ahern]. *The Turkish Bloodbath*. New York Ace-Charter, 1980.

———. [pseud.: Leon Lazarus]. *The Turncoat*. New York: Award, 1976; London: Tandem, 1978.

————. [ ]. *Weapon of the Night.* New York: Award, 1978.

————. [ ]. *Zero-Hour Strike Force.* New York: Charter, 1984.

Cartwright, Justin. *The Horse of Darius.* London: H. Hamilton, 1980 New York: Macmillan, 1980.

Case, Jim. *Cody's Army: Assault into Libya.* New York, Warner, 1986.

————. *Cody's Army: Sword of the Prophet.* New York: Warner, 1988.

Castle, John [pseud.: John William Garrod and Ronald Charles Payne]. *The Seventh Fury.* London: Souvenir, 1961; New York: Walker, 1963.

Cawley, Robert. *Shockwave.* London: Sphere, 1979.

Chafets, Zev. *Hang Time.* New York, Time Warner, 1996.

————. *The Project.* New York: Time Warner, 1997.

Chambers, Philip. *Bullets to Baghdad.* London, Fleetway, 1960.

Charles, Robert [pseud.: Robert Charles Smith]. *Clash of Hawks.* New York: Pinnacle, 1975; London: Hale, 1976.

————. [pseud.: Robert Charles Smith]. *The Counter-Terror Mission Trilogy: The Flight of the Raven; The Hour of the Wolf; The Scream of the Dove.* London: Hale, 1975; New York: Pinnacle, 1975.

————. *Stamboul Intrigue.* London: Hale, 1968; New York: Roy, 1968.

Chase, Philip [pseud.: Philip Friedman]. *Deadly Crusade.* New York: Dell, 1976.

Chesbro, George C. *City of Whispering Stone.* New York: Simon and Schuster, 1978; London: Severn, 1981.

Childs, Marquis. *Taint of Innocence.* New York: Harper and Row, 1967 London: Cassell, 1968.

Christian, John. *Five Gates to Armageddon.* London: Harwood-Smart, 1975; New York: St. Martin's Press, 1975.

————. *Persian Death Trap.* London: Harwood, 1976.

Christie, Agatha. *Appointment with Death.* London: Collins, 1938; New York: Dodd, 1938.

————. *Death on the Nile.* London: Collins, 1937; New York Dodd, 1938.

————. *Murder in Mesopotamia.* London: Collins, 1936; New York Dodd, 1936.

————. *Destination Unknown.* London: Collins 1954; also published as *So Many Steps to Death.* New York: Dodd, 1955.

————. *They Came to Baghdad.* London: Collins, 1951; New York Dodd, 1951.

Christie, William. *The Warriors of God.* New York: Lyford Books, 1995.

Chubin, Barry. *The Feet of a Snake.* New York: Tom Doherty, 1984.

Clancy, Tom. *Patriot Games.* New York: Putnam, 1987.

————. *The Sum of All Fears.* New York: Putnam, 1991.

Clancy, Tom and Steve Pieczenik. *Tom Clancy's Op-Center: Acts of War.* New York, Berkley, 1997.

Clarkson, Geoffrey. *Jihad.* New York: Pinnacle, 1981.

Cleary, Jon. *Season of Doubt.* London: Collins, 1968; New York William Morrow, 1968

Cobb, Belton. *Corpse at Casablanca*. London, W.H. Allen, 1956.

Cohen, Willliam S. *One-Eyed Kings*. New York: Doubleday, 1991.

Coles, Manning [pseud.: Francis Oke Manning and Cyril Henry Coles]. *Search for a Sultan*. London: Hodder, 1961; Garden City, N. Y.: Doubleday, 1961.

Collin, Richard Oliver. *The Man with Many Names*. New York: St. Martin's Press, 1995.

Collins, Larry, and Dominique Lapierre. *The Fifth Horseman*. New York: Simon and Schuster, 1980; London: Granada, 1980.

Connelly, Marc (Marcus Cook). *A Souvenir from Qam*. New York Holt, 1965.

Cook, Nick. *Aggressor*. New York: St. Martin's Press, 1993.

Cook, Robin. *Sphinx*. New York, G.P. Putnam's Sons, 1979.

Coonts, Stephen. *Find Flight*. New York: Doubleday, 1988.

———. *The Red Horseman*. Pocket Books, 1993.

Cooper, Charles [pseud.: Arnold Charles Cooper Lock]. *The Turkish Spy*. London: Stockwell, 1932.

Copeland, William. *Five Hours from Isfahan*. New York: Putnam, 1975; London: Hart-Davis, 1976.

Coppel, Alfred [pseud.: A. C. Marin]. *The Apocalypse Brigade*. New York: Holt, 1981.

———. *Show Me a Hero*. New York: Harcourt Brace Jovanovich, 1987.

———. *Thirty-Four East*. New York: Harcourt, 1974; London: Macmillan, 1974.

Corrigan, Mark. *Baby Face*. London: Wenner Laurie, 1952.

Couch, Dick. *Pressure Point*. New York: Putnam, 1992.

Cox, Richard. *Sam 7*. London: Hutchinson, 1977; New York: Reader's Digest, 1977.

———. *Ground Zero*. New York: Stein and Day, 1984.

Coyle, Harold. *Bright Star*. New York, Simon and Schuster, 1990.

———. *Sword Point*. New York: Simon and Schuster, 1988.

Crane, Frances. *The Coral Princess Murders*. New York: Random House, 1954; London: Hammond, 1955.

Creasey, John. *The Hounds of Vengeance*. London: Long, 1945.

Cronin, Michael [pseud.: Brendan Leo Cronin]. *The Marksman*. London: Hale, 1974.

Crosby, John. *An Affair of Strangers*. New York: Stein and Day, 1975; London: Cape, 1977.

Crowder, Herbert. *Ambush at Osirak*. Novato, California, Presidio Press, 1988.

———. *Missile Zone*. New York: Putnam, 1991.

Cullen, Robert. *Cover Story*. New York: Simon and Schuster, 1994.

———. *Heirs of the Fire*. New York: Ballantine, 1997.

Cunningham, Richard. *A Ceremony in the Lincoln Tunnel*. Kansas City, Mo.: Sheed, Andrews, and McMeel, 1978; London: Arrow, 1980.

Cussler, Clive. *Sahara*. New York: Simon and Schuster, 1992.

———. *Treasure*. New York, Pocket Books, 1988.

Dan, Uri, and Peter Manor. *Carlos Must Die*. New York: Leisure, 1978.

————. *Ultimatum: PU 94*. New York: Leisure, 1977.

Daniel, Roland. *The Death House*. London, Wright and Brown, 1941.

Davidson, Lionel. *A Long Way from Shiloh*. London: Gollancz, 1966; also published as *The Menorah Men*. New York: Harper and Row, 1966.

————. *The Sun Chemist*. London: Cape, 1976; New York: Knopf, 1976.

Davis, Maggie. *Rommel's Gold*. Philadelphia: Lippincott, 1971; London: Barrie, 1972.

————. *The Sheik*. New York: William Morrow, 1977.

Davison, Geoffrey. *The Chessboard Spies*. London: Hale, 1969; New York: Roy, 1969.

Deighton, Len (Leonard Cyril Deighton). *City of Gold*. New York, Harper Collins, 1992

————. *The Ipcress File*. London: Hodder, 1962; New York: Simon and Schuster, 1963.

————. *Twinkle, Twinkle Little Spy*. London: Cape, 1976; also published as *Catch a Falling Spy*. New York: Harcourt, 1976.

Delacorte, Peter. *Levantine*. New York: Norton, 1985.

DeMille, Nelson. *By the Rivers of Babylon*. New York: Harcourt, 1978; London: Hart-Davis, 1978.

————. *The Lion's Game*. New York: Warner Books, 2000.

————. *Night Fall*. New York: Warner, 2004.

Dempsey, Al. *The Stendal Raid*. New York: Tom Doherty, 1985.

De Villiers, Gerard. *Malko: Kill Kissinger*. New York: Pinnacle, 1974.

————. *Malko: The Man From Kabul*. New York: Pinnacle, 1973.

————. *Versus the CIA*. London: New English Library, 1969; New York: Pinnacle, 1974.

————. *West of Jerusalem*. London: New English Library, 1969; New York: Pinnacle, 1973.

Dewar, Evelyn. *Perfumes of Arabia*. London: Bles, 1973; New York: Walker, 1974.

Dickinson, Peter. *The Poison Oracle*. London: Hodder, 1974; New York: Pantheon, 1974.

Dickson, Carter [pseud.: John Dickson Carr]. *Behind the Crimson Blind*. New York: William Morrow, 1952; London: Heinemann, 1952.

DiMercurio, Michael. *Phoenix Sub Zero*. New York: Donald Fine, 1994.

Dinallo, Greg. *Purpose of Evasion*. New York: St. Martin's Press, 1990.

Dixon, Roger [pseud.: John Christian]. *Going to Jerusalem*. London: Collins, 1977; New York: Coward McCann, 1977.

Drummond, Ivor [pseud.: Roger (Erskine) Longrigg]. *A Stench of Poppies*. London: Joseph, 1978; New York: St. Martin's Press, 1978.

————. *The Tank of Sacred Eels*. London: Joseph, 1976; New York St. Martin's Press, 1976.

Duncan, Patrick. *Courage under Fire*. New York: Putnam, 1996.

Dye, Dale. *Outrage*. Boston: Little, Brown, 1988.

Easterman, Daniel. *The Final Judgement*. New York: HarperCollins, 1996.

————. *The Last Assassin*. London: Hodder and Stoughton, 1984; Garden City, N. Y.: Doubleday, 1985.

————. *Name of the Beast*. New York: HarperCollins, 1992; London: Grafton, 1993.

————. *Night of the Apocalypse*. New York: HarperCollins, 1995.

————. *The Seventh Sanctuary*. Garden City: Doubleday, 1987; London: Grafton, 1987.

Eden, Matthew. *The Murder of Lawrence of Arabia*. London: New English Library, 1980; New York: Crowell, 1980.

Edwards, Paul [pseud.: Robert Lory]. *John Eagle Expediter: The Fist of Fatima*. New York: Pyramid, 1973; London: New English Library, 1976.

Edwards, Samuel [pseud.: Noel B(ertram) Gerson]. *The Exploiters*. New York: Praeger, 1974; London: Heinemann, 1975.

Egleton, Clive. *The Eisenhower Deception*. New York: Atheneum, 1981.

————. *Skirmish*. London: Hodder, 1975; New York: Coward, McCann, 1975.

————. *Warning Shot*. New York: St. Martin's Press, 1996.

Eisenberg, Dennis, Eli Landau, and Menahem Portugali. *Operation Uranium Ship*. New York: New American Library, 1978.

Eliot, Anne [pseud.: Lois Dwight Cole]. *Incident at Villa Rahmana*. New York: Hawthorn, 1972; London: Hale, 1975.

Elkins, Aaron. *Dead Men's Hearts*. New York, Mysterious Press, 1994.

Elsworthy, A. L. *Death Glides In*. London: Hutchinson, 1935.

Epstein, Edward Jay. *Cartel*. New York: Putnam, 1978; London: Arrow, 1979.

Erdman, Paul E. *The Billion Dollar Sure Thing*. New York: Berkley, 1982.

————. *The Crash of '79*. New York: Simon and Schuster, 1976.

————. *The Silver Bears*. New York: Scribner's, 1974; London Hutchinson, 1974.

Evans, Jonathan. *Misfire*. London: Joseph, 1980; New York Pinnacle, 1982.

Evans, Kenneth. *No Cause for Dying*. London: Hale, 1969.

————. *Oasis of Fear*. London: Hale, 1968; New York: Roy, 1968.

————. *A Rich Way to Die*. London: Hale, 1973.

————. *Shadows of Violence*. London: Hale, 1971.

Falkirk, Richard [pseud.: Derek William Lambert]. *The Twisted Wire*. Garden City, New York.: Doubleday, 1971; London: Corgi, 1972.

Faqir, Nadia. *Nisanit*. London: Ellis, 1987; New York Penguin, 1990.

Farhi, Moris. *The Last of Days*. New York: Crown, 1983.

Farnsworth, Clyde H. *Shadow Wars*. New York: Donald I. Fine, 1998.

Fergusson, Bernard E. *The Rare Adventure*. London: Collins, 1954; New York: Rinehart, 1955.

Ferro, James. *Death Wish*. New York: Berkley, 2002.

————. *Fort Apache*. New York: Berkley, 2000.

————. *Going Deep.* New York: Berkley Books, 1999.

————. *Hog Down.* New York: Berkley, 1999.

————. *Snake Eaters.* New York: Berkley, 2001.

————. *Target: Saddam.* New York: Berkeley, 2001.

Fisher, David E. and Col. Ralph Albertazzie. *Hostage One.* New York: Random House, 1989.

Fitzgerald, Gregory and John Dillon. *The Druze Document.* Oakland: Cliffhanger Press, 1989.

Fitzsimmons, Christopher. *Early Warning.* London: Hodder, 1978; New York: Viking, 1978.

Flagg, John [pseud.: John Gearon]. *The Persian Cat.* Greenwich, Conn.: Fawcett, 1950.

————. *Woman of Cairo.* Greenwich, Conn.: Fawcett, 1953; London: Muller, 1954.

Flannery, Sean. [pseud.: David Hagberg]. *The Hollow Men.* New York: Charter, 1982.

————. *Kilo Option.* New York: Forge, 1996.

Flem-Ath, Rose. *Field of Thunder.* Stoddart, 1997.

Fleming, Joan. *Nothing Is the Number When You Die.* London: Collins, 1965; New York: Washburn, 1965.

————. *When I Grow Rich.* London: Collins, 1962; New York: Washburn, 1962.

Flett, Alfred. *Never Shake a Skeleton.* London: Joseph, 1973; New York: Walker, 1978.

Flynn, Vince. *Separation of Power.* New York: Pocket Books, 2001.

Follett, Ken. *The Key to Rebecca.* New York: William Morrow, 1980; London: H. Hamilton, 1980.

————. *Lie Down With Eagles.* New York: William Morrow, 1986.

————. *Triple.* London: Macdonald, 1979; New York: Arbor House, 1979.

Forbes, Colin [pseud.: Raymond H. Sawkins]. *Year of the Golden Ape.* London: Collins, 1974; New York: Dutton, 1974.

Forsyte, Charles [pseud.]. *Diplomatic Death.* London: Cassell, 1961; New York: William Morrow, 1961.

————. *Murder with Minarets.* London: Cassell, 1968.

Forsyth, Frederick. *The Afghan.* New York: Putnam, 2006.

————. *The Deceiver.* New York: Bantam, 1991.

————. *The Fist of God.* New York: Bantam, 1994.

————. *The Negotiator.* New York: Bantam, 1989.

Foss, John [pseud.: James Gordon]. *Flesh and Blood.* London: Dobson, 1951.

Frankel, Sandor, and Webster Mews [pseud.]. *The Aleph Solution.* New York: Stein and Day, 1978.

Franklin, Jo. *The Wing of the Falcon.* Nashville: Atlantis, 1995.

Freemantle, Brian. *The Run Around.* New York: Bantam, 1989.

Fulton, E.G. *Vengeance My Love.* New York: Tom Doherty, 1982.

Fry, Pete [pseud.: James Clifford King]. *The Grey Sombrero*. London: Boardman, 1958; New York: Roy, 1958.

Garbo, Norman. *Cabal*. New York: Norton, 1978; London: W.H. Allen, 1979.

Garner, William. *The Andra Fiasco*. London: Collins, 1971; also published as *Strip Jack Naked*. New York: Bobbs-Merrill, 1971.

Garve, Andrew [pseud.: Paul Winterton]. *The Ascent of D-13*. London: Collins, 1969; New York: Harper and Row, 1969.

Gerard, Francis. *The Prince of Paradise*. London: Rich, 1938; New York: Dutton, 1941.

Gibbs, George F. *The Road to Baghdad*. New York: Appleton-Century, 1938.

Gilbert, Michael. *The Ninety-Second Tiger*. London: Hodder, 1973; New York: Harper and Row, 1973.

Gilman, Dorothy. *The Amazing Mrs. Pollifax*. Garden City, N. Y.: Doubleday, 1970; London: Hale, 1971.

———. *Mrs. Pollifax and the Whirling Dervish*. New York: Doubleday, 1990.

———. *Mrs. Pollifax, Innocent Tourist*. New York: Ballantine, 1997.

———. *Mrs. Pollifax Unveiled*. New York: Ballantine, 2000.

Gluck, Sinclair. *Red Emeralds*. London: Mills, 1932.

Golan, Matti. *The Geneva Crisis*. New York: A&W, 1981.

Goodchild, George. *The Road to Marrakesh*. London: Hodder, 1931; New York: Houghton, 1932.

———. *The Last Secret*. London: Rich and Cowan, 1956.

Goodkin, Michael. *Paper Gold*. New York: Macmillan, 1981.

Gordon, Alexander [pseud.: Gordon Cotler]. *The Cipher*. New York: Simon and Schuster, 1961; London: Boardman, 1962.

Gordon, Mildred, and Gordon Gordon. *Tiger on My Back*. Garden City, N. Y.: Doubleday, 1960; London: MacDonald, 1960.

Gough, Laurence. *Sandstorm*. New York: Viking, 1992.

Graham, Burton. *Spy or Die*. London: Dent, 1972.

Graham, David. *Down to a Sunless Sea*. New York: Simon and Schuster, 1981.

Graham, James. *Bloody Passage*. London: Macmillan, 1974; also published as *The Run to Morning*. New York: Stein and Day, 1974.

———. *The Khufra Run*. London: Macmillan, 1972; Garden City, N.Y.: Doubleday, 1973.

Graham, Mark. *The Fire Theft*. New York: Viking, 1993.

Gram, Dewey and Duane Dell'Amico. *True Lies*. New York: Signet, 1994.

Graves, Richard. *Cobalt 60*. New York: Stein and Day, 1975.

Green, William Mark. *The Man Who Called Himself Devlin*. New York: Bobbs-Merrill, 1978.

Grenier, Richard. *The Marrakesh One-Two*. Boston: Houghton Mifflin, 1983.

Griffith, Glyn. *Fire over Baghdad*. London: Long, 1939.

Griswold, George [pseud.: Robert George Dean]. *Red Pawns*. New York: Dutton, 1954; London: Eyre, 1955.

Gruber, Frank. *Bridge of Sand*. New York: Dutton, 1963; London: Boardman, 1964.

Guenter, C G. [pseud.: K H. Gunther]. *Death in Aqaba*. New York: Manor, 1978.

Gur, Batya. *Bethlehem Road Murder*. New York: HarperCollins, 2004.

———. *Literary Murder: A Critical Case*. New York: HarperCollins, 1993.

———. *Murder Duet: A Musical Case*. New York: HarperCollins, 1999.

———. *Murder on a Kibbutz: A Communal Case*. New York: HarperCollins, 1994.

———. *The Saturday Morning Murder: A Psychoanalytic Case*. New York: HarperCollins, 1992.

Haddad, C. A. *Bloody September*. New York: Harper and Row, 1976.

———. *The Moroccan*. New York: Harper and Row, 1975; London: W.H. Allen, 1977.

———. *Operation Apricot*. New York: Harper and Row, 1978.

Hadley, Joan. *The Night-Blooming Cereus*. New York: St. Martin's, 1986.

Hagberg, David. *Countdown*. New York: St. Martin's Press, 1990.

———. *Desert Fire*. New York: Tom Doherty, 1993.

———. *Joshua's Hammer*. New York: Tom Doherty, 2001.

Haggard, William [pseud.: Richard Henry Michael Clayton]. *The Bitter Harvest*. London: Cassell, 1971; also published as *Too Many Enemies*. New York: Walker, 1971.

———. *The Median Line*. London: Cassell, 1979; New York: Walker, 1981.

———. *The Mischief Makers*. New York: Walker, 1982.

———. *The Powder Barrel*. London: Cassell, 1965; New York: Washburn, 1965.

———. *Season of Doubt*. New York: William Morrow, 1968.

———. *Visa to Limbo*. London: Cassell, 1978; New York: Walker, 1979.

Hall, Adam [pseud.: Elleston Trevor]. *The Tango Briefing*. London: Collins, 1973; Garden City, N.Y.: Doubleday, 1973.

Hamilton Adam [pseud. Marilyn Granbeck and Arthur Moore]. *The Peacemaker: The Yashar Pursuit*. New York: Berkley, 1974.

Hamizrachi, Yoram. *The Golden Lion and the Sun*. New York: Dutton, 1982.

Hammonds, Michael. *The OPEC Objective*. Suspense, 1981.

Hannah, Janet. *The Wish to Kill*. New York: Soho, 1999.

Harrington, Kent. *The Gift of a Falcon*. New York: McGraw-Hill, 1988.

Harris, Leonard. *The Masada Plan*. New York: Crown, 1976; London Joseph, 1977.

Harris, Thomas. *Black Sunday*. New York: G.P. Putnam's Sons, 1975; London: Hodder, 1975.

Harrison, Harry. *Queen Victoria's Revenge*. Garden City, N. Y.: Doubleday, 1975; London: Severn, 1977.

Harrison, Payne. *Black Cipher*. New York, Crown Publishers, 1994.

Hartov, Steven. *The Devil's Shepherd*. New York: Morrow, 2000.

———. *The Heat of Ramadan*. New York: Harcourt, 1992.

———. *The Nylon Hand of God*. New York: William Morrow, 1996.

Harvester, Simon [pseud.: Henry St. John Clair Gibbs]. *A Breastplate for Aaron*. London: Rich and Cowan, 1949.

———. *Assassin's Road*. London: Jarrolds, 1965; New York: Walker, 1965.

———. *Lucifer at Sunset*. London: Jarrolds, 1953.

———. *Sahara Road*. London: Jarrolds, 1972; New York: Walker,1972.

———. *Treacherous Road*. London: Jarrolds, 1966; New York: Walker, 1967.

———. *Unsung Road*. London: Jarrolds, 1960; New York: Walker, 1961.

———. *Zion Road*. London: Jarrolds, 1968; New York: Walker, 1968.

Harwood, Ronald. *The Genoa Ferry*. London: Secker, 1976; New York: Mason/Charter, 1977.

Hashan. *Shanidar*. New York: Wynwood Press, 1990.

Hastings, Michael. *The Sands of Khali*. London: Macdonald, 1964.

———. *Veiled Isis*. London: Macdonald, 1960.

Hastings, Michael [pseud: Michael Bar Zohar]. *The Devil's Spy*. New York: Scribners, 1988.

Hayes, Ralph. *Agent for COMINSEC: The Bloody Monday Conspiracy*. New York: Belmont-Tower Books, 1974.

Heckstall-Smith, Anthony. *The Man with Yellow Shoes*. London: Wingate, 1957; New York: Roy 1958.

Hedges, Sidney George. *Diamond Duel*. London: Jenkins, 1935.

Heim, Michael. *Aswan*. New York: Knopf, 1972.

Hemingway, Joan, and Paul Bonnecerre. *Rosebud*. London: Ellis, 1974; New York: Morrow, 1974.

Henissart, Paul. *Margin of Error*. London: Hutchinson, 1980; New York: Simon and Schuster, 1980.

———. *Narrow Exit*. London: Hutchinson, 1974; New York: Simon and Schuster, 1974.

Herman, Richard, Jr. *Against All Enemies*. New York: Avon, 1998.

———. *Firebreak*. New York: William Morrow, 1991

———. *The Warbirds*. New York: Donald I. Fine, Inc., 1989.

Hernon, Peter. *Earthly Remains*. New York: Carol, 1989.

Hesky, Olga. *A Different Night*. London: Longmans, 1970; New York Random House, 1971.

———. *The Sequin Syndicate*. London: Longmans 1969; New York: Dodd, Mead, 1969.

———. *The Serpent's Smile*. London: Longmans, 1967; New York: Dodd, Mead, 1967.

———. *Time for Treason*. London: Longmans, 1967; New York: Dodd, Mead, 1968.

Higgins, Jack. *Edge of Danger*. New York: Putnam, 2001.

———. *The President's Daughter*. New York: Putnam, 1997.

———. *Seven Pillars to Hell*. London: Abelard-Schuman, 1963.

———. *Sheba*. New York: Berkley, 1995.

Highsmith, Patricia. *The Tremor of Forgery*. Garden City, N.Y.: Doubleday, 1969; London: Heinemann, 1969.

Hild, Jack. *Jihad*. New York: Gold Eagle, 1986.

————. *The Plains of Fire*. New York: Gold Eagle, 1984.

Hocking, Anne [pseud.: Mona Naomi Anne Messer]. *Death Loves a Shining Mark*. Garden City, N.Y.: Doubleday, 1943; also published as *Nile Green*. London: Bles, 1943.

Hoffenberg, Jack. *17 Ben Gurion*. New York: G.P. Putnam's Sons, 1977.

Hoffman, Andrew Jay. *Beehive*. Sag Harbor: Permanent Press, 1992.

Holden, J. Railton. *Spider Flies Again*. London: Newnes, 1937.

————. *Suez Patrol*. London: Newnes, 1936.

————. *Suez Side Ace*. London: Newnes, 1938.

Holt, Robert Lawrence. *Good Friday*. Blue Ridge Summit, P.A.: TAB, 1987.

Home. Michael [pseud.: Christopher Bush]. *Attack in the Desert*. New York: William Morrow, 1942.

————. *The Place of Little Birds*. London: Methuen, 1941.

————. *The House of Shade*. London: Methuen, 1942; New York: William Morrow, 1942.

Hone, Joseph. *The Private Sector*. London: H. Hamilton, 1971; New York: Dutton, 1972.

Household, Geoffrey. *Arabesque*. London: Chatto, 1948; Boston: Little, Brown, 1948.

————. *Doom's Caravan*. London: Joseph, 1971; Boston: Little, Brown, 1971.

————. *The High Place*. London: Joseph, 1950; Boston: Little, Brown, 1950.

————. *Olura*. London: Joseph, 1965; Boston: Little, Brown, 1965.

Houston, Robert. *Ararat*. New York: Avon, 1982.

Howlett, John. *Murder of a Moderate Man*. London: Arrow, 1985; New York: St. Martin's Press, 1986.

Hunt, E. Howard. *The Gaza Intercept*. New York: Stein and Day, 1981.

Hunter, Jack D. *The Terror Alliance*. New York: Leisure, 1980.

Hunter, James H. *Banners of Blood*. Toronto: Evangelical Publishers, 1947.

————. *The Mystery of Mar Saba*. New York: Evangelical Publishers, 1940.

Hunter, Robin. *The Fourth Angel*. New York: Arbor House, 1984.

Hunter, Stephen. *The Second Saladin*. New York: William Morrow, 1982.

Hymers, John. *Utter Death*. London: Gifford, 1952; New York: Detective Book Club, 1953.

Ignatius David. *Agents of Innocence*. New York: Norton, 1987.

————. *The Bank of Fear*. New York: William Morrow, 1994.

Imber, Hugh. *On Helle's Waves*. London: Hodder and Stoughton, 1930.

Ing, Dean. *Butcher Bird*. New York: Tom Doherty, 1993.

————. *Skins of Dead Men*. New York: Forge, 1998.

Innes, Hammond. *The Black Tide*. Garden City, N.Y.: Doubleday, 1983.

————. *The Doomed Oasis*. London: Collins, 1960; New York: Knopf, 1960.

————. *The Strange Land*. London: Collins, 1954; also published as *The Naked Land*. New York: Knopf, 1954.

Irwin, Robert. *The Arabian Nightmare*. London: Penguin, 1983.

————. *The Mysteries of Algiers*. London: Penguin, 1988.

Iverson, Marc. *Persian Horse: A Novel of War in the Gulf*. New York: Orion Books, 1991.

Jackman, Stuart. *A Game of Soldiers*. New York: Atheneum, 1982.

————. *Operation Catcher*. London: H. Hamilton, 1980; also published as *Sandcatcher*. New York: Atheneum, 1980.

Jacont, Amnon. *Borrowed Time*. London: Hamish Hamilton, 1986.

Jackson, Clarence J.L. [pseud.: Richard W. Bulliet]. *Kicked to Death by a Camel*. New York: Harper and Row, 1973.

James, Leigh [pseud.]. *The Caliph Intrigue*. New York: Dodd, Mead, 1979.

James, Stuart. *The Spy is Falling*. New York: Bantam, 1989.

Janson, Frank. *Soft Cargo*. London: Compact Books, 1964.

Jason, Stuart [House name]. *Appointment in Iran*. New York: Pinnacle, 1977.

————. *Blood Debt*. New York: Pinnacle, 1972.

————. *Sealed with Blood*. New York: Pinnacle, 1973.

Jay, Charlotte [pseud.: Geraldine Mary Jay Halls]. *Arms for Adonis*. London: Collins, 1960; New York: Harper, 1961.

Jefferies, Ian [pseud.: Peter Hays]. *Thirteen Days*. London: Cape, 1959.

Jepson, Selwyn. *The Death Gong*. London: Harrap, 1927; New York: Watt, 1927.

————. *A Noise in the Night*. London: Hart-Davis, 1957; New York: Lippincott, 1957.

John, Owen. *Dead on Time*. London: Joseph, 1969; New York: Paperback Library, 1969.

Johnson. James L. *Code Name Sebastian*. New York: Lippincott, 1967.

Johnston. Ronald. *The Black Camels of Qashran*. London: Collins, 1970; also published as *The Black Camels*. New York: Harcourt Brace, 1969.

Jones, Dennis. *Rubicon One*. New York: Beaufort Books, 1983.

————. *Winter Palace*. Boston: Little Brown, 1988.

Jones, Harry. *Shadow in a Weary Land*. New York: Permanent Press, 1992.

Jones, Scott. *Heaven's War*. Waterbrook Press, 1998.

Jordan, David [pseud.: A. Joshua Sherman]. *Nile Green*. London: Joseph, 1973; New York: Stein and Day, 1974.

Jordan, Eric. *Operation Hebron*. London: International Media, 2000.

Kabal, A.M. [pseud., H.S. Bhabra]. *The Adversary*. New York: Walker, 1987.

Kalb, Marvin, and Ted Koppel. *In the National Interest*. New York: Simon and Schuster, 1977; London: Bodley, 1978.

Kane. Henry. *The Tripoli Documents*. New York: Simon and Schuster, 1976; London: Hamlyn, 1979.

Kaplan, Andrew. *Scorpion*. London: Arrow Books, 1985; New York: Macmillan, 1985.

Kaplan, Howard. *The Damascus Cover*. New York: Dutton, 1977; London: Hodder, 1978.

Karlin, Wayne. *The Extras.* New York: Holt, 1989.

Kartun, Derek. *Megiddo.* New York: Walker, 1987.

Katz, Robert. *The Spoils of Ararat.* Boston: Houghton Mifflin, 1978; London: Sphere,1979.

Keane, Christopher. *The Heir.* New York: William Morrow, 1977 London: Hamlyn, 1979.

Keller, Beverly. *The Baghdad Defections.* New York: Bobbs-Merrill, 1973.

Kellerman, Jonathan. *The Butcher's Theatre.* New York: Bantam, 1988.

Kelly, Orr. *Seals Eagle Force: Desert Thunder.* New York: Morrow, 1998.

Kemelman, Harry. *Monday the Rabbi Took Off.* New York: Putnam, 1972; London: Hutchinson, 1972.

———. *One Fine Day the Rabbi Bought a Cross.* New York: Morrow, 1987.

Keneally, Thomas. *Flying Hero Class.* New York: Harper, 1984.

Kenmore, Frank J. *The Frankincense Trail.* New York: Pinnacle, 1989.

Kennedy, W.P. *Toy Soldiers.* New York: St. Martin's Press, 1988.

Kenyon, Michael. *Deep Pocket.* London: Collins, 1978; also published as *The Molehill File.* New York: Coward, McCann, 1978.

Kilgore, Axel. *The Afghan Penetration.* New York: Kensington, 1983.

King, Frank. *Raya.* New York: Richard Marek, 1980.

King, Laurie R. *O Jerusalem.* New York: Bantam, 1999.

Kinsolving, William. *The Diplomat's Daughter.* New York: Doubleday, 1993.

Klawans, Harold L. *The Jerusalem Code.* New York: New American Library, 1988.

Klein, Z. *No Saving Grace.* New York: Ivy, 1993.

Klinger, Henry. *Essence of Murder.* New York: Permabooks, 1963.

———. *Lust for Murder.* New York: Trident, 1966.

———. *Murder Off Broadway.* New York: Permabooks, 1962.

———. *Wanton for Murder.* New York: Permabooks, 1961.

Kneale, Bruce. *Appointment in Cairo.* London: Evans Bros, Ltd., 1950.

Koenig, Joseph. *Brides of Blood.* New York: Grove Press, 1993.

Koperwas, Sam. *The Flash Effect.* New York: William Morrow and Company, 1994.

Laflin, Jack. *The Temple at Ilumquh.* New York: Award, 1970.

Lancaster, Graham. *The Nuclear Letters.* London: Eyre, 1979; New York: Atheneum, 1979.

Land, Jon. *The Pillars of Solomon.* New York: Tom Doherty, 1999.

———. *The Walls of Jericho.* New York: Tom Doherty, 1997.

———. *A Walk in the Darkness.* New York: Tom Doherty, 2000.

Landon, Christopher. *A Flag in the City.* London: Heinemann, 1953; New York: Macmillan, 1954.

Landsborough, Gordon. *The Glasshouse Gang.* New York: Manor, 1967.

Lane, Kendall. *Gambit.* Greenwich, Conn.: Fawcett. 1966.

Lange, John [pseud.: Michael Crighton]. *Easy Go.* New York: Signet, 1968; London: Sphere, 1972; also published as *The Last Tomb.* New York: Bantam, 1974.

Latham, Aaron. *Double, Double Oil and Trouble*. New York: Simon and Schuster, 1978.

———. *Orchids for Mother*. Boston: Little, Brown, 1977.

Law, J. Patrick. *The Assistant*. New York: Simon and Schuster, 2000.

Lawrence, Sheila. *A Million Tears*. New York: Dell, 1977.

Leader, Charles [pseud.: Robert Charles Smith]. *Murder in Marrakech*. London: Hale, 1966.

———. *Nightmare on the Nile*. London: Hale, 1967.

Leasor, James. *Never Had a Spanner on Her*. London: Heinemann, 1970.

———. *Passport for a Pilgrim*. London: Heinemann, 1968; Garden City, N.Y.: Doubleday, 1969.

———. *Passport to Oblivion*. London: Heinemann, 1964; Philadelphia: Lippincott, 1965; also published as *Where the Spies Are*. New York: Signet, 1965; London: Pan, 1965.

Le Carré, John [pseud.: David John Moore Cornwell]. *The Little Drummer Girl*. London: Hodder and Stoughton, 1983; New York: Knopf, 1983.

Lee, Elsie. *The Drifting Sand*. New York: Lancer, 1966.

Lee, John. *Assignation in Algeria*. New York: Walker, 1971; also published as *The Killing Wind*. London: Longmans, 1972.

Leib, Franklin Allen. *Fire Arrow*. Novato, California: Presidio Press, 1988.

Leigh, James. *The Caliph Intrigue*. New York: Dodd, Mead, 1979.

Leighton, Tom. *Night of the Sphinx*. New York: Dell, 1979.

Leonard, Charles L. [pseud.: Mary Violet Heberden]. *Expert in Murder*. Garden City, N. Y.: Doubleday, 1945.

———. *Fanatic of Fez*. Garden City, N. Y.: Doubleday, 1943.

Leonard, Elmore. *The Hunted*. New York: Delacorte, 1977; London: Secker, 1978.

Leopold, Christopher. *Casablack*. London: H. Hamilton, 1978; Garden City, N. Y.: Doubleday, 1979.

Lichtman, Charles. *The Last Inauguration*. Hollywood, Florida: Lifetime Books, Inc., 1998.

Littell, Blaine. *The Dolorosa Deal*. New York: Saturday Review Press, 1973; London: Collins, 1973.

Livingston, Harold. *To Die in Babylon*. New York: St. Martin's Press, 1993.

Litvinoff, Emanuel. *Falls the Shadow*. New York: Stein and Day, 1984.

Llewellyn, Richard [pseud.: Richard David Vivian Uewellyn Lloyd]. *White Horse to Banbury Cross*. Garden City, N. Y.: Doubleday, 1970; London: Joseph, 1972.

Loraine, Philip. *Loaded Questions*. New York: St. Martin's Press, 1985.

Louvish, Simon. *The Silencer*. New York: Interlink Books, 1993.

Luard, Nicholas. *The Robespierre Serial*. London: Weidenfeld, 1975; New York: Harcourt, 1975.

———. *The Shadow Spy*. New York: Harcourt, Brace, 1979; also published as *The Dirty Area*. London: H. Hamilton, 1979.

————. *The Traveling Horseman*. London: Weidenfeld, 1975.

Ludlum, Robert. *The Icarus Agenda*. New York, Random House, 1988.

————. *The Scorpio Illusion*. New York: Bantam, 1993.

Luther, Ray [pseud.: Arthur Gordon Ley]. *Intermind*. Banner, 1967; Dobson, 1969.

Lyall, Gavin. *Judas Country*. London: Hodder 1975; New York: Viking, 1975.

————. *Uncle Target*. London: Hodder and Stoughton, 1988.

MacAlister, Ian [pseud.: Marvin H. Albert]. *Valley of the Assassins*. Greenwich, Conn.: Fawcett, 1975; London: Coronet, 1976.

MacKenzie, Nigel. *Murder Over Karnak*. London: Wright, 1949.

MacKinnon, Alan. *Assignment in Iraq*. London: Collins, 1960; Garden City, N.Y.: Doubleday, 1960.

————. *Cormorant's Isle*. London: Longmans, 1962; Garden City, N.Y.: Doubleday, 1962.

————. *Red-Winged Angel*. London: Collins 1958; also published as *Summons From Baghdad*. Garden City, N.Y.: Doubleday, 1958.

MacKinnon, Colin. *Finding Hoseyn*. New York: Arbor House, 1986.

MacLean, Alistair. *Goodbye California*. London: Collins 1977; Garden City, NY: Doubleday, 1978.

MacLean, Arthur. *Pursuit to Algeria*. Amalgamated Press, 1961.

MacLean, Robinson. *The Baited Blonde*. New York: Mill, 1949; London: Barker, 1950.

MacLeish, Roderick. *The Man Who Wasn't There*. New York: Random House, 1976; also published as *Carnaby Rex*. London: Weidenfeld, 1976.

MacLeod, Robert. *Place of Mists*. London: Longmans 1969; New York: McCall, 1970.

Manchester, William. *Beard the Lion*. New York: M.S. Mill Co., 1959; London: Cassell, 1959; also published as *Cairo Intrigue*. New York: Pocket Books, 1959.

Mann, Jessica. *Death Beyond the Nile*. New York: St. Martin's Press, 1988.

Mann, Paul. *The Libyan Contract*. New York: Macmillan, 1988.

Mantel, Hilary. *Eight Months on Ghazzah Street*. New York: Henry Holt and Company, 1988.

Marcinko, Richard and John Weisman. *Rogue Warrior: Green Team*. New York: Pocket Books, 1995.

Mark, Ted. *The Man from ORGY*. New York: Lancer Books, 1965.

Marlowe, Hugh. *Seven Pillars to Hell*. London and New York: Abelard-Schuman, 1963.

Marlowe, Stephen [pseud.: Milton A. Lesser]. *Manhunt Is My Mission*. Greenwich, Conn.: Fawcett, 1961; London: Muller, 1961.

Martyn, Wyndham. *Cairo Crisis*. London: Jenkins, 1945.

Mason, Colin. *Hostage*. London: Macmillan, 1973; New York: Walker, 1973.

Mason, David. *Shadow over Babylon*. New York: Dutton, 1993.

Mason, F. van Wyck. *The Cairo Garter Murders*. Garden City, N.Y.: Doubleday, 1938; London: Jarrolds, 1938.

————. *The Dardanelles Derelict*. Garden City, N Y: Doubleday, 1949; London: Barker, 1950.

————. *The Deadly Orbit Mission*. Garden City, N.Y.: Doubleday, 1968; London: Hale, 1968.

————. *Two Tickets for Tangier*. Garden City, N.Y.: Doubleday, 1955; London: Hale, 1956.

Mason, Robert. *Arab Agent*. London: Hurst, 1944.

————. *Cairo Communiqué*. London: Hurst, 1942.

————. *More News from the Middle East*. London: Hurst, 1943.

Mather, Arthur. *The Mind Breaker*. London: Hodder, 1980; New York Delacorte, 1980.

Mather, Berkeley [pseud.: John Evan Weston Davies]. *The Achilles Affair*. London: Collins, 1959; New York: Scribner's, 1959.

————. *With Extreme Prejudice*. London: Collins, 1975; New York: Scribner's, 1976.

Maudsley, Jere. *Hunter*. Sag Harbor: Permanent Press, 1985.

Maugham, Robin [pseud.: Robert Cecil Romer Maugham]. *The Man with Two Shadows*. London: Longmans, 1958; New York: Harper and Row, 1959.

Maxim, John R. *Haven*. New York: Avon, 1997.

Maybury, Ann [pseud.: Anne Buxton]. *The Midnight Dancers*. New York: Random House, 1973; London: Collins, 1974.

Mayo, James [pseud. Stephen Coulter]. *Once in a Lifetime*. London: Heinemann, 1968; also published as *Sergeant Death*. New York: William Morrow, 1968.

McCarry, Charles. *The Better Angels*. New York: Dutton, 1979; London: Hutchinson, 1979.

————. *Second Sight*. New York: Avon, 1991.

McCarthy, Mary. *Cannibals and Missionaries*. New York: Harcourt Brace, 1979; London: Weidenfeld, 1979.

McConnell, Malcolm. *Clinton Is Assigned*. New York: Paperback, 1978; London: Hamlyn, 1979.

McCurtin, Peter. *Soldier of Fortune: Spoils of War*. New York: Belmont-Tower, 1976; London: New English Library, 1978.

McCutchan, Philip. *Sladd's Evil*. London: Harrap, 1965; New York: John Day, 1967.

McCutcheon, Hugh. *Yet She Must Die*. London: Longmans, 1962; Garden City, N.Y.: Doubleday, 1962.

McFarlane, Ian. *The Jerusalem Conspiracy*. London: Rigby, 1984.

McGrath, H. *Carpet from Baghdad*. New York: Bobbs, 1911.

McKean, Thomas. *Moroccan Mystery*. New York: Avon, 1986.

McKinley, F(rances). *Death Sails the Nile*. Boston: Stratford, 1933.

Meade, Glenn. *The Sands of Sakkara*. New York: St. Martin's Press, 1999.

Meiring, Desmond. *A Talk with the Angels*. London: Secker and Warburg, Ltd., 1985; New York: St. Martin's Press, 1985.

————. *The Wildcatter*. New York: St. Martin's Press, 1988.

Melville-Ross, Antony. *Blindfold*. London: Collins, 1978; New York: Harper and Row, 1978.

Merek, Jack. *Blackbird*. Chicago: Contemporary Books, 1990.

———. *Target Stealth*. New York: Warner, 1989.

Michelson, Bennett. *The Chosen People*. New York: Belmont-Tower Books, 1982.

———. *The Perfect Weapon*. New York: Tower, 1980.

Moore, Robin [pseud.: Robert Lowell Moore, Jr.]. *Dubai*. Garden City, N. Y.: Doubleday, 1976; London: Barrie, 1976.

Morris, M. E. *Sword of the Shaheen*. Novato, California: Presidio Press, 1990.

Morris, T. B. *Crash into Murder*. London, Hale, 1961.

Mosley, Leon. *The Cat and the Mice*. New York: Harper, 1958; also published as *Foxhole in Cairo*. New York: Belmont, 1961.

Moss, William Stanley. *Bats with Baby Faces*. London: Boardman, 1951; New York: Harlequin, 1952.

Moyzisch, L. C. *Operation Cicero*. London: Pocket Books, 1952.

Mundy, Talbot [pseud.: William Lancaster Gribbon]. *Jimgrim and Allah's Peace*. London: Hutchinson, 1933; New York: Appleton Century, 1936.

———. *The King in Check*. London: Hutchinson, 1933; also published as *Affair in Araby*. New York: Appleton Century, 1934.

———. *The Lion of Petra*. London: Hutchinson, 1932; New York: Appleton Century, 1933.

———. *The Mystery of Khufu's Tomb*. London: Hutchinson, 1933; New York: Appleton Century, 1935.

———. *The Woman Ayisha*. London: Hutchinson, 1930.

Munro, James [pseud.: James William Mitchell]. *The Innocent Bystanders*. London: Jenkins,1969; New York: Knopf, 1970.

———. *The Man Who Sold Death*. London: Hammond, 1964; New York: Knopf, 1965.

Munslow, Bruce. *Deep Sand*. London: Hodder, 1955.

———. *No Safe Road*. London: Longmans, 1959; New York: Walker, 1962.

Murphy, Tom. *The Panther Throne*. New York: Signet, 1982.

Murphy, Warren. *Red Moon*. New York: Fawcett, 1982.

Murphy, Warren, and Richard Sapir. *The Destroyer #104: Angry White Mailmen*. New York: Worldwide, 1996.

———. *The Destroyer #116: The Final Reel*. New York: Worldwide, 1999.

———. *The Destroyer #120: The Last Monarch*. New York: Worldwide, 2000.

———. *The Destroyer #16: Oil Slick*. New York: Pinnacle, 1974.

Murray, Paul. *The Free Agent*. New York: Holt, 1952; London: Bles, 1953.

Nadel, Barbara. *Belshazzar's Daughter*. London: Headline, 1999.

———. *A Chemical Prison*. London: Headline, 2000; also published as *The Ottoman Cage*. Thomas Dunne, 2005.

Nance, John J. *Scorpion Strike*. New York: Crown Publishers, 1992.

Nelson, Walter. *The Minstrel Code*. London: Secker, 1979; also published as *The Siege of Buckingham Palace*. Boston: Little, Brown, 1980.

Newman, Oscar. *Unmasking a King*. New York: Macmillan, 1981.

Niesewand, Peter. *The Underground Connection*. London: Secker and Warburg, Ltd., 1978; New York: Stein and Day, 1985.

North, Oliver and Joe Musser. *The Assassins*. Nashville: Boardman and Hellman, 2005.

———. *The Jericho Sanction*. Nashville: Boardman and Hellman, 2003.

———. with Joe Musser. *Mission Compromised*. Nashville: Boardman and Hellman, 2002.

O'Brine, (Padriac) Manning. *Corpse to Cairo*. London: Hammond, 1952.

———. *Dagger Before Me*. London: Hammond, Hammond and Company, 1957.

———. *Deadly Interlude*. London: Hammond, 1954.

O'Connor, Dermot. *The Slender Chance*. London: Longmans, 1973.

O'Donnell, Peter. *Sabre Tooth*. London: Souvenir, 1966; Garden City, NY: Doubleday, 1966.

———. *A Taste for Death*. London: Souvenir, 1969; Garden City, N.Y.: Doubleday, 1969.

O'Keefe, Bernard J. *Trapdoor*. Boston: Houghton Mifflin, 1988.

O'Neill, Archie [pseud.: Jim Henaghan]. *Da Vinci Road*. New York: Bantam, 1973.

O'Neill, Edward A. *The Rotterdam Delivery*. New York: Coward-McCann, 1975; London: Gollancz, 1976.

O'Neill, Frank. *Agents of Sympathy*. New York: G Putnam's Sons, 1985.

———. *Roman Circus*. New York: Simon and Schuster, 1990.

O'Neill, Will(iam Daniel III). *The Libyan Kill*. New York: Norton, 1980.

Operator 1384 [pseud.: John H. Harvey]. *The Black Arab*. New York: Rich, 1939.

———. *The Catacombs of Death*. London: Hutchinson, 1936.

———. *The Devil's Diplomats*. London: Hutchinson, 1935.

———. *Jackals of the Secret Service*. New York: Rich, 1938.

———. *Queen of the Riffs*. London: Lane, 1937.

———. *The Scourge of the Desert*. New York: Rich, 1936.

———. *The Son of Allah*. London: Rich, 1937.

———. *Spies and Rebels*. New York: Rich, 1939.

———. *Spies of the Sahara*. London: Sampson and Low, Marston and Company, 1936.

———. *The White Tuareg*. London: Rich, 1936.

Osborne, Helena [pseud.: Mary Galbraith Moore]. *Pay-Day*. London: Hoddard, 1972; also published as *My Enemy's Friend*. New York: Coward, McCann, 1972.

Osmond, Andrew. *Saladin*. London: Hutchinson, 1975. Garden City, NY: Doubleday, 1976.

Ostrovsky, Victor. *Lion of Judah—A Novel of the Mossad*. New York: St. Martin's Press, 1993.

Pace, Eric. *Any War Will Do*. New York: Random House, 1973; London: Deutsch, 1974.

———. *Nightingale*. New York: Random House, 1979; London: Collins, 1980.

———. *Sabrelegs*. New York: World Publishing, 1970; London: Deutsch, 1971.

Pape, Gordon, and Tony Aspler. *The Scorpion Sanction*. New York: Viking, 1980.

Parry, David and Patrick Withrow. *The Jacamar Nest*. New York: St. Martin's Press, 1992.

Parsons, Anthony. *Death by the Nile*. London: Wright, 1955.

Patterson, James. *The Jericho Commandment*. New York: Crown, 1979; London: Hamlyn, 1980.

Pearce, Michael. *The Camel of Destruction: A Mamur Zapt Mystery*. London: Harper-Collins, 1993.

———. *A Cold Touch of Ice: A Mamur Zapt Mystery*. London: HarperCollins, 2000.

———. *Death of An Effendi: A Mamur Zapt Mystery*. London: HarperCollins, 1999.

———. *The Face in the Cemetery*. London: HarperCollins, 2001.

———. *The Fig Tree Murder: A Mamur Zapt Mystery*. London: HarperCollins, 1996.

———. *The Last Cut: A Mamur Zapt Mystery*. London: HarperCollins, 1998.

———. *The Mamur Zapt and the Donkey-Vous: A Suspense Tale of Old Cairo*. London: HarperCollins, 1990.

———. *The Mamur Zapt and the Girl in the Nile: A Suspense Tale of Old Cairo*. London: HarperCollins, 1992.

———. *The Mamur Zapt and the Men Behind: A Suspense Tale of Old Cairo*. London: Collins, 1991; New York: Mysterious Press, 1991.

———. *The Mamur Zapt and the Night of the Dog*. London: Collins 1991; New York: Doubleday Crime Club, 1991.

———. *The Mamur Zapt and the Return of the Carpet*. London: Collins, 1988.

———. *The Mamur Zapt and the Spoils of Egypt: A Suspense Tale of Old Cairo*. London: HarperCollins, 1992; New York: Mysterious Press, 1992.

———. *The Mingrelian Conspiracy: A Mamur Zapt Mystery*. London: HarperCollins, 1995.

———. *The Snake Catcher's Daughter: A Mamur Zapt Mystery*. London: HarperCollins, 1994.

Peel, Colin. *Covenant of the Poppies*. New York: St. Martin's Press, 1993.

———. *Dark Armada*. New York: St. Martin's Press, 1995.

———. *Flameout*. London: Hale, 1976; New York: St. Martin's Press, 1976.

Pendleton, Don. *The Beirut Payback*. New York: Worldwide Library, 1984.

———. *The Iranian Hit*. New York: Worldwide Library, 1982.

———. *Risk Factor*. New York: Worldwide Library, 2000.

———. *Don Pendleton's Mack Bolan-Vengeance*. New York: Worldwide Library, 1999.

Pendower, Jacques. *Mission in Tunis*. London: Hale, 1958; New York: Paperback Library, 1967.

Pentecost, Hugh [pseud.: Judson Pentecost Philips]. *The Deadly Friend*. New York: Dodd, 1961; London: Boardman, 1962.

Perdue, Lewis. *Queen's Gate Reckoning*. New York: Pinnacle, 1982.

Peters, Elizabeth [pseud.: Barbara Mertz]. *The Ape Who Guards the Balance: An Amelia Peabody Mystery*. New York: Avon, 1998.

———. *Crocodile on the Sandbank*. New York: Dodd, Mead, 1975; London: Cassell, 1976.

———. *The Curse of the Pharaohs*. New York: Mysterious Press 1981.

———. *Dead Sea Cipher*. New York: Dodd, Mead, 1970; London: Cassell, 1975.

———. *The Deeds of the Disturber*. New York: Atheneum, 1988.

———. *The Falcon at the Portal: An Amelia Peabody Mystery*. New York: Avon, 1999.

———. *He Shall Thunder in the Sky: An Amelia Peabody Mystery*. New York: William Morrow, 2000.

———. *The Hippopotamus Pool*. New York: Warner,1996.

———. *The Jackal's Head*. New York: Meredith Press, 1968; London: Jenkins, 1969.

———. *The Last Camel Died at Noon*. New York: Warner, 1991.

———. *Lion in the Valley*. New York: Morrow, 1986.

———. *The Mummy Case*. New York: Warner, 1985.

———. *Night Train to Memphis*. New York: Warner, 1994.

———. *Seeing a Large Cat*. New York: Warner, 1997.

———. *The Snake, the Crocodile and the Dog*. New York: Warner, 1992.

Peters, Ralph. *The Devil's Garden*. New York: Avon, 1998.

Petschull, Jürgen. *The Martyr*. San Francisco: Mercury House, 1988.

Pineiro, R.J. *Retribution*. New York: Tom Doherty, 1995.

———. *Ultimatum*. New York: Tom Doherty, 1994.

Pollitz, Edward R. *The Forty-First Thief*. New York: Delacorte, 1975; London: Hart-Davis, 1976.

Pollock, Daniel. *Lair of the Fox*. New York: Walker, 1989.

Ponthier, Francois. *Assignment Basra*. London: Cassell, 1969; New York: McKay, 1969.

Pope, Liston. *Redemption*. New York: N.A. Gilbert, 1994.

Portugali, M. *Khamsin*. London: MacDonald Futura, 1981.

Poyer, David. *Black Storm*. New York: St. Martin's Press, 2002.

———. *The Gulf*. New York: St. Martin's Press, 1990.

———. *The Med*. New York: St. Martin's Press, 1988.

Price, Anthony. *The Alamut Ambush*. London: Gallancz, 1972; Garden City, N. Y.: Doubleday, 1972.

Pugh, Marshall. *A Murmur of Mutiny*. London: Deutsch, 1962; New York: Harper and Row, 1972.

Quinn, Derry. *The Solstice Man*. London: Harrap, 1977; New York: St. Martin's Press, 1977.

Quinnell, A. J. *The Mahdi*. London: Macmillan, 1981; New York: William Morrow, 1982.

————. *The Snap*. New York: William Morrow, 1982; also published as *Snap Shot*. London: Macmillan, 1982.

Randall, John D. *The Jihad Ultimatum*. Dallas: Saybrook, 1988.

Rathbone, Julian. *Diamonds Bid*. London: Joseph, 1967; New York: Walker, 1967.

————. *Hand Out*. London: Joseph, 1968; New York: Walker, 1968.

————. *Kill Cure*. London: Joseph, 1975; New York: St. Martin's Press, 1975.

————. *Sand Blind*. London: Serpent's Tail, 1993.

————. *Trip Trap*. London: Joseph, 1972; New York: St. Martin's Press, 1972.

————. *With My Knives I Know I'm Good*. London: Joseph, 1969; New York: Putnam, 1970.

Raynor, William. *Eating the Big Fish*. London: Collins, 1977; also published as *The Interface Assignment*. New York: Atheneum, 1977.

Reich, Christopher. *The Devil's Banker*. New York: Delacorte, 2003.

Reich, Tova. *The Jewish War*. New York: Pantheon, 1995.

Reid, MacDonald. *Jihad: World War in 2036*. Authorhouse, 2000.

Reiss, Bob. *Divine Assassin*. Boston: Little Brown, 1985.

Rhodes, Kathlyn. *It Happened in Cairo*. London: Hutchinson, 1944.

Rhodes, Russell. *The Herod Conspiracy*. New York: Dodd Mead, 1980.

Rider, Rick. *Dyed for Death*. New York: Belmont-Tower, 1980.

Ritner, Peter. *Red Carpet for the Shah*. New York: William Morrow, 1975; London: Weidenfeld, 1976.

Rivers, Gayle, and James Hudson. *The Teheran Contract*. Garden City, N.Y.: Doubleday, 1981.

Rizzi, Timothy. *The Phalanx Dragon*. New York: Donald I. Fine, 1994.

————. *Strike of the Cobra*. New York: Donald I. Fine, 1993.

Roberts, David. *Journey from Baghdad*. Garden City, N.Y.: Doubleday, 1969.

Roberts, Thomas A. *The Heart of the Dog*. New York: Random House, 1972.

Robertson, Charles. *The Elijah Conspiracy*. New York: Bantam, 1980.

Rogers, Barbara. *The Doomsday Scroll*. New York: Dodd Mead, 1979.

Rohmer, Richard. *Periscope Red*. New York: Beaufort, 1980.

Rohmer, Sax [pseud: Arthur Henry Sarsfield Ward]. *The Bat Flies Low*. London: Cassell, 1935; Garden City, N.Y.: Doubleday, 1935.

————. *Brood of the Witch Queen*. London: 1918.

————. *Daughter of Fu Manchu*. London: Cassell, 1931; Garden City, N.Y.: Doubleday, 1931.

————. *Egyptian Nights*. London: Hale, 1944; also published as *Bimbashi Baruk of Egypt*. New York: Robert McBride, 1944.

————. *The Mask of Fu Manchu*. Garden City, N.Y.: Doubleday, 1932; London: Cassell, 1933.

————. *Sand and Satin*. London: Jenkins, 1955; also published as *Return of Sumuru*. GM, 1954.

————. *She Who Sleeps*. London: Cassell, 1929; Garden City, N.Y.: Doubleday, 1929.

———. *Tales of East and West*. Garden City, N.Y.: Doubleday, 1922; London: Cassell, 1932.

———. *Tales of Secret Egypt*. London: Methuen, 1920.

———. *White Velvet*. New York: Doubleday,1936; London: Cassell, 1936.

Rosenberg, Joel C. *The Copper Scroll*. Wheaton: Tyndale, 2006.

———. *The Ezekiel Option*. Wheaton: Tyndale, 2005.

———. *The Last Days*. New York: Tom Doherty, 2003.

———. *The Last Jihad*. New York: Tom Doherty, 2002.

Rosenberg, Robert. *An Accidental Murder*. New York: Simon and Schuster, 1999.

———. *Crimes of the City*. New York: Simon and Schuster, 1991.

———. *House of Guilt*. New York: Scribner, 1996.

Rosenberger, Joseph. *Death Merchant #56: Afghanistan Crashout*. New York: Pinnacle, 1983.

———. *Death Merchant #18: Nightmare in Algeria*. New York: Pinnacle, 1976.

———. *Death Merchant #3: The Psychotron Plot*. New York: Pinnacle, 1972; London: Corgi, 1981.

———. *Vengeance of the Golden Hawk*. New York: Pinnacle, 1976.

Ross, Frank [pseud.: Colin Northway and Michael Eweings]. *Dead Runner*. London: Macmillan, 1977; New York: Atheneum, 1977.

Rosten, Leo. *A Most Private Intrigue*. New York: Atheneum, 1967; London: Gollancz, 1967.

Rothberg, Abraham. *The Heirs of Cain*. New York: Putnam, 1966.

Rothstein, Raphael. *The Hand of Fatima*. New York: Manor, 1979.

Roudybush, Alexandra. *A Sybaritic Death*. Garden City, N.Y.: Doubleday, 1972.

Rougvie, Cameron. *Tangier Assignment*. London: Barker, 1965; New York: Ballantine, 1965.

Rowe, John. *The Aswan Solution*. Garden City, N.Y.: Doubleday, 1979.

Royce, Kenneth. *10,000 Days*. London: Hodder, 1981; New York: McGraw Hill, 1981.

Rudd, Colin. *The Violent Dawn*. London: Hale, 1971.

Ryan, Will Harrison. *Nile Nightmare*. McKinleyville: Fithian Press, 1993.

Sachar, Howard M. *The Man on the Camel*. New York: Times Books, 1981.

Sadler, Barry. *Casca: Desert Mercenary*. New York: Charter, 1986.

Saltmarsh, Max. *Highly Inflammable*. London: Joseph, 1936; Boston: Little, 1936.

San Antonio [pseud.: Frederic Dard]. *Knights of Arabia*. London: Duckworth, 1969; New York: Paperback Library, 1970.

Sandys, James. *A Stripe for a Stripe*. London: Paul, 1938.

Sapir, Richard Ben. *The Body*. Garden City, N.Y.: Doubleday, 1983.

Saxon, Peter. *The Violent Hours*. London: Amalgamated Press, 1957.

Scanlon, Noel. *Quinn*. London: John Murray, 1973.

———. *Quinn and the Desert Oil*. London: John Murray, 1975.

Schiff, Barry and H. Fishman. *The Vatican Target*. New York: St. Martin's Press, 1979; London: Severn, 1980.

Seton, Graham [pseud.: Graham Seton Hutchinson]. *Colonel Grant's Tomorrow.* London: Butterworth, 1931; New York: Farrar, 1932.

Settle, Mary Lee. *Blood Tie.* New York: Houghton Mifflin, 1977.

Seymour, Gerald. *At Close Quarters.* London: Collins Harvill, Ltd., 1987; also published as *An Eye for an Eye.* New York: William Morrow, 1987.

———. *Condition Black.* New York: William Morrow, 1990.

———. *The Glory Boys.* London: Collins, 1976; New York: Random House, 1976.

———. *In Honor Bound.* New York: W.W. Norton, 1984.

———. *A Line in the Sand.* New York: Simon and Schuster, 1999.

———. *Running Target.* New York: William Morrow, 1989.

Seymour, Henry [pseud.: Helmut Henry Hartmann] *Intrigue in Tangier.* London: Gifford, 1958.

Shabtai, Sabi. *Five Minutes to Midnight.* New York: Delacorte, 1980; London: Dent, 1980.

Shagan, Steve. *The Formula.* New York: William Morrow, 1979; London: Joseph, 1980.

———. *Pillars of Fire.* New York: Pocket Books, 1989.

Shakespeare, L.M. *Utmost Good Faith.* New York: St. Martin's Press, 1987.

Shedley, Ethan I. *The Medusa Conspiracy.* New York: Viking Press, 1980.

Sheehan, Edward. *The Kingdom of Illusion.* New York: Random House, 1964.

Shelton, Dan. *Assault on the Venture.* Boulder: Intrigue Press, 1996.

Sheraton, Neil [pseud.: Norman Edward Mace Smith]. *Cairo Ring.* London: Hale, 1958.

Sherwood, John. *Undiplomatic Exit.* London: Hodder, 1958; Garden City, N.Y.: Doubleday, 1958.

Sigel, Efrem. *The Kermanshah Transfer.* New York: Macmillan, 1973.

Silva, Daniel. *The Kill Artist.* New York: Random House, 2000.

———. *The Mark of the Assassin.* New York: Villard, 1998.

Simon, Frank. *Veiled Threats.* Wheaton: Good News, 1996.

———. *Walls of Terror.* Wheaton: Good News, 1997.

Simon, Roger. *Raising the Dead.* New York: Villard Books, 1988.

Sinclair, Frederic. *Drop One, Carry Four.* Garden City, NY; Doubleday, 1947.

Singer, Sally M. *For Dying You Always Have Time.* New York: Putnam, 1971.

Smith, Colin. *The Cut-Out.* London: Deutsch, 1980; New York Viking, 1981.

Smith, Don. *The Libyan Contract.* New York: Award, 1974.

———. *Secret Mission: Cairo.* New York: Award, 1970.

———. *Secret Mission: Istanbul.* New York: Award, 1972.

———. *Secret Mission: Morocco.* New York: Award, 1968; London: Tandem, 1968.

Smith, Robert C. *The Flight of the Raven.* New York: Pinnacle, 1975.

———. *The Hour of the Wolf.* New York: Pinnacle, 1975.

———. *The Scream of the Dove.* New York: Pinnacle, 1975.

Smith, Wilbur. *Wild Justice.* London: Heinemann, 1979; also published as *The Delta Decision.* Garden City, NY: Doubleday, 1979.

Sofer, Barbara. *The Thirteenth Hour*. New York: Dutton, 1996.

Somerville-Large, Peter. *Couch of Earth*. London: Gollancz, 1975.

Spark, Muriel. *The Mandlebaum Gate*. New York: Knopf, 1965.

Spillane, Mickey. *The Body Lovers*. New York: Dutton, 1967; London: Barker, 1967.

St. Clair, Leonard. *A Fortune in Death*. Greenwich, Conn.: Fawcett, 1972; London: Constable, 1976.

St. James, Ian. *The Balfour Conspiracy*. New York: Atheneum, 1981.

Stacey, Tom. *Deadline*. New York: St. Martin's Press, 1989.

Stagg, James [pseud.: Gilbert Johns]. *Assignment in Beirut*. New York: Amalgamated Press, 1956.

———. *Desert Intrigue*. London: Fleetway, 1960.

Starnes, Richard. *The Flypaper War*. New York: Trident Press, 1969; London: Hutchinson, 1970.

Stead, Philip John. *In the Street of the Angel*. Art and Education Publications, 1947.

Stein, Aaron Marc. *Deadly Delight*. Garden City, N.Y.: Doubleday, 1967; London: Hutchinson, Hale, 1969.

Stein, Benjamin, and Herbert Stein. *On the Brink*. New York: Ballantine, 1977.

Stevens, G. *Do Not Go Gentle*. New York: St. Martin's Press, 1988.

Stevens, Serita and Rayanne Moore. *Red Sea, Dead Sea*. Hard Shell Word Factory, 1991.

Stevenson, William. *Booby Trap*. New York: Zebra, 1989.

Stewart, Chris. *The Kill Box*. M Evans, 1998.

———. *The Third Consequence*. New York: Evans, 2000.

Stewart, Desmond. *Leopard in the Grass*. London: Farrar, Straus, and Young, 1951.

Stewart, Mary. *The Gabriel Hounds*. London: Hoddes 1967; New York: Nil, 1967.

Stivers, Dick. *Able Team: Cairo Countdown*. New York: Worldwide Library, 1983.

Stokes, Donald. *Captive in the Night*. New York: Coward, McCann, 1951.

Stone, Robert. *Damascus Gate*. Boston, Houghton Mifflin, 1998.

Sugar, Andrew. *Israeli Commandos: The Alps Assignment*. New York: Manor, 1975.

———. *Israeli Commandos: The Aswan Assignment*. New York: Manor, 1974.

———. *Israeli Commandos: The Fireball Assignment*. New York: Manor, 1974.

———. *Israeli Commandos: The Kamikaze Plot*. New York: Manor, 1975.

Sulzberger, C. L. *The Tooth Merchant*. Chicago: Quadrangle, 1973; London: Collins, 1973.

Summers, Keith. *Design for Death*. London: Boardman, 1957.

Summerton, Margaret. *The Sand Rose*. London: Collins, 1969; Garden City. N.Y.: Doubleday, 1969.

Tabori, George. *Original Sin*. Boston: Houghton Mifflin, 1947.

Tanenbaum, Robert K. *Justice Denied*. New York: Penguin, 1994.

———. *Reckless Endangerment*. New York: Dutton, 1998.

Tannous, Peter, and Paul Rubinstein. *The Petrodollar Takeover*. New York: Putnam, 1975; London: Deutsch, 1976.

Taylor, Walker. *Murder in the Suez Canal*. London: Butterworth, 1937.

Teed, G. H. *Bottom of Suez*. London: Columbine, 1939.

Temple, Paul. *East of Algiers*. London: Hodder and Stoughton, 1959.

Thomas, Gordon. *Deadly Perfume*. London: Chapmans Publishers, Ltd., 1991; New York: HarperCollins, 1992.

Thomas, Michael M. *Green Monday*. New York: Wyndham Books, 1980; London: Hutchinson, 1980.

Thomas, Ross. *The Mordida Man*. New York: Simon and Schuster, 1981.

Thorne, E. P. *Chinese Poker*. London: Wright, 1964.

———. *They Never Came Back*. London: Wright, 1961.

———. *White Arab*. London: Wright, 1936.

Tiger, John [pseud.: Walter Wager]. *Doomdate*. New York: Popular Library, 1967.

Topol, Allan. *Fourth of July War*. New York: William Morrow, 1978.

———. *Spy Dance*. New York: Onyx, 2001.

———. *A Woman of Valor*. New York: William Morrow, 1980.

Townend, Paul. *The Road to El Saida*. London: Collins, 1961.

Tranter, Nigel [pseud.: Nye Tredgold]. *The Enduring Flame*. London: Hodder, 1957.

Traylor, Ellen Gunderson. *The Priest*. New York: Thomas Nelson, 1998.

Trevanian [pseud.: Rodney W. Whitaker]. *Shibumi*. New York: Crown, 1979; London: Granada, 1979.

Trew, Antony. *Ultimatum*. London: Collins, 1976; New York: St. Martin's Press, 1976; also published as *The Soukour Deadline*. London: Fontana, 1977.

Tripp, Miles. *Kilo Forty*. London: Macmillan, 1963; New York: Holt, 1964.

Tucker, Wilson. *This Witch*. Garden City, N.Y.: Doubleday, 1971; London: Gollancz, 1972.

Turner, Elaine. *Our Secret Is in a Well*. New York: Manor, 1977.

Tute, Warren. *The Cairo Sleeper*. London: Constable, 1977.

Tyndall, John. *Death in Lebanon*. London: Bles, 1971.

———. *Death in the Jordan*. London: Bles, 1970.

Underwood, Michael. *The Shadow Game*. London: MacDonald, 1969.

Unsworth, Barry. *Pascali's Island*. London: Joseph, 1980; also published as *The Idol Hunter*; New York: Simon and Schuster, 1980.

Vance, John Holbrook. *The Man in the Cage*. New York: Random House, 1960; London: Boardman, 1960.

Vange, Norman. *A Spy in Damascus*. London: Sampson Low, Marston, 1940.

Verner, Gerald [pseud.: Donald Stuart]. *The Faceless Ones*. London: Wright, 1964.

Wadham, Ruth. *Weekend in Baghdad*. London: Gollancz, 1958; New York: Macmillan, 1959.

Wallace, Edgar. *The Man from Morocco*. London: Longmans, 1925; also published as *The Black*; Garden City, NY: Doubleday, 1930.

Walsh, J. M. *Death at His Elbow*. London: Collins, 1941.

———. *King's Messenger*. London: Collins, 1933.

Warmbold, Jean. *The Third Way*. Sag Harbor, NY: The Permanent Press, 1990.

Warren, Christopher. *The Allah Conspiracy*. New York: Scribner's, 1981.

Waugh, Alec. *The Mule on the Minaret*. New York: Farrar, Straus, 1966.

Weatherby, W.J. *Goliath*. New York: Bantam, 1981.

Webb, Geoffrey. *Prince of the Furies*. London: Mandeville Publications, 1949.

Webster, Leslie. *The Yellow Turban*. London: Eldon, 1936.

Weigall, Arthur. *The King Who Preferred Moonlight*. London: Hutchinson and Company, 1928.

Weil, Barry. *Dossier IX*. London: H. Hamilton, 1969; New York: Bobbs Merrill, 1969.

Weinstein, Sol. *Loxfinger*. New York: Pocket Books, 1965.

———. *Matzohball: An Adventure of Hebrew Secret Agent Oy-Oy 7 Israel Bond*. New York: Pocket Books, 1966.

———. *On the Secret Service of His Majesty, the Queen: A Thrilling Adventure of Oy-Oy 7 Israel Bond*. New York: Pocket Books, 1966.

———. *You Only Live Until You Die: The Last Adventure of Oy-Oy 7 Israel Bond*. London: Trident Press, 1968.

West, Morris L. *The Tower of Babel*. London: Heinemann, 1968; New York: William Morrow, 1968.

Weston, Garrett. *The Hidden Portal*. Garden City, N.Y.: Doubleday, 1946.

Wheatley, Dennis. *The Eunuch of Stamboul*. London: Hutchinson, 1935; Boston: Little, Brown, 1935.

———. *The Quest of Julian Day*. London: Hutchinson, 1939.

———. *The Sword of Fate*. London: Hutchinson, 1941; New York: Macmillan, 1944.

White, Percy. *Cairo*. London: Constable, 1914.

White, Robin A. *Angle of Attack*. New York: Crown, 1992.

———. *The Sword of Orion*. New York: Crown, 1993

Whitney, Phyllis. *Black Amber*. New York: Appleton Century-Crofts, 1964; London: Hale, 1965.

Wilkinson, Laurence. *Appointment in Tangier*. London: Collins, 1955.

William, Peter. *Affair at Abu Mina*. London: McCrae Smith, 1944; also published as *Death at Abu Mina*. New York: Thriller Novel Classic, 1944.

Williams, Alan. *Barbouze*. London: Blond, 1964; also published as *The False Beards*. New York: Harper and Row, 1963.

———. *Long Run South*. London: Blond, 1962; Boston: Little Brown, 1962.

———. *Shah-Mak*. London: Blond, 1976; also published as *A Bullet for the Shah*. New York: Coward, McCann, 1976.

Williamson, Sherman. *The Glory Trap*. London: New English Library, 1977; New York: Walker, 1977.

Williamson, Tony. *The Doomsday Contract*. London: Collins, 1977; New York: Simon and Schuster, 1978.

Wilson, Ger. *Phoenix Force: Aswan Hellbox*. New York: Worldwide Library, 1983.

Wingate, William [pseud.: Ronald Ivan Grbich]. *Bloodbath*. London: Hutchinson, 1978; New York: St. Martin's Press, 1980.

Winston, Peter. *The Adjusters: Assignment to Bahrein*. New York: Award, 1967; London: Tandem, 1967.

Wood, Barbara. *Hounds and Jackals*. Garden City, N.Y.: Doubleday, 1978; London: Eyre, 1979.

Wood, Clement. *Death in Ankara*. New York: Mystery House, 1944.

Wynne, Fred E. *A Mediterranean Mystery*. London: Jenkins, 1923; New York: Duffield and Company, 1923.

Yerby, Frank. *The Voyage Unplanned*. New York: Dial Press, 1974.

York, Andrew. *The Combination*. Garden City: Doubleday, 1983.

Young, George. *The Man Called Lenz*. London: Hutchinson, 1954; New York: Coward, McCann, 1955.

Zeno [pseud.]. *Grab*. London: Macmillan, 1970; New York: Stein and Day, 1970.

Zeyv, Sender. *Aleph Shin—A Novel for the Sixth Millennium*. Lakewood, N.J.: TMS Publishing Company, 2000.

Nonfiction Works
Cited and Consulted

Reference Works

Hagen, Ordean. *Who Done It? A Guide to Detective, Mystery, and Suspense Fiction.* New York: Bowker, 1969.

Herbert, Rosemary, ed. *The Oxford Companion to Crime and Mystery Writing.* New York: Oxford University Press, 1999.

Hubin, Allen J. *Crime Fiction 1749–1980: A Comprehensive Bibliography.* New York: Garland, 1984.

———. *Crime Fiction II: A Comprehensive Bibliography 1949– 1990.* New York: Garland, 1994.

McCormick, Donald and Katy Fletcher. *Spy Fiction: A Connoisseur's Guide.* New York: Facts on File, 1990.

McCormick, D. *Who's Who in Spy Fiction.* New York: Taplinger, 1977.

Polmar, Norman and Thomas B. Allen. *Spy Book: The Encyclopedia of Espionage.* New York: Random House, 1997.

Reilly, John M. *Twentieth-Century Crime and Mystery Writers.* New York: St. Martin's Press, 1980.

Smith, Myron J., Jr. *Cloak and Dagger Bibliography: An Annotated Guide to Spy Fiction 1937–1975.* Metuchen, N.J.: Scarecrow Press, 1976; 2nd ed. Santa Barbara: ABC Clio, 1982.

Smith, Myron J., Jr. and Terry White. *Cloak and Dagger Fiction: An Annotated Guide to Spy Thrillers.* 3rd edition. Westport: Greenwood Press, 1995.

———. *Cloak and Dagger Fiction: An Annotated Guide to Spy Thrillers.* 2nd edition. Santa Barbara: ABC Clio, Inc., 1982.

Books and Articles

Aisenberg, Nadya. *A Common Spring: Crime Novel and Classic.* Bowling Green, Ohio: Bowling Green University Popular Press, 1979.

Allen, Dick and David Chacko. *Detective Fiction: Crime and Compromise.* New York: Harcourt Brace Jovanovich, 1974.

Allen, L. David. "Sax Rohmer," in E. F. Bleiler, ed. *Supernatural Fiction Writers: Fantasy and Horror.* New York: Charles Scribner's Sons, 1985.

Allport, Gordon W. *The Nature of Prejudice.* 25th ed. Reading, Mass.: Addison Wesley, 1981.

Al Shailkh-Alif, Anas S. "Islam in British and American Popular Fiction 1970–1996: Conspiracy of Fashion." *The Diplomat.* October, 1996, 44–49.

Ambler, Eric, ed. "Introduction," *To Catch A Spy: An Anthology of Favorite Spy Stories.* New York: Atheneum, 1965.

Anderson, David M. and David Killingray. *Policing the Empire: Government, Authority, and Control, 1830–1940.* Manchester: Manchester University Press, 1991.

Antonini, Fausto. "The Psychoanalysis of 007," in Oreste del Buono and Umberto Eco., eds. *The Bond Affair.* London: Macdonald, 1966.

Apostolou, John L and Martin H. Greenberg, eds. *Murder in Japan: Japanese Stories of Crime Fiction.* New York: December Books, 1987.

Aronoff, Myron J. *The Spy Novels of John le Carré: Balancing Ethics and Politics.* New York: St. Martin's Press, 1999.

Atkins, John. *The British Spy Novel: Styles in Treachery.* London: John Calder, 1984.

Aydelotte, William. "The Detective Story as a Historical Source," *Yale Review* 39(1949–1950), 76–95.

Bacevich, Andrew J. *The New American Militarism: How Americans Are Seduced by War.* New York: Oxford University Press, 2005.

Ball, John, ed. *The Mystery Story.* New York: Penguin, 1978.

Barber, Benjamin R. *Jihad vs McWorld.* New York: Ballantine, 1995.

Barkun, Michael. *The Culture of Conspiracy: Apocalyptic Visions in Contemporary America.* Berkeley: University of California Press, 2003.

Barzun, Jacques. "Meditations on the Literature of Spying," *American Scholar* 34(1965), 167–178.

Barzun, Jacques and W.H. Taylor. *A Catalogue of Crime.* New York: Harper and Row, 1971.

Baudet, Henri. *Paradise on Earth: Some Thoughts on European Images of Non-European Man.* New Haven: Yale University Press, 1965.

Bedell, Jeanne F. "Romance, Adventure and Mechanization: Attitudes Towards Technology in Espionage Fiction," *Lamar Journal of the Humanities* 5(1979), 54–62.

———. "Romance and Moral Certainty: The Espionage Fiction of John Buchan," *The Midwest Quarterly* 22(1981), 230–241.

Bennett, Tony and Janet Woollacott. *Bond and Beyond: The Political Career of a Popular Hero.* London: Macmillan Education, Ltd., 1987.

Bettleheim, Bruno. *The Uses of Enchantment: The Meaning and Importance of Fairy Tales.* New York: Vintage, 1977.

Bhabha, Homi. *The Location of Culture.* London: Routledge, 1994.

Birner, Louis. "The James Bond Phenomenon," *Journal of Contemporary Psychotherapy* 1(1968):13–18.

Bjorgo, Tore, ed. *Terror from the Extreme Right.* London: Frank Cass, 1995.

Black, Ian and Benny Morris. *Israel's Secret Wars: A History of Israel's Intelligence Services.* New York: Grove and Weidenfeld, 1991.

Blodgett, Jan. *Protestant Evangelical Literary Culture and Contemporary Society.* Westport: Greenwood Press, 1997.

Bloom, Clive. *Cult Fiction: Popular Reading and Pulp Theory.* New York: St. Martin's Press, 1996.

Boyer, Paul. *When Time Shall Be No More: Prophecy Belief in Modern American Culture.* Cambridge: Harvard University Press, 1992.

Bragg, Melvyn. "*The Little Drummer Girl:* An Interview with John LeCarré." In Matthew J. Bruccoli and Judith S. Baughman, eds. *Conversations with John LeCarré.* Jackson: University of Mississippi Press, 2004.

Brandt, Bruce E. "Reflections of the 'Paranoid Style' in the Current Suspense Novel. *Clues* 3(1982), 62–69.

Brantlinger, Patrick. *Rule of Darkness: British Literature and Imperialism, 1830–1914.* Ithaca: Cornell University Press, 1988.

Breen, Jon L. and Martin Harry Greenberg. *Murder off the Rack: Critical Studies of Ten Paperback Masters.* Metuchen: The Scarecrow Press, 1989.

Breines, Paul. "The Rambowitz Syndrome," *Tikkun* 5(1990), 17–20.

———. *Tough Jews: Political Fantasies and the Moral Dilemma of American Jewry.* New York: Basic Books, 1990.

Briney, Robert, "Death Rays, Demons, and Worms Unknown to Science," in John Ball, ed. *The Mystery Story.* New York: Penguin, 1976.

———. "Sax Rohmer: An Informal Survey," in Francis M. Nevins, Jr., ed., *The Mystery Writer's Art.* Bowling Green: Bowling Green University Popular Press, 1970.

Briney, R.E. and Francis M. Nevins, Jr., eds. *Multiplying Villainies: Selected Mystery Criticism 1942–1968 by Anthony Boucher.* Boston: Bouchercon, 1973.

Bristow, Joseph. *Empire Boys: Adventures in a Man's World.* London: Harper Collins Academic, 1991.

Brod, Harry. "Of Mice and Supermen: Images of Jewish Masculinity," In T. M. Rudavsky, ed. *Gender and Judaism: The Transformation of Tradition.* New York: New York University Press, 1995.

Brodkin, Karen. *How Jews Became White Folks and What That Says about Race in America.* New Brunswick: Rutgers University Press, 1999.

Bronowski, J. *The Face of Violence*. New York: World, 1967.

Brown, Judith M. and Wm Roger Louis, eds. *The Oxford History of the British Empire: The Twentieth Century*. Oxford: Oxford University Press, 1999.

Buchan, James. "*Greenmantle*, John Buchan and the Near East," *The John Buchan Journal* (1992), 2–11.

Buchan, John. *Nelson's History of the War. Vol. XIII: The Position at Sea, the Fall of Erzerum, and the First Battle of Verdun*. London: Thomas Nelson and Sons, Ltd., 1916.

Butler, William Vivian. *The Durable Desperadoes*. London: Macmillan, 1973.

Byrd, Max. "The Detective Detected: From Sophocles to Ross MacDonald," *Yale Review* 64(1974).

Cannadine, David. "Fantasy, Ian Fleming and the Realities of Escapism," in David Cannadine, ed. *In Churchill's Shadow: Confronting the Past in Modern Britain*. New York : Oxford University Press, 2003.

————. "James Bond and the Decline of England," *Encounter* 53(1979), 46–55.

Carvajal, Doreen. "The Spy Who Fell Onto the Remainder Table," *The New York Times*. December 22, 1998.

Castle, Kathryn. *Britannia's Children: Reading Colonialism Through Children's Books and Magazines*. Manchester: Manchester University Press, 1996.

Caton, Steven C. *Lawrence of Arabia: A Film's Anthopology*. Berkeley: University of California Press, 1999.

Cawelti, John G. *Adventure, Mystery, and Romance: Formula Stories as Art and Popular Culture*. Chicago: University of Chicago Press, 1976.

Cawelti, John G. and Bruce A. Rosenberg. *The Spy Story*. Chicago: University of Chicago Press, 1987.

Çelik, Zeynep. *Empire, Architecture, and the City: French-Ottoman Encounters, 1830–1914*. Seattle: University of Washington Press, 2008.

Chabon, Michael. *The Amazing Adventures of Kavalier and Clay*. New York: Picador, 2000.

Chandler, Raymond. "The Simple Art of Murder," *The Atlantic Monthly*. December, 1944.

Chapman, James. *License to Thrill*. New York: Columbia University Press, 2000.

Chastain, Thomas "Q. Who Cares Who Killed Roger Ackroyd? A. Millions of Readers Do," *Publishers Weekly* 213(1978), 58.

Clark, Arthur. "Agatha Christie: Mysteries and the Middle East." *Aramco World* (1990), 45–48.

Cohen, Michael J. "The Strategic Role of the Middle East after The War," in Michael J. Cohen and Martin Kolinsky, eds. *Demise of the British Empire in the Middle East: Britain's Responses to Nationalist Movements 1943–1955*. London: Frank Cass, 1998.

Cooper, Artemis. *Cairo in the War 1939–1945*. London: Hamish Hamilton, 1989.

Crider, Bill. "The Western," in Rosemary Herbert, ed. *The Oxford Companion to Crime and Mystery Writing*. New York: Oxford University Press, 1999.

Curl, James Stevens. *Egyptomania: The Egyptian Revival—A Recurring Theme in the History of Taste.* Manchester: Manchester University Press, 1994.

Daniel, Norman. *Islam and the West: The Making of an Image.* Edinburgh: Edinburgh University Press, 1960.

———. *Islam, Europe and Empire.* Edinburgh: Edinburgh University Press, 1966.

Daniell, David. *The Interpreter's House: A Critical Assessment of John Buchan.* London: Thomas Nelson and Sons, Ltd., 1975.

Dann, Uri and Eli Landau. *The Mossad: Israel's Secret Intelligence Service.* London: Paddington Press, 1978.

Darnton, Robert. "The Meaning of Mother Goose," *The New York Review of Books.* February 2, 1984.

Davis, Curtis Carroll. "The Figure Behind the Landscape: The Emergence of the Secret Agent in British Belles Lettres" *The Southern Humanities Review* 1(1967): 223–235.

Davis, Kenneth C. *The Two Bit Culture: The Paperbacking of America.* Boston: Houghton Mifflin, 1984.

Dawson, Graham. *Soldier Heroes: British Adventure, Empire and the Imaginings of Masculinities.* London: Routledge, 1994.

Deacon, Richard. *The Israeli Secret Service.* New York: Taplinger, 1977.

De Camp, Sprague. *Literary Swordsmen Sorcerers: The Masters of Heroic Fantasy.* Sauk City, Wisconsin: Arkham House, 1976.

Del Buono, Oreste, and Umberto Eco, eds. *The Bond Affair.* London: Macdonald, 1966.

Denning, Michael. *Cover Stories: Narrative Ideology in the British Spy Thriller.* London: Routledge and Kegan Paul, 1987.

Dixon, Wheeler Winston. "The Colonial Vision of Edgar Wallace," *The Journal of Popular Culture.* 32 (Summer 1998): 121–139.

Drew, Bernard A. "Adventurer and Adventuress," in Rosemary Herbert, ed. *The Oxford Companion To Crime and Mystery Writing.* New York: Oxford University Press, 1999.

Dubose, Mike S. "Holding Out for the Heroic: Reaganism, Comic Book Vigilantes, and Captain America," *The Journal of Popular Culture* 40 (2007), 915–935.

Durgnat, A. "Spies and Ideologies" *Cinema* 2(1969): 5–13.

East, Andy. "The Spy in the Dark: A History of Espionage Fiction," *The Armchair Detective* 19(Winter 1986), 23–40.

Eco, Umberto. "James Bond: une combinatoire narrative," *Communications 8* (1966), 77–93.

Edwards, David B. "Mad Mullahs and Englishmen: Discourse in The Colonial Encounter," *Comparative Studies in Society and History* 31 (1989), 649–670.

Eisenberg, Dennis and Menachem Portugali. *Operation Uranium Ship.* London: Corgi, 1978.

El Wakil, Safia. "Egypt in American and British Popular Fiction." *Images of Egypt in Twentieth Century Literature.* Proceedings—International Symposium on Comparative Literature, 1989. Cairo, 1991.

Fagan, Brian M. *The Rape of the Nile: Tomb Robbers, Tourists and Archaeologists in Egypt*. London: Moyer Bell, 1975.

Fischer, Fritz. *Germany's Aims in the First World War*. New York: W.W. Norton, 1967.

Fletcher, Katy. "Evolution of the Modern American Spy Novel," *Journal of Contemporary History* 22 (1987), 319–331.

Follett, Ken. "The Spy as Hero and Villain." In Lucy Freeman, ed. *The Murder Mystique: Crime Writers on Their Art*. New York: Frederick Ungar, 1982.

Frayling, Christopher. "Sax Rohmer and the Devil Doctor," *London Magazine* 13(1973), 65–80.

Freeman, Lucy. *The Murder Mystique: Crime Writers on Their Art*. New York: Frederick Ungar, 1982.

Freeth, Zahra and Victor Winstone. *Explorers of Arabia: From the Renaissance to the Victorian Era*. New York: Holmes and Meier, 1978.

Frykholm, Amy Johnson. *Rapture Culture: Left Behind in Evangelical America*. New York: Oxford University Press, 2004.

Gal, Allon, ed. *Envisioning Israel: The Changing Ideals and Images of North American Jews*. Jerusalem: Magnes Press, 1996.

Gasiorowski, Mark. "The 1953 *Coup d'Etat* in Iran," *International Journal of Middle East Studies* 19 (1987), 261–286.

Genter, Robert. "With Great Power Comes Great Responsibility": Cold War Culture and the Birth of Marvel Comics," *The Journal of Popular Culture* 40 (2007), 953–978.

Gerges, Fawaz. *America and Political Islam: Clash of Cultures Or Clash of Interests?* New York: Cambridge University Press, 1999.

Ghareeb, Edmund, ed. *Split Vision: The Portrayal of Arabs in the America Media*. Washington,D.C.: American Arab Affairs Council, 1983.

Gibson, James William. *Warrior Dreams: Violence and Manhood in Post-Vietnam America*. New York: Hill and Wang, 1994.

Gilbert, Michael. "The Spy in Fact and Fiction," in J. Ball, ed. *The Mystery Story*. New York: Penguin, 1978.

Glover, David and Cora Kaplan. "Guns in the House of Culture? Crime Fiction and the Politics of the Popular," in Lawrence Grossberg, Cary Nelson, and Paula A. Treichler, ed. *Cultural Studies*. New York: Routledge, 1992.

Goh, Robbie B.H. "Peter O'Donnell, Race Relations and National Identity: The Dynamics of Representation in 1960s and 1970s Britain," *Journal of Popular Culture* 32(Spring 1999), 29–43.

Goode, Greg. "The Oriental in Crime Fiction: The Sinister Oriental." *The Armchair Detective* 15(1982).

Gorenberg, Gershom. *The Accidental Empire: Israel and the Birth of the Settlements 1967–1977*. New York: Times Books, 2006.

———. "Book Review: *The Remnant*." *The American Prospect* 13 (September 23, 2002).

Greco, Albert. *The Book Publishing Industry.* 2nd ed. Lawrence Erlbaum, 2004.

Green, Martin. "John Buchan," in Rosemary Herbert, ed. *The Oxford Companion to Crime and Mystery Writing.* New York: Oxford University Press, 1999.

———. *Dreams of Adventure, Deeds of Empire.* London: Routledge and Kegan Paul, 1980.

———. *Transatlantic Patterns: Cultural Comparisons of England with America.* New York: Basic Books, 1977.

Greenberger, Allen J. *The British Image of India: A Study in the Literature of Imperialism 1880–1960.* London: Oxford University Press, 1969.

Grenander, M.E. "The Heritage of Cain: Crime in American Fiction." *The Annals of the American Academy of Political and Social Science.* 423(1976), 47–66.

Grieves, Keith. "*Nelson's History of the War:* John Buchan as a Contemporary Military Historian 1915–22," *Journal of Contemporary History* 28 (1993), 533–551.

Hagen, Gottfried. "German Heralds of Holy War: Orientalists And Applied Oriental Studies," *Comparative Studies of South Asia, Africa and the Middle East* 24 (2004), 145–162.

Hall, Stuart and Paddy Whannel. *The Popular Arts.* London: Hutchinson, 1964.

Harper, Ralph. *The World of the Thriller.* Cleveland: The Press of Case Western Reserve University, 1969.

Hawkins, Harriett. *Classics and Trash: Traditions and Taboos in High Literature and Popular Modern Genres.* New York: Harvester, 1990.

Haycraft, Howard. *The Art of the Mystery Story: A Collection of Critical Essays.* New York: Grosset and Dunlap, 1946.

Henissart, Paul. "Of Spies and Stories." *The Writer* 91(1978).

Hodson, Joel C. *Lawrence of Arabia and American Culture: The Making of a Transatlantic Legend.* Westport: Greenwood Press, 1995.

Hofstadter, Richard. *The Paranoid Style in American Politics and Other Essays.* Chicago: University of Chicago Press, 1965.

Holquist, Michael. "Whodunit and Other Questions: Metaphysical Detective Stories in Post-War Fiction," *New Literary History* 31(1971), 135–156.

Hopkins, Joel. "An Interview with Eric Ambler." *Journal of Popular Culture* 9(1975), 285–293.

Hopkirk, Peter. *Like Hidden Fire: The Plot to Bring Down the British Empire.* New York: Kodansha International, 1994.

———. *The Great Game: The Struggle for Empire in Central Asia.* New York: Kodansha International, 1994.

Hoppenstand, Gary C. *In Search of the Paper Tiger: A Sociological Perspective of Myth, Formula, and the Mystery Genre in the Entertainment Print Mass Media.* Bowling Green: Bowling Green State University Popular Press, 1987.

Hopwood, Derek and Diana Grimwood Jones. "Servants of the Empire: Sidelights on the British in Egypt," in B. C. Bloomfield, ed. *Middle East Studies and Libraries: A Felicitation Volume For Professor J.D. Pearson.* London: Mansell, 1980.

Howard, Michael. "Empire, Race and War in Pre-1914 Britain" in Hugh Lloyd-Jones, Valerie Pearl, and Blair Worden, eds. *History and Imagination: Essays in Honour of H.R. Trevor-Roper*. London: Duckworth, 1981.

Howarth, Patrick. *Play Up and Play the Game: The Heroes of Popular Fiction*. London: Methuen, 1973.

Hugo, Grant. "The Political Influence of the Thriller," *Contemporary Review* 221(1972), 284–289.

Isaacs, Harold R. *Scratches on Our Minds: American Views of China and India*. Armonk, New York: Sharpe, Inc., 1980.

Jeffords, Susan. *The Remasculinization of America: Gender and the Vietnam War*. Bloomington: Indiana University Press, 1989.

———. *Hard Bodies: Hollywood Masculinity in the Reagan Era*. New Brunswick: Rutgers University Press, 1994.

Jewett, Robert and John Shelton Lawrence. *Captain America and the Crusade Against Evil: The Dilemma of Zealous Nationalism*. Grand Rapids, MI: William B. Eerdmans Publishing Company, 2003.

Jones, Gerard. *Men of Tomorrow: Geeks, Gangsters and the Birth of the Comic Book*. New York: Basic Books, 2004.

Juergensmeyer, Mark. *Terror in the Mind of God: The Global Rise of Religious Violence*. Berkeley: University of California Press, 2000.

Kabbani, Rana. *Europe's Myths of Orient*. Bloomington: University of Indiana Press, 1986.

Kaplan, Arie. *From Krakow to Krypton: Jews and Comic Books*. Philadelphia: Jewish Publication Society, 2008.

Karabell, Zachary. "Shepheard's Hotel," in Reeva S. Simon, Philip Mattar, and Richard Bulliet, eds. *Encyclopedia of the Modern Middle East*. New York: Macmillan, 1996.

Keating, H.R.E. *WHODUNIT: A Guide to Crime, Suspense, and Spy Fiction*. New York: Van Nostrand Reinhold, 1982.

Kelly, George. "Paperbacks," in Rosemary Herbert, ed. *The Oxford Companion to Crime and Mystery Writing*. New York: Oxford University Press, 1999.

Kinzer, Stephen. *All the Shah's Men: An American Coup and the Roots of Middle East Terror*. Hoboken: John Wiley and Sons, Inc., 2003.

Kitteredge, William and Steven M. Krauzer. "The Evolution of the Great American Detective: The Reader as Detective Hero." *The Armchair Detective* 11(1978): 318–333.

Klapp, Orrin E. *Heroes, Villains and Fools: The Changing American Character*. Englewood Cliffs, N.J.: Prentice-Hall, 1962.

Klein, Gerard. "A Petition by Agents of the Dominant Culture for The Dismissal of Science Fiction." *Science Fiction Studies* 7(1980), 115–123.

Klein, Kathleen Gregory. *The Woman Detective: Gender and Genre*. 2nd ed. Urbana: University of Illinois Press, 1995.

Klinghoffer, Judith A. *Vietnam, Jews and the Middle East: Unintended Consequences.* New York: St. Martin's Press, 1998.

Knight, Stephen. *Form and Ideology in Crime Fiction.* London: Macmillan, 1980.

Knox, Father Ronald, ed. *The Best English Detective Stories of 1928.* New York, 1928.

Kolinsky, Martin. *Britain's War in the Middle East: Strategy and Diplomacy 1936–1942.* New York: St. Martin's Press, 1999.

Kuklick, Bruce. "Myth and Symbol in American Studies," *American Quarterly* 24(1972), 435–450.

La Farge, Christopher. "Mickey Spillane and his Bloody Hammer," in Bernard Rosenberg and David Manning White, eds. *Mass Culture: The Popular Arts in America.* Glencoe, Illinois: The Free Press, 1960.

Lamy, Philip. "Millennialism in the Mass Media: The Case of *Soldier of Fortune* Magazine," *Journal for the Scientific Study of Religion* 31 (1992), 408–424.

Landrum, Larry N., et al. *Dimensions of Detective Fiction.* Bowling Green, Ohio: The Popular Press, 1976.

Laqueur, Walter. "Le Carré's Fantasies," *Commentary* 75(1983), 62–67.

Larsen, M.T. "Orientalism and the Ancient Near East," *Culture and History* 2(1987), 96–115.

Lawrence, John Shelton and Robert Jewett. *The Myth of the American Superhero.* Grand Rapids, MI: William B. Eerdmans Publishing Company, 2002.

Lawrence, T.E. *The Seven Pillars of Wisdom.* New York: Dell, 1962.

Lee, Robert G. *Orientals: Asian Americans in Popular Culture.* Philadelphia: Temple University Press, 1999.

Lekachman, Robert. "Super Thrillers and Superpowers," *The New York Times Book Review* (February 19, 1984).

———. "The Thriller Connection." *The Nation* 231 (1980), 677–678.

Lesch, David W. *1979: The Year that Shaped the Modern Middle East.* Boulder: Westview Press, 2001.

Leuchtenberg, William E. "The American Perception of the Arab World." In George Atiyeh, ed. *Arab and American Culture.* Washington, DC: American Enterprise Institute, 1977.

Levine, Lawrence W. "AHR Forum: The Folklore of Industrial Society: Popular Culture and Its Audiences," *American Historical Review* 97(1992), 1369–1399.

Lewis, George H. "Spy Fiction American Style." *Journal of Communication* 25(1975), 132–137.

Lipset, Seymour Martin and Earl Rabb. *The Politics of Unreason: Right-wing Extremism in America 1790–1970.* New York: Harper and Row, 1970.

Little, Douglas. *American Orientalism: The United States and the Middle East since 1945.* Chapel Hill: University of North Carolina Press, 2002.

Lownie, Andrew. *John Buchan: The Presbyterian Cavalier.* Rev. ed. Boston: David R. Godine, 2003.

Louis, Wm Roger. "The British Withdrawal from the Gulf, 1967–71," *The Journal of Imperial and Commonwealth History* 31 (2003), 83–108.

MacKenzie, John M. "Heroic Myths of Empire" in John M. MacKenzie, ed., *Popular Imperialism and the Military 1850–1950*. Manchester: Manchester University Press, 1992.

————. *Orientalism: History, Theory and the Arts*. Manchester: Manchester University Press, 1995.

————. "The Popular Culture of Empire in Britain," in Judith M. Brown and Wm Roger Louis, eds. *Oxford History of the British Empire: The Twentieth Century*. Oxford: Oxford University Press, 1999.

————. *Propaganda and Empire: The Manipulation of British Public Opinion 1880–1960*. Manchester: Manchester University Press, 1984.

————. "T. E. Lawrence: The Myth and the Message" in Robert Giddings, ed. *Literature and Imperialism*. London: Macmillan, 1991.

Mahdy, Hossam M. "Travellers, Colonisers and Conservationists," in Paul Starkey and Janet Starkey, eds. *Travellers in Egypt*. London: I.B. Tauris, 1998.

Mangen, J.A. "'The Grit of Our Forefathers': Invented Traditions, Propaganda and Imperialism," in John M. MacKenzie, ed. *Imperialism and Popular Culture*. Manchester: Manchester University Press, 1986.

Mart, Michelle. "Tough Guys and American Cold War Policy Images of Israel 1948–1960," *Diplomatic History* 20 (1996), 357–380.

McAlister, Melani. *Epic Encounters: Culture, Media, and U.S. Interests in the Middle East, 1945–2000*. Berkeley: University of California Press, 2001.

McAllister, Matthew P., Edward H. Sewell, Jr., and Ian Gordon. *Comics and Ideology*. New York: Peter Lang, 2001.

————. "Prophecy, Politics, and the Popular: The *Left Behind* Series and Christian Fundamentalism's New World Order," *The South Atlantic Quarterly* 102 (2003), 773–798.

McCarus, Ernest. *The Development of Arab-American Identity*. Ann Arbor: University of Michigan Press, 1994.

McDowell, Edwin. "James Bond Making 'Wild Comeback'," *The New York Times*. June 5, 1982.

————. "Paperback Publishers: Survival Versus Taste." *New York Times*. December 29, 1983.

————. "Western Novels Ride High Again." *The New York Times*. September 16, 1985.

Meade, Walter Russell. *Special Providence: American Foreign Policy and How It Changed the World*. New York: Routledge, 2002.

Melka, R.L. "Max Frieherr von Oppenheim: Sixty Years of Scholarship and Political Intrigue in the Middle East," *Middle Eastern Studies* 9 (1973), 81–93.

Melvin, David Skene. "The Secret Eye: The Spy in Literature; The Evolution of Espionage Literature—A Survey of the History and Development of the Spy and Espionage Novel," *Pacific Quarterly* 3 (1978), 11–26.

Merry, Bruce. *Anatomy of the Spy Thriller*. Montreal: McGill-Queens University Press, 1977.

Meyers, Annette, "Murder is Their Business." *The Armchair Detective* 38(1997).

Meyers, Jeffrey. *Fiction and the Colonial Experience.* Totowa, N.J.: Rowman and Littlefield, 1973.

Michalak, Laurence. "The Arab in American Crime: A Century of Otherness," *Cineaste* 17(1989), 3–9.

———. "Cruel and Unusual: Negative Images of Arabs in Popular American Culture." *ADC American-Arab Anti-Discrimination Committee Issues.* January, 1984.

Mitchell, Timothy. *Colonizing Egypt.* Berkeley: University of California Press, 1991.

Mitgang, Herbert. "The Thrilling Eric Ambler." *The New York Times Book Review.* September 13, 1981.

Moore, Deborah Dash. "From David to Goliath: American Representations of Jews around the Six Day War," in Eli Lederhendler, ed. *The Six Day War and World Jewry.* University Press of Maryland, 2000.

Morgenthau, Henry. *Secrets of the Bosphorus.* 2nd ed. London: Hutchinson and Company, 1918.

Most, Glenn W. and William Stowe. *The Poetics of Murder: Detective Fiction and Literary Theory.* New York: Harcourt Brace Jovanovich, 1983.

Mukerji, Chandra and Michael Schudson, eds., *Rethinking Popular Culture: Contemporary Perspectives in Cultural Studies.* Berkeley: University of California Press, 1991.

Murray, Will. "The Executioner Phenomenon," in Jon L. Breen and Martin Harry Greenberg,eds. *Murder Off the Rack: Critical Studies of Ten Paperback Masters.* Metuchen: The Scarecrow Press, 1989.

———. "The Saga of Nick Carter, Killmaster," *The Armchair Detective* 15(1982): 316–329.

Nasir, Sari J. *The Arabs and the English.* London: Longman, 1979.

Neilson, Keith. "Dennis Wheatley (1897–1977)" in E.F. Bleiler, ed. *Supernatural Fiction Writers: Fantasy and Horror.* New York: Charles Scribner's Sons, 1985.

Neuse, Steven M. "Teaching Political Science with Chillers and Thrillers," *Teaching Political Science* 7(1980), 153–167.

Nevins, Francis M., Jr., ed. *The Mystery Writer's Art.* Bowling Green: Bowling Green University Press, 1970.

Nye, Russel. *The Unembarrassed Muse: The Popular Arts in America.* New York: Dial Press, 1970.

O'Donnell, Peter. "Becoming Modesty," in Dilys Winn, ed., *Murder Ink: The Mystery Reader's Companion.* New York: Workman Publishing, 1977.

Oppenheim, Jean-Marc R. "The Twilight of a Colonial Ethos: The Alexandria Sporting Club 1890–1956. PhD Dissertation, Columbia University, 1991.

Ossman, Susan. *Picturing Casablanca: Portraits of Power in a Modern City.* Berkeley: University of California Press, 1994.

Palmer, Jerry. *Potboilers: Methods, Concepts and Case Studies in Popular Fiction.* London: Routledge, 1991.

————. *Thrillers: Genesis and Structure of a Popular Genre*. London: Edward Arnold, 1978.

Panek, LeRoy L. *Probable Cause: Crime Fiction in America*. Bowling Green: Bowling Green State University Popular Press, 1990.

————. *The Special Branch: The British Spy Novel 1890–1980*. Bowling Green: Bowling Green University Popular Press, 1981.

Parry, Benita. *Delusions and Discoveries: Studies on India in the British Imagination*. Berkeley: University of California Press,1972.

Pawling, Christopher, ed. *Popular Fiction and Social Change*. London: Macmillan Press, 1984.

Peters, Rudolph. *Jihad in Classical and Modern Islam: A Reader*. Princeton: Marcus Wiener, 1996.

Powers, Richard Gid. "J. Edgar Hoover and the Detective Hero." *Journal of Popular Culture* 9(1975), 257–278.

Price, Thomas J. "Spy Stories, Espionage and the Public in the Twentieth Century," *Journal of Popular Culture* 30(1996), 84–89.

Pryce-Jones, David. "A Demonological Fiction: *The Little Drummer Girl* by John le Carré." *The New Republic*. April 18, 1983.

Pyrhonen, Heta. *Murder from an Academic Angle: An Introduction to the Study of the Detective Narrative*. Columbia, South Carolina: Camden House, 1994.

Radway, Janice A. *A Feeling for Books: The Book-of-the-Month Club, Literary Taste, and Middle Class Desire*. Chapel Hill: University of North Carolina Press, 1997.

————. *Reading the Romance: Women, Patriarchy, and Popular Literature*. Chapel Hill: University of North Carolina Press, 1984.

Rausch, G. Jay and Diane K. Rausch. "Developments in Espionage Fiction." *Kansas Quarterly* 10(1978), 71–82.

Ray, P.E. "The Villain in the Spy Novels of John Buchan." *English Literature in Transition* 24(1981), 81–90.

Reid, Donald Malcolm. "Cromer and the Classics: Imperialism, Nationalism and the Greco-Roman Past In Modern Egypt," *Middle Eastern Studies* 32(1996), 1–29.

————. "French Egyptology and the Architecture of Orientalism: Deciphering the Façade of Cairo's Egyptian Museum," in L. Carl Brown and Matthew S. Gordon, eds. *Franco-Arab Encounters: Studies in Memory of David C. Gordon*. Beirut: American University of Beirut, 1996.

Reilly, John M. "Publishing, History of the Books," in Rosemary Herbert ed. *The Oxford Companion to Crime and Mystery Writing*. New York: Oxford University Press, 1999.

Reimer, Michael J. "Colonial Bridgehead: A Social and Spatial Change in Alexandria 1850–1882," *International Journal of Middle East Studies* 20 (1988), 531–553.

————. "Urban Government and Administration in Egypt, 1805–1914," *Die Welt des Islams* 39(1999), 289–318.

Reitz, Caroline. *Detecting the Nation: Fictions of Detection and the Imperial Venture.* Columbia: The Ohio State University Press, 2004.

Richards, Jeffrey. "Popular Imperialism and the Image of the Army in Juvenile Literature" in John M. MacKenzie, ed. *Popular Imperialism and the Military 1850–1950.* Manchester: Manchester University Press, 1992.

Richelson, Jeffrey T. *A Century of Spies: Intelligence in the Twentieth Century.* New York: Oxford University Press, 1995.

———. "The Mossad Imagined: the Israeli Secret Service in Film and Fiction," *International Journal of Intelligence and Counterintelligence* 20 (2007), 136–166.

Richler, Mordecai. "James Bond Unmasked" in Bernard Rosenberg and David Manning White, eds. *Mass Culture Revisited.* New York: Van Nostrand Reinhold, 1971.

Roberts, Thomas J. *On Aesthetics of Junk Fiction.* Athens: University of Georgia Press, 1990.

Robinson, Jane. *Unsuitable for Ladies: An Anthology of Women Travellers.* Oxford: Oxford University Press, 1995.

Rockwell, Joan. "Normative Attitudes of Spies in Fiction" in Bernard Rosenberg and David Manning White, eds. *Mass Culture Revisited.* New York: Van Nostrand Reinhold, 1971.

Rodenbeck, Max. *Cairo: The City Victorious.* New York: Knopf, 1999.

Rodinson, Maxime. *Europe and the Mystique of Islam.* Translated by Roger Veinus. Seattle: University of Seattle Press, 1987.

Rosen, Judith. "Sleuthing in the Stores," *Publishers Weekly.* April 22, 2002.

Rosenberg, Bernard and David Manning White. *Mass Culture: The Popular Arts in America.* Glencoe, Illinois: The Free Press, 1960.

———. *Mass Culture Revisited.* New York: Van Nostrand Reinhold, 1971.

Rosenthal, Michael. *The Character Factory: Baden-Powell and the Origins of the Boy Scout Movement.* New York: Pantheon Books, 1984.

Roucek, Joseph S. "The American Detective, Murder and Violent Novel in Its Sociological Aspects," *Indian Journal of Social Research* 2(1964), 178–186.

Rudgers, David F. "The Origins of Covert Actions," *Journal of Contemporary History* 35 (2000), 249–262.

Sabbagh, Suha J. *Sex, Lies and Stereotypes: The Image of Arabs in American Popular Fiction.* Washington, D.C.: ADC, 1990.

Said, Edward. *Orientalism.* New York: Pantheon, 1978.

Sandison, Alan. *The Wheel of Empire: A Study of the Imperial Idea in Some Late 19th and Early 20th-Century Fiction.* New York: St. Martin's Press, 1967.

Sarna, Jonathan D. *American Judaism: A History.* New Haven: Yale University Press, 2004.

———. "A Projection of America as It Ought to Be: Zion in the Mind's Eye of American Jews," in Allon Gal, ed. *Envisioning Israel: The Changing Ideals and Images of North American Jews.* Detroit: Wayne State University Press, 1996.

Satia, Priya. *Spies in Arabia: The Great War and the Cultural Foundations of Britain's Covert Empire in the Middle East.* New York: Oxford University Press, 2008.

Sauerberg, Lars Ole. "Literature in Figures: An Essay on the Popularity of Thrillers," *Orbis Litterarum* 38(1983), 93–107.

———. *Secret Agents in Fiction: Ian Fleming, John le Carré and Len Deighton.* London: Macmillan, 1984.

Sawhill, Raw. "In Japanese Novels, Its Business as Usual." *The New York Times Book Review.* October 13, 1996.

Schlesinger, Arthur, Jr. "He Won't Tell. Should We Care?" *The New York Times.* January 9, 2000.

Schwarz, Benjamin. "Divided Attention: Britain's Perception of a German Threat to Her Eastern Frontier in 1918," *Journal of Contemporary History* 28 (1993), 103–122.

Seymour, Gerald. "Craft Notes," in Myron J. Smith, Jr. and Terry White, eds. *Cloak and Dagger Fiction: An Annotated Guide to Spy Thrillers.* Westport: Greenwood Press, 1995.

Shaheen, Jack G. "Arab Images in American Comic Books," *Journal of Popular Culture* 28(Summer 1994), 123–133.

———. "The Image of the Arab on American Television" in Edmund Ghareeb, ed. *Split Vision: The Portrayal of Arabs in the American Media.* Washington, DC: American Arab Affairs Council, 1983.

———. *Reel Bad Arabs: How Hollywood Vilifies A People.* New York: Olive Branch Press, 2001.

Sheffy, Yigal. *British Military Intelligence in the Palestine Campaign 1914–1918.* London: Frank Cass, 1998.

Shipler, David K. "The Arab-American Counts His Stereotypes." *The New York Times.* December 31, 1985.

Sick, Gary. *All Fall Down: America's Tragic Encounter with Iran.* New York: Random House, 1985.

Siemion, Piotr. "No More Heroes: The Routinization of the Epic in Techno-Thrillers," in Joseph Tabbi and Michael Wutz, eds. *Reading Matters: Narrative in the New Media Ecology.* Ithaca: Cornell University Press, 1997.

Silet, Charles L.P. "The First Angry White Male—Mickey Spillane's Mike Hammer." *The Armchair Detective.* 29(1996), 195–199.

Simon, Reeva S. "Gore by Gur." *Jewish Book World* 13(Fall 1995), 4–5.

———. *Iraq Between the Two World Wars: The Militarist Origins of Tyranny.* New York: Columbia University Press, 2004.

———. *The Middle East in Crime Fiction: Mysteries, Spy Novels, and Thrillers from 1916 to the 1980s.* New York: Lilian Barber Press, Inc., 1989.

———. "*The Tomb of the Twelfth Imam*" and other Tales of Crime," in Neguin Yavari, Lawrence G. Potter, and Jean-Marc Oppenheim, eds. *Views from the Edge: Essays in Honor of Richard W. Bulliet.* New York: Columbia University Press, 2004.

Skene, Melvin. "The Secret Eye: The Spy in Literature—A Survey of the History and Development of the Spy and Espionage Novel," *Pacific Quarterly* 3(1978).

Slade, Shelly. "The Image of the Arab in America: Analysis of a Poll on American Attitudes," *Middle East Journal* 35 (1981), 143–162.

Slotkin, Richard. *Gunfighter Nation: The Myth of the Frontier in Twentieth Century America*. New York: Atheneum, 1992.

Smith, Dinitia, "Apocalyptic Potboiler is Publisher's Dream," *The New York Times*. June 8, 2000.

Smith, Erin A. "How the Other Half Read: Advertising, Working-Class Readers, and Pulp Magazines," *Book History* 3 (2000), 204–230.

Smith, Jane. *Islam in America*. New York: Columbia University Press, 1999.

Snow, Peter and David Phillips. *The Arab Hijack War*. New York: Ballantine, 1970.

Southern, R.W. *Western Views of Islam in the Middle Ages*. Cambridge, Mass.: Harvard University Press, 1962.

Stafford, David A.T. *The Silent Game: The Real World of Imaginary Spies*. Athens, Georgia: University of Georgia Press, 1991.

———. "Spies and Gentlemen: The Birth of the British Spy Novel, 1893–1914." *Victorian Studies* 24(1981), 491–509.

Stearn, Roger T. "War Correspondents and Colonial War, c. 1870–1900," in John M. MacKenzie, ed. *Popular Imperialism and the Military 1850–1950*. Manchester: Manchester University Press, 1992.

Sterling, Claire. *The Terror Network: The Secret War of International Terrorism*. New York: Holt Rinehart and Winston, 1981.

Steven, Stewart. *The Spymasters of Israel*. New York: Macmillan, 1980.

Stockton, Ronald. "Ethnic Stereotypes and the Arab Image," in Ernest McCarus, ed. *The Development of Arab-American Identity*. Ann Arbor: University of Michigan Press, 1994.

Storey, John. *Cultural Theory and Popular Culture: An Introduction*. 5th ed. New York: Pearson Education Limited, 2009.

Stowe, William W. "Critical Investigations: Convention and Ideology in Detective Fiction." *Texas Studies in Literature and Language* 31 (1989), 570–591.

Straus, Neil. "Wal-Mart's CD Standards are Changing Pop Music." *The New York Times*. November 12, 1996.

Street, Brian V. *The Savage in Literature: Representations of 'Primitive' Society in English Fiction 1858–1920*. London: Routledge and Kegan Paul, 1975.

Suleiman, M. "Stereotypes, Public Opinion and Foreign Policy: The Impact on American-Arab Relations." *Journal of Arab Affairs* 1 (1982), 147–166.

Sutherland, John. *Best-sellers: Popular Fiction of the 1970s*. London: Routledge and Kegan Paul, 1981.

———. *Reading the Decades: Fifty Years of the Nation's Best-Selling Books*. London: BBC Worldwide, 2002.

Symons, Julian. *Bloody Murder: From the Detective Story to the Crime Novel*. London: Penguin, 1974.

————. *Mortal Consequences: A History from the Detective Story to the Crime Novel*. New York: Schocken Books, 1973.

Taylor, Jessica. "And You Can be My Sheikh: Gender, Race, and Orientalism in Contemporary Romance Novels," *The Journal of Popular Culture* 40 (2007), 1032–1051.

"Terrorists Take over Thrillers." *Time*. April 14, 1980.

Terry, Janice J. "Arab Stereotypes in Popular Fiction." *Arab Perspectives* (April 1982).

————. "The Arab-Israeli Conflict in Popular Literature." *Arab-American Affairs* (Fall 1982).

————. "Images of the Middle East in Contemporary Fiction" in Edmund Ghareeb, ed. *Split Vision: The Portrayal of Arabs in the American Media*. Washington, DC: American-Arab Affairs Council, 1983.

————. *Mistaken Identity: Arab Stereotypes in Popular Writing*. Washington, DC: American-Arab Affairs Council, 1985.

Thomas, G.W. "Murder in Mesopotamia: Agatha Christie in the Middle East," *The Armchair Detective* 27(1994): 277–283.

Thomas, Martin. *Empires of Intelligence: Security Services and Colonial Disorder after 1914*. Berkeley: University of California Press, 2007.

Thomas, Robert McG., Jr. "Don Pendleton, 67, Writer Who Spawned a Genre." *The New York Times* (October 28, 1995).

Thompson, Jon. *Fiction, Crime and Empire: Clues to Modernity and Postmodernism*. Urbana: University of Illinois Press, 1993.

Tidrick, Kathryn. *Heary-beguiling Araby*. Cambridge: Cambridge University Press, 1981.

Tinnin, David. B. *The Hit Team*. Boston: Little, Brown, 1976.

Todorov, Tsvetan. *The Fantastic: A Structural Approach to a Literary Genre*. Translated by Richard Howard. Ithaca: Cornell University Press, 1975.

Tollefson, Harold. *Policing Islam: The British Occupation of Egypt and the Anglo-Egyptian Struggle over Control of the Police, 1882–1914*. Westport: Greenwood Press, 1999.

Tolstiakov, George. "The Man Who Was Quiller," *The Armchair Detective* 29(1996): 81–84.

Trahair, R.C.S. "A Psychological Study of the Modern Hero: The Case of James Bond." *Australian and New Zealand Journal of Psychiatry* 8(1974): 155–165.

————. "A Contribution to the Psychoanalytic Study of the Modern Hero." *La Trobe Sociology Papers* (Bundoora, Vic. Australia), 1976.

Trotter, David. "The Politics of Adventure in the Early British Spy Novel," In Wesley K. Wark, ed. *Spy Fiction, Spy Films and Real Intelligence*. London: Frank Cass, 1991.

Turnbaugh, Roy. "Images of Empire: George Alfred Henty and John Buchan." *Journal of Popular Culture* 9(1975): 734–740.

Vail, Jeffrey W. "The Standard of Revolt: Revolution and National Independence in Moore's *Lalla Rookh*," *Romanticism on the Net* 40(2005).

Van Ash, Cay and Elizabeth Sax Rohmer. *Master of Villainy: A Biography of Sax Rohmer*. Bowling Green, Bowling Green University Popular Press, 1972.

Van Dover, J. Kenneth. *Murder in the Millions: Erle Stanley Gardner, Mickey Spillane, Ian Fleming*. New York: Frederick Ungar, 1984.

Varma. Devendra P. *The Gothic Flame: Being a History of the Gothic Novel in England: Its Origins, Efflorescence, Disintegration, and Residuary Influence*. New York: Russell and Russell, 1966.

Wagner, Donald. "Reagan and Begin, Bibi and Jerry: The Theopolitical Alliance of the Likud Party with the American Christian 'right'," *Arab Studies Quarterly* 20 (1998), 33–52.

Wark, Wesley K. "Introduction: Fictions of History," *Intelligence and National Security* 5 (1990), 1–16.

———. *Spy Fiction, Spy Films and Real Intelligence*. London: Frank Cass, 1991.

Watson, Colin. *Snobbery With Violence*. London: Eyre and Spottswade, 1971.

Weber, Eugen. *Apocalypses: Prophecies, Cults and Millennial Beliefs through the Ages*. Cambridge: Harvard University Press, 1999.

Weber, Timothy P. *On the Road to Armageddon: How Evangelicals Became Israel's Best Friend*. Grand Rapids: Baker Academic, 2004.

Whitney, Phyllis A. "Gothic Mysteries" in John Ball, ed. *The Mystery Story*. New York: Penguin, 1976.

Wills, Gary. "John Wayne's Body." *The New Yorker* (August 19, 1996), 39–49.

Wilson, Edmund. "Who Cares Who Killed Roger Ackroyd." *Classics and Commercials* (1950), 257–265.

Winks, Robin, ed. *Detective Fiction*. Englewood Cliffs, N.J.: Prentice-Hall, 1980.

———. "The Genre of Mystery and Spy Fiction Should Get Serious Study but It Must Be for the Right Reasons," *The Chronicle of Higher Education* (August 2, 1989), 131–132.

———. *The Historian as Detective*. New York: Harper, 1968.

———. *Modus Operandi: An Excursion into Detective Fiction*. Boston: David R. Godine, 1982.

———. "Sinister Orientals: Everybody's Favorite Villains" in Dilys Winn, ed. *Murder Ink: The Mystery Reader's Companion*. New York: Workman Publishing, 1977.

Winks, Robin and James R. Rush, eds. *Asia in Western Fiction*. Manchester: Manchester University Press, 1990.

Winn, Dilys. *Murder Ink: The Mystery Reader's Companion*. New York: Workman Publishing, 1977.

———. *Murder Ink: Revived, Revised, Still Unrepentent*. New York: Workman Publishing, 1984.

Winstone, H.V.F. *The Illicit Adventure*. London: Jonathan Cape, 1982.

Wright, Bradford W. *Comic Book Nation: The Transformation of Youth Culture in America*. Baltimore: Johns Hopkins University Press, 2001.

Wu, William F. *The Yellow Peril: Chinese Americans in American Fiction 1850–1940*. Hamden, C.T.: Archon Books, 1982.

Young, William H. *A Study of Action-Adventure Fiction:* The Executioner *and Mack Bolan*. Lewiston: The Edwin Mellon Press, 1996.

Zogby, James J. "ADC Issues No. 3: The Other Anti-Semitism: The Arab as Scapegoat" American-Arab Anti-Discrimination Committee, n.d.

Index

Milton Keynes UK
Ingram Content Group UK Ltd.
UKHW010705280324
439889UK00010B/158